LAWYER'S MODEL LETTER BOOK

OTHER BOOKS BY ROBERT SELLERS SMITH

HANDBOOK OF LAW OFFICE FORMS
ALABAMA LEGAL FORMS ANNOTATED
MODERN OFFICE FORMS FOR LAWYERS
ALABAMA LAW FOR THE LAYMAN
FORMS UNDER A.R.C.P.

LAWYER'S MODEL LETTER BOOK

Robert Sellers Smith

PRENTICE-HALL, INC.
ENGLEWOOD CLIFFS, N.J.

Prentice-Hall International, Inc., *London*
Prentice-Hall of Australia, Pty. Ltd., *Sydney*
Prentice-Hall of Canada, Ltd., *Toronto*
Prentice-Hall of India Private Ltd., *New Delhi*
Prentice-Hall of Japan, Inc., *Tokyo*
Prentice-Hall of Southeast Asia Pte. Ltd., *Singapore*
Whitehall Books, Ltd., *Wellington, New Zealand*

Fourth Printing . . . . . February, 1980

Library of Congress Cataloging in Publication Data

Smith, Robert Sellers.
    Lawyer's model letter book.

    Includes index.
    1. Legal correspondence. 2. Legal secretaries—
United States—Handbooks, manuals, etc. I. Title.
KF320.L48S58   651.7'5'024344   78-3835
ISBN 0-13-526897-4

Printed in the United States of America

How This Book Will Help You

This book will benefit your law practice in two ways:

It will help you write better letters

It will help you write your letters in less time

Consider how many letters you write in the course of your practice. Suppose, for example, you write 20 letters a week. That comes to over 1000 letters a year. Right now, you probably spend over 300 hours a year writing letters. Improvement of only 10% to 20% in the quality and speed of your letter writing will produce enormous dividends in client satisfaction and office income.

What if you had to sit down and draft an entirely new deed or complaint every time you needed one, without reference to prior deeds or complaints? We know that pleading and practice forms help. The same logic applies to specimen or model letters. That is the purpose of this book: To make available to you a comprehensive collection of model or specimen letters for your use in letter writing. You should use them in almost the same way you now use form books when drafting pleading and practice instruments.

Over 400 model letters are reproduced in this book. Lawyers from large firms, small firms and one-man offices throughout the United States contributed their best letters to this book. Each letter was written by a practicing lawyer. Each letter was written to accomplish a specific purpose found necessary or desirable in actual practice. There are 175 letters to clients, 51 letters to opposing and other parties, 9 letters to witnesses, 40 letters to lawyers, 83 letters to public officials, 8 letters to friends, and 48 letters to other addressees.

All practice situations are covered in this book. Here are examples.

CONTRACTS

Thirty-seven letters cover insurance claims, collection efforts for clients, leases, rent collection, and clients' problems with creditors.

CORPORATIONS AND OTHER BUSINESS ENTITIES

There are 34 letters transmitting corporate documents and giving advice on such subjects as limited partnerships, buy-sell agreements, and sale of stock.

CRIMINAL LAW

There are 14 important letters to district attorneys and clients. Included is the hard-to-write letter in which the attorney withdraws from the case.

ESTATE PLANNING AND PROBATE

Thirty-eight letters on wills, codicils, trusts and settlement of estates are addressed to clients, bank trust officers, insurance companies and clerks of court. Four of the letters give the client a detailed review of his estate plan and make recommendations for the estate plan.

FAMILY LAW

Forty letters cover divorce, including negotiations for settlement; post-divorce matters; juvenile cases; and adoption.

LAW OFFICE MANAGEMENT

There are 21 letters requesting payment of accounts, congratulating new lawyers, and acknowledging applications for positions.

NEGLIGENCE LAW

Ninety-seven letters cover all aspects of negligence cases. There are letters to clients, opposing parties, attorneys, insurance companies, witnesses, clerks of court, and the department of public safety. Several letters have special enclosures of instruction to the client on depositions, interrogatories and medical examinations.

PROPERTY LAW

Fifty-six letters cover real estate transactions, SBA loans, mortgages, rental property, encroachment on property, etc.

TAX LAW

There are 19 letters, many to the IRS on tax problems of clients. Others are on pension and profit sharing plans.

MISCELLANEOUS

Fifty-eight letters include general letters such as "Notice of Date of Trial" and letters on workmen's compensation, social security, and bankruptcy.

The letters in this book were carefully selected, in each case, as best demonstrating the successful use of a letter by a lawyer in his practice. They will help you in a large variety of practice situations. The letters, of course, are only raw material for you to use to suit your purpose, and they will not detract from your creativity, spontaneity, or sincerity. We know that Shakespeare fashioned his plays from existing themes and materials. He seems not to have suffered from it. Neither will you from using these letters as specimens or models.

As an example of how this book will help you, assume that your client wants to execute the will you prepared for him at home, and you must write to him to explain the proper procedure. Locate a similar letter in this book and use it to aid you in drafting your letter. Other examples include letters proposing terms for divorce settlements, distributing settlement proceeds, explaining the purpose of discovery depositions, or requesting medical reports.

You may wish to use some of the letters almost verbatim. Others, you may want to use simply as points of departure to help you compose or begin letters you need to write to suit your particular needs. The final product, in each case, is your letter.

Robert Sellers Smith

THE AUTHOR

Robert Sellers Smith is a practicing attorney and an expert on legal forms and law office management. He is a partner in the firm of Smith, Huckaby & Graves, P.A., in Huntsville, Alabama, and has authored five previous books, including the Handbook of Law Office Forms (Prentice-Hall). He received his L.L.B. degree from the University of Virginia Law School and in addition to being in general practice for 15 years, served as Assistant Counsel of the Special Committee to Investigate Campaign Expenditures for the House of Representatives, and Counsel to the U.S. Senate Committee on Labor and Public Welfare from 1961-1963.

Acknowledgments

The following practicing lawyers gave me suggestions and specimen letters for use in this book:

Richard P. Beck, Wilmington, DE; Bernard P. Chamberlain, Charlottesville, VA; Richard G. Clemens, Chicago, IL; William Byron Darden, Las Cruces, NM; Herbert Hafif, Claremont, CA; Dale R. Larabee, San Diego, CA; J. D. Lee, Madisonville, TN; James B. Lovelace, High Point, NC; Irwin Owen, Shawnee, OK; George E. Ray, Dallas, TX; Ralph H. Scheuer, Santa Fe, NM; Claude L. Stuart, Greenville, MS; Neva B. Talley-Morris, Little Rock, AR; and James R. Accardi, Norman Bradley, Patrick H. Graves, Jr., John M. Heacock, Jr., Ralph W. Hornsby, Gary C. Huckaby, Douglas Claude Martinson, Dan Moran, Ernest L. Potter, Jr., Robert M. Shipman, and John S. Somerset, all of Huntsville, AL.

Mrs. Marcia Bargeron handled the correspondence in connection with soliciting specimen letters and typed much of the original draft of the book. Mrs. Christine Berryman, Mrs. Virginia Mobbs, and Mrs. Margaret Wunderlich typed the manuscript.

Mrs. Joan McIntyre, Legal Assistant with Smith, Huckaby & Graves, P.A., Huntsville, AL, read and helped improve the entire manuscript. She is a published author and experienced book editor. Without her outstanding help it would have been difficult, if not impossible, to complete the book within the time allowed for preparation.

Robert Sellers Smith

Contents

HOW THIS BOOK WILL HELP YOU

GROUP A

Giving Notice or Information   41

17

SECTION I   LETTERS TO CLIENTS *(continued)*

SECTION I   LETTERS TO CLIENTS *(continued)*

SECTION I   LETTERS TO CLIENTS *(continued)*

GROUP C

Explaining Procedure   131

GROUP D

Giving Advice   147

SECTION I LETTERS TO CLIENTS *(continued)*

SECTION I   LETTERS TO CLIENTS *(continued)*

SECTION I LETTERS TO CLIENTS *(continued)*

SECTION II.   LETTERS TO OPPOSING AND OTHER PARTIES (*continued*)

GROUP B

Requesting Information   221

GROUP C

Requesting or Demanding Action   227

GROUP A

Giving Notice or Information   255

SECTION III. LETTERS TO WITNESSES *(continued)*

GROUP B

Requesting Report or Information 257

SECTION IV. LETTERS TO LAWYERS 265

GROUP A

Giving Notice or Information 267

SECTION IV.   LETTERS TO LAWYERS *(continued)*

GROUP B

Requesting Information   283

GROUP C

Negotiating Agreement or Settlement   289

SECTION IV.   LETTERS TO LAWYERS *(continued)*

GROUP A

Giving Notice or Information   303

CONTENTS

SECTION V. LETTERS TO PUBLIC OFFICIALS *(continued)*

GROUP B

Requesting Information   329

SECTION V.   LETTERS TO PUBLIC OFFICIALS *(continued)*

GROUP C

SECTION V.   LETTERS TO PUBLIC OFFICIALS *(continued)*

SECTION VI.   LETTERS TO FRIENDS

GROUP A

"Thank You" Letters   365

SECTION VI.   LETTERS TO FRIENDS *(continued)*

CONTENTS

SECTION VII.   LETTERS TO OTHER ADDRESSEES *(continued)*

SECTION VII.   LETTERS TO OTHER ADDRESSEES *(continued)*

SECTION VII.   LETTERS TO OTHER ADDRESSEES *(continued)*

LAWYER'S MODEL LETTER BOOK

SECTION 1
LETTERS TO CLIENTS

Letters to clients are most important as they materially help the lawyer maintain good relationships with his clients. A lawyer should keep his clients informed of the status of the cases and matters he is handling for them. Letters keeping the client informed include those giving notice, reporting the status of the matter, explaining procedures, giving recommendations, and giving opinion.

Other types of letters lawyers write to their clients include letters requesting information, letters requesting a review by a client, letters requesting action, and letters requesting a decision by a client.

It is a good idea to send copies of all correspondence received by a lawyer in connection with a case to the client, as well as copies of all pleadings and other legal instruments. It is most important that the client knows at all times that the lawyer is taking care of his matter. Letters do a very good job of keeping the client knowledgeable of what is happening and coordinating those things a client can do to assist in connection with his case.

Letters to clients should be friendly, written in plain language, informative and convey to the client that his case or matter is being taken care of in a professional way.

GROUP A
Giving Notice or Information

1.

TRANSMITTAL OF CERTIFICATE OF INCORPORATION

Dear Mr. Johnson:

Enclosed is the original Certificate of Incorporation for ABC Company, Inc. This should be placed in the corporate records and permanently retained.

Sincerely yours,

COMMENT:

1. The lawyer organizing a new corporation should ascertain from the client who will maintain the originals of important corporate legal documents. In this case it appears the client will be maintaining them, and the letter simply transmits the original Certificate of Incorporation.

2. There are advantages which may result from the lawyer maintaining the corporate kit or file of important corporate documents. For example, the originals of all documents will be on hand in the lawyer's office for use in connection with subsequent transactions.

3. In the event the lawyer retains the original of important corporate papers, it is suggested that copies of each paper be transmitted to the client for his files.

2.

TRANSMITTAL OF STOCK CERTIFICATES

Dear Charles:

Enclosed you will find the following:

1. The ABC Corporation Stock Certificate No. 1247 for 1400 shares of common stock;

2. XYZ Company Stock Certificate No. 6389 for 2500 shares of preferred stock.

This completes the transfer of all stock owned by your mother.

Very truly yours,

COMMENT:

1. The above letter is a rather standardized letter of transmittal. Many lawyers still use the phrase "Enclosed you will find," or "Enclosed please find." Variations, if desired, include, "I am enclosing," "We are enclosing," or "Enclosed are."

3.

TRANSMITTAL OF MINUTES OF ANNUAL MEETING OF STOCKHOLDERS AND BOARD OF DIRECTORS

Dear Mr. Brown:

I am enclosing the Minutes for the Annual Meeting of Stockholders and the Meeting of the Board of Directors of ABC Company, Inc. If you and Frank Jones would please sign the originals and return them to me for my files, I will file them in your corporate kit.

I am also enclosing a copy of these minutes for your records.

Sincerely yours,

COMMENT:

1. The above letter is a standard letter of transmittal of corporate minutes.

2. The letter could be further personalized by reference to the contents of the minutes or matters contained in them of particular interest to the clients.

4.
NOTICE OF DATE TO APPEAR IN COURT IN CONNECTION
WITH SUSPENDED SENTENCE

Dear Dave:

I enjoyed seeing you on Thursday, and I am glad we were able to work your case out to your satisfaction.

This letter is to remind you that you are due back in Judge Hunter's Court, the District Court, on March 5, at 10:00 a.m. In the event you have any problems in connection with your school or anything arises in connection with your case that you don't understand, please let me know. Unless I hear from you to the contrary, I do not intend to be in court on March 5th.

Thank you very much. Please give my best to your mother.

Very sincerely,

COMMENT:

1. The writer could, if appropriate, comment more about the case.

5.
NOTICE OF WITHDRAWAL AS ATTORNEY IN CRIMINAL CASE

Dear Mr. Wilson:

In June 19___ , you were charged with grand larceny of an automobile. In that case, as you recall, you applied for youthful offender status, the hearing was had on your application, and you were adjudged a youthful offender by Judge Johnson. On that case, as of August, 19___ , there was a balance of $1,750 owing. That is, from June, 19___ , until October, 19___ , you have paid a total of $250 into this office. In addition, in September, 19___ , you were charged with grand larceny of an automobile. Again we went to court two times on that case, and the felony charge was dismissed, and that particular case is over. I now understand that the state has elected to take you to a grand jury and secure a new case against you in that incident.

Although I would like to represent you, it is economically impossible to do so. I cannot make court appearances, prepare for trial, etc., on the basis of a $250 payment. As you know, I quoted you a retainer fee on the second case which has not been paid, and in all seriousness it should have been paid by October. All cases in which I have engaged in court action are terminated. I feel at this time it is advisable for you to seek other counsel as to any other charge brought against you.

Yours truly,

COMMENT:

1. The above letter explains in detail and in a personal way the exact reason the lawyer is withdrawing from further representation of the client in a criminal case.

6.
TRANSMITTAL OF DRAFTS OF WILLS AND REQUEST
FOR APPOINTMENT TO EXECUTE WILLS

Dear John and Irene:

I am enclosing drafts of your wills which we have prepared in accordance with your instructions. Please read each will carefully, noting particularly that all names are correctly spelled and that the wills contain every provision that you desire. In the event there are any corrections to be made, or there are any portions of the wills that you do not understand, please call me or come to the office to discuss the matter.

In the event the wills are in proper form for execution, please call our office and arrange an appointment at your convenience to execute them.

Sincerely,

COMMENT:

1. The above letter is a good example of a satisfactory transmittal letter for will drafts. The procedure of forwarding will drafts to clients for review prior to execution is recommended.

2. The letter could be further personalized by the lawyer for the client by commenting on specific provisions of the wills.

7.
TRANSMITTAL OF DRAFT OF WILL CODICIL

Dear Mrs. West:

Enclosed is a draft of the first codicil to your will, which I believe accomplishes the changes we have discussed. When you have had a chance to review it, we can make such changes in it as you wish, and, after that, I believe it would be desirable to let the Bank Trust Department have a copy of it for their review and suggestions.

Sincerely,

COMMENT:

1. The above letter could be further personalized by describing the particular changes made to the will by the codicil.

8.

TRANSMITTAL OF LETTER REGARDING AMENDMENT TO TRUST AGREEMENT AND COPY OF CODICIL TO WILLS

Dear Bob:

Enclosed is a letter we received from Tom Clark.

In accordance with Tom's letter, we have retyped the first page of your First Amendment to Revocable Life Insurance Trust Agreement and enclosed a copy which we would appreciate your attaching to your copy of the Fifth Amendment in place of the previous page.

We have also typed a Second Codicil to your Last Will and Testament and enclose a copy for your review. If the Second Codicil meets with your approval, please call my secretary and make an appointment to come in and execute it. If you have any questions, please call me.

Sincerely,

COMMENT:

1. The above letter relates to an amendment to an intervivos trust. The letter transmits a changed first page of the amendment, which obviously has not been executed.

2. The letter also transmits a proposed second codicil to the client's will for his review.

3. It is a good idea for the lawyer to send drafts or copies of all wills, codicils, trusts, and amendments to trusts for review by the client prior to scheduling a conference with the client for execution. This gives the client an opportunity to carefully read and review the document in the privacy of his own home and to discuss it at home. Unless this is done, the client may come to the office and hastily sign a very complicated document without fully understanding it or without having actually read it.

9.
TRANSMITTAL OF CODICILS TO WILLS AND COPY OF
LETTER FORWARDING CODICILS TO BANK

Dear Mr. and Mrs. Brown:

We are enclosing the original of your codicils, which you both executed last night. These codicils should be appended to the originals of your wills. We have retained copies for our file and forwarded copies to First National Bank at Carson City for their records.

Also enclosed is the cover letter which we forwarded to Don Johnson today, together with the enclosures.

Thank you very much for giving us the opportunity to work on this matter. Best wishes.

Sincerely yours,

COMMENT:

1. The writer could suggest periodic review of the wills and codicils.

2. The writer could also suggest additional estate planning matters or items that should be considered or taken care of by the client from time to time.

10.
TRANSMITTAL OF COPIES OF WILLS AND STATEMENT
FOR SERVICE

Dear Tom:

Enclosed are the originals and one conformed copy of the new wills for you and Joan. Also enclosed is our statement in connection with this work. We hope that you will find it satisfactory as to amount and want to assure you and Joan how much we appreciate your confidence in us and the opportunity you have given us to be of service to you in these matters.

Very sincerely,

COMMENT:

1. The lawyer in the above letter has combined transmittal of the original and copies of wills with the statement for services rendered. The approach to the statement for services is both personal and respectful. The approach to the client is cordial and warm.

11.
TRANSMITTAL OF COPIES OF WILLS, NOTICE OF MAILING ORIGINAL WILLS, STATEMENT FOR SERVICE AND SEASON'S GREETINGS

Dear Mr. Hunt:

Enclosed is a conformed copy of your will, together with our statement for services in connection with the matters which we have been handling for you recently. We hope you find the amount satisfactory. We have mailed the original of the will to Tom Clark at XYZ Bank for safekeeping, and he will send you a receipt for it.

It was a pleasure to work on these matters with you, and we appreciate very much your confidence in us.

With many thanks and very warmest good wishes to you and the family for Christmas and the New Year.

Sincerely yours,

COMMENT:

1. The above letter personalizes the transaction and indicates the lawyer's cordial and warm regard for his client.

12.

TRANSMITTAL OF INSURANCE POLICIES

Dear Mr. Brown:

We are enclosing the following insurance policies:

1. Your ABC Insurance Company policy, together with your change of alternate beneficiary designation attached to it.

2. Your DEF Company policy, together with your change of alternate beneficiary designation attached to it.

3. Your GHI Insurance Company policy, together with your change of alternate beneficiary designation attached to it.

4. Your JKL Insurance Company Certificate of Insurance, together with your change of alternate beneficiary designation attached to it.

5. Your new MNO Company policy, indicating your wife as primary beneficiary, and your estate as contingent beneficiary.

6. Your PXR Insurance Company policy. I have no recent correspondence in my file since August 3, the date we forwarded additional information to them. Please check your records to see if perhaps the alternate beneficiary change was forwarded directly to you. If you do not have any recent correspondence from them regarding it, we need to write them again.

7. Your XYZ Insurance Policy. Enclosed with it is a copy of our last correspondence with this company. You should receive a designation of your alternate beneficiary change on this policy very shortly.

Best wishes to you.

Yours truly,

COMMENT:

1. The above letter transmitting insurance policies states in a simple way an obviously fairly involved transaction in connection with estate planning for the client.

2. Letters such as the above are helpful in documenting steps taken in connection with a transaction, such as the change of beneficiaries in insurance policies.

3. More comment could be made regarding the matter if desired.

13.
REVIEW OF ESTATE PLAN AND RECOMMENDATIONS FOR ESTATE PLAN

Dear Henry and Ethel:

The purpose of this letter is to review your estate plan and make recommendations.

First, a little preliminary comment. It appears that in the event of your death, total family assets which would be available to your family would be something over one million dollars. The total amount of insurance of which you are the insured is $920,000 (excluding the policy with ABC Insurance Company owned by your employer and payable to your employer). Although I do not have current figures, I am estimating your net estate, excluding your insurance, at $100,000. Therefore, your total insurance program together with estimated net assets would give your family something over $1,000,000 in the event of your death. This is outstanding.

One of the primary vehicles for your estate plan is the Trust Agreement which you executed on April 15, 19___ . This Trust Agreement was amended on October 12, 19___ , to name the XYZ Bank of Granville as successor Trustee.

1. The general terms of your Trust Agreement executed April 15, 19___ , as modified by the Amendment of October 12, 19___ , are as follows:

(a) *Marital Deduction Share*. Trust A under the Trust Agreement consists of the marital deduction share for the benefit of Ethel. Ethel receives all income from this Trust during her lifetime. The Trustee may invade principal for Ethel's benefit. Ethel has the right to appoint to herself, children, grandchildren or spouses of such descedants, any or all of the property in this Trust. Ethel may dispose of the remaining principal by her Will; otherwise, remaining principal goes to the Family Trust.

(b) *Family Trust*. The remainder of your estate going into this Trust at your death goes to the Family Trust, or Trustee. The Trustee of the Trust is given the authority and duty to spray the income from Trustee to Ethel and your children in such amounts as he deems to be in the best interest of them. This Trust expressly states that Ethel is the primary beneficiary and her needs are to be given priority. The Trustee may encroach on principal of Trust B for support and education of the children at any time. On Ethel's death, Trust B is continued for the benefit of your children. When your youngest child is 21, the property in Trust B is divided into shares, with an equal share for each child (with appropriate provisions in the event of death of a child) and with the further provision that after the division of Trust B into shares, each child may receive his share as follows: one-third at age 21; one-third at age 25; and the balance at age 30.

2. Your Will was executed on April 15, 19___ . There was a Codicil to your Will on October 12, 19___ . Under your Will, all tangible, personal property (automobile, furniture, etc.) goes to Ethel if she is living, otherwise to your children with the provision that in the event any of your children are minors, their shares may be received by the Trustee and held in the Family Trust described above. The remainder of your estate goes approximately one-half to the Marital Trust and one-half to the Family Trust. Other provisions in your will are as follows:

(a) *Executor*. Ethel and the XYZ Bank of Granville.

(b) *Guardian*. Ethel would be guardian if she survived you. Next would be your sister, Leah; next, Homer Adams; and next, Albert Adams.

3. Ethel's Will was executed on April 15, 19___ , and her Codicil to the Will was executed on October 12, 19___ . Ethel's Will as modified by the Codicil provides as follows:

(a) All of Ethel's property goes to Henry if he survives her by thirty (30) days; otherwise, her tangible, personal property goes to the children with the provision that the shares of any child who is a minor may be received by the Trustee and held in Trust under Trust B, the Family Trust described above. The remainder of Ethel's property would go to Trust B, also.

(b) *Guardian*. The guardians named in Ethel's Will are the same as those named in Henry's. Henry, of course, in the event he survived Ethel, would be guardian of the children.

(c) *Executor*. Henry is named as Executor, and the Alternate Executor is the XYZ Bank of Granville.

4. *Life Insurance*. Henry is the insured, as stated above, for $920,000 of life insurance (excluding the policy owned and payable to his employer). Henry's life insurance is further described as follows:

(a) Total face amount $920,000.

(b) Amount of insurance that is ordinary life, $370,000; amount which is term insurance, $550,000. Percentage of total insurance program that is ordinary life, 40%.

(c) Total annual premium, $7,148. (This includes insurance owned and paid for by DEF Company, Inc., Employee Pension and Profit Sharing Plan). Total premium in relation to income is approximately 7%, which is considered a sound figure. This assumes an annual income of approximately $100,000.

(d) Ownership of life insurance.

(1) Henry, $120,000. This includes Policy Number 10, described hereinafter, which is owned by the employer and payable to Ethel, face amount $50,000, but which would be deemed to be owned by Ethel for estate tax purposes in the event of his death.

(2) Amount of Henry's insurance owned by Ethel, $200,000.

(3) Amount of life insurance owned by Clifford Trust, payable to Clifford Trust for the benefit of the children, $300,000.

(4) Amount of insurance owned by Employer's Pension and Profit Sharing Plans, $300,000.

(e) Beneficiaries of life insurance. Ethel is the beneficiary of $320,000, the Trustee of the Employer's Pension and Profit Sharing Plans is the beneficiary of $300,000 and the Trustee of your Clifford Trust is the beneficiary of $3000,000.

(f) The individual policies are as follows:

(1) ABC Insurance Company, Policy No. 1000, face amount $100,000. This policy was lapsed.

(2) DEF Insurance Company, Policy No. 2000, face amount $25,000, annual premium $430 (est.), owner: Henry; beneficiary: Ethel. This policy is located at ABC National Bank where it is pledged as collateral security.

(3) GHI Insurance Company, Policy No. 3000, face amount $25,000, annual premium $431, owner: Henry; beneficiary: Ethel. This policy is located at ABC National Bank where it is pledged as collateral security.

(4) JKL Insurance Company, Policy No. 4000, face amount, $20,000, annual premium $333, owner: Henry; beneficiary: Ethel.

(5) MNO Insurance Company, Policy No. 5000, face amount, $198,000, annual premium $2680, owner: Trustee of ABC Employees Pension Plan; beneficiary: Trustee of ABC Employees Pension Plan.

(6) MNO Insurance Company, Policy No. 6000, face amount, $102,000, annual premium $1481, owner: Trustee of ABC Employees Pension Plan; beneficiary: Trustee of ABC Employees Pension Plan.

(7) MNO Insurance Company, Policy No. 4000, face amount $200,000, annual premium $600, owner: Ethel, beneficiary: Ethel.

(8) MNO Insurance Company, Policy No. 8000, face amount $200,000, annual premium $581, owner: Clifford Trust; beneficiary: Clifford Trust, Trustee of which the beneficiaries are the children, Sarah and Barbara (in the event you have additional children, you should consider making a similar arrangement to what you have already done for Sarah and Barbara).

(9) MNO Insurance Company, Policy No. 9000, face amount $100,000, annual premium $298, owner: Clifford Trust; beneficiary: Trustee of Clifford Trust.

(10) PQR Insurance Company, Policy No. 10,000, face amount $50,000, annual premium $150 year paid by employer, owner: Employer, beneficiary: Ethel.

(11) PQR Insurance Company, Policy No. 11,000, face amount, unknown, annual premium $165 paid by employer; owner: Employer, beneficiary: Employer.

5. *Recommendations*:

(a) Assign policies number 2, 3, 4 and 10, as described above, to Ethel. Ethel is already the beneficiary of these policies and the effect of such an assignment would be to remove the face amount of them from Henry's gross estate. This total would be $120,000 and would save a substantial amount of estate taxes. Indeed, under your existing situation, in the event this recommendation is followed, it is estimated that there would be no estate taxes in the event of your death. Considering your total assets which would go to your family would be something like $1,000,000, this is the ultimate accomplishment so far as estate planning is concerned.

(b) I understand the beneficiary of funds in Henry's account held by ABC Employees Pension and Profit Sharing Plans is the Trustee of Trust B, described hereinabove. I suggest you consider changing this to provide that one-half of funds coming from the plans go to the Marital Trust and one-half to the Family Trust. The reason for this recommendation is not to save taxes but to continue the general scheme whereby approximately one-half of your assets go to Ethel directly or in Trust and the other half go in Trust for the children. Under your present situation, there is $300,000 of insurance that would be payable to your Clifford Trust for your children and in the event my recommendation regarding the transfer of policies above described is taken, Ethel would be the owner and the beneficiary of $320,000 of insurance. My thought is not to overload the assets in favor of the children. This is a value judgment and I would be happy to discuss it further with Bill Boone and Adam McHenry in the event they differ with this recommendation. I would also be happy to discuss it further with you, of course.

(c) In reviewing your Trust Agreement, I noted that the Trustee has the right to encroach on corpus of Trust B, the Family Trust, at any time prior to Ethel's death, as well as after her death "in such amounts as the Trustee may deem necessary in its judgment to provide for the proper support and education (including college and postgraduate education) of the children." No express power is given to encroach the corpus of the Family Trust for Ethel. While the possibility of need to encroach for Ethel's benefit is remote (in view of overall family assets), I recommend you consider amending the Trust Agreement to authorize the Trustee to invade the corpus of the Trust B in the event of actual need on the part of Ethel.

(d) I concur with Bill Boone's recommendation that you not make a voluntary contribution to the ABC Pension or Profit Sharing Plan, whichever one is the one designated for voluntary contributions. I further agree with his suggestion in the event you did want to make some type of tax-sheltered investment that you consider purchasing high quality tax exempt bonds or shares of a mutual fund of tax exempt bonds in the same amount that you would have made for a voluntary contribution to the qualified plan. I like this idea better as it is simpler, and it would be easier for you to handle, and the yield should approximately equal the amount in the qualified plan.

(e) I recommend that Adam McHenry review your major medical insurance coverage for the purpose of avoiding over-lapping coverage, if any, while maintaining high total coverage.

(f) I recommend that Adam McHenry review your disability income coverage to assure that the amount is adequate.

6. *Comments:*

(a) Your estate is in excellent shape. There appear to be ample assets to maintain your family in the event of your death. Please consider the above recommendations and let me know what decision you make. I am sending copies of this letter to Bill Boone and Adam McHenry as we discussed during our last conference with the hope that they will let us have whatever suggestions and ideas that may occur to them after reading this letter.

One last thing I want to say is that it is working with outstanding people like you and Ethel that make practicing my profession much more pleasant. You have my best wishes for next year and always.

Very sincerely,

COMMENT:

1. The above letter contains a thorough review of an estate plan. Letters such as this go a long way in simplifying and clarifying for a client the status of his estate plan.

2. The lawyer has also included specific recommendations for changes in the estate plan and has also listed the reasons for the recommendations.

3. The personalized closing paragraph helps promote warm and cordial lawyer-client relations.

4. All tax consequences should be reviewed in light of current law.

14.
REVIEW OF ESTATE PLAN AND RECOMMENDATIONS FOR ESTATE PLAN

Dear James and Roberta:

This letter is to review your estate plan and make recommendations. The reason for the delay is it seems I never have all of the information in front of me when I have time to make a thorough review. (I still need some information which I will mention later on.)

You have an estimated adjusted gross estate of about $600,000. In addition, there is about $144,000 which would not be in your gross estate but which would be an asset to your family in the event of your death. Therefore, in the event of your death, your total family assets, after payment of debts, would be upwards of $750,000. This is outstanding.

Your Will was executed on June 15, 19___ . The first Codicil was executed on April 8, 19___ .

1. Terms of Will as modified by Codicil.

(a) *Marital Deduction Share*. This is given in trust for the benefit of Roberta. Roberta receives all income from this trust during her lifetime. Trustee may invade principal for Roberta's benefit. Roberta has right to appoint to herself, children, grandchildren or spouses of such descendants, up to one-half of the total property in this trust. Roberta may dispose of remaining principal by her will; otherwise, remaining principal goes to Family Trust.

(b) *Family Trust*. Remainder of estate goes to Family Trust. Income from this trust is appointed by Trustee among Roberta, James Jr., Joan and Peggy. The Trustee has discretion for tax purposes but the will states that the preference is to be given to Roberta. Trustee may encroach principal of the trust for Roberta and the children in the event of need. After Roberta dies and the youngest child is at least twenty-one, this trust is divided into shares. Each child receives one-half of his share at age 25 and the balance at age 30.

(c) *Household Furniture and Furnishings*. These go to Roberta if she survives, otherwise to children. The will recites that the household furniture, furnishings and automobile used in and about the home are already the property of Roberta.

(d) *Trustee*. ABC Bank of Mason City is the Trustee.

(e) *Executor*. Roberta and ABC Bank of Mason City are the co-executors. Evelyn White Jones is an alternate to Roberta and Wanda Sullivan is an alternate to Evelyn.

(f) *Guardian of Minor Children*. Roberta. First alternate is Evelyn, and second alternate is Wanda.

Roberta's will was executed about the time of your will, on October 15, 19___ , but I do not have the date nor the names of the witnesses. Please check this and call it to me so we can make a notation in the file.

1. Terms of Roberta's Will.

(a) *Primary Gift*. Entire estate goes to husband if he survives by thirty days.

(b) *Contingent Gift*. In the event husband does not survive by thirty days, entire estate goes to Family Trust created in husband's will dated October 15, 19___ .

(c) *Executor*. Husband. Alternate executor is Evelyn White Jones, and second alternate is Wanda Sullivan. Next alternate executor is ABC Bank of Mason City.

Life Insurance. James is the insured of the following life insurance:

1. Total face amount of $403,000.

2. Total annual premium $2,329 plus premium for $100,000 ABC Insurance Company policy and premium for $75,000, ABC Insurance Company Policy, which is in the Pension Plan.

3. Ownership of life insurance.

(a) Insured. $328,000.

(b) Pension Plan. $75,000.

4. Beneficiaries of life insurance.

(a) Wife of insured, $178,000.

(b) Testamentary trusts, $225,000.

5. The individual policies are as follows:

(a) ABC Insurance Company, Policy No. 1000, face amount $100,000, owner: James Wells; beneficiary: Trustee of Testamentary Trust (I understand this policy is pledged to secure your home mortgage loan but have been unable to verify it.)

(b) ABC Insurance Company, Policy No. 2000, face amount $50,000, owner: Wells Manufacturing Company; beneficiary: ABC Bank of Mason City as Trustee of Testamentary Trust.

(c) ABC Life Insurance Company, Policy No. 3000, face amount $25,000, owner: James Wells; beneficiary: Roberta Wells.

(d) DEF Life Insurance Company, Policy No. 4,000, face amount $50,000, owner: James Wells; beneficiary: Roberta Wells.

(e) DEF Life Insurance Company, Policy No. 5,000, face amount $5,000, owner: James Wells; beneficiary: Roberta Wells.

(f) GHI Life Insurance Company, Policy No. 6000, face amount $100,000, owner: Trustee of Wells Manufacturing Company Employees Trust; beneficiary: Trustee of Family Trust created in the Will of James Wells.

Recommendations:

1. Assign $100,000 ABC Life Insurance Company Policy to Roberta. (I would recommend putting it in Pension & Profit Sharing Plans except I understand this policy is pledged to secure payment of your home mortgage loan.)

2. Assign $50,000, ABC Life Insurance Company Policy, $25,000, ABC Life Insurance Company Policy and $50,000 DEF Life Insurance Company policy to Trustee of the Wells Manufacturing Company Employees Trust, approximately equally divided between Pension Plan and Profit Sharing Plan, considering the existing $100,000 GHI Life Insurance Policy which is in the Pension Plan. This would facilitate payment of premiums equalling almost $2,000 per year out of before-tax dollars going into the plans rather than from after-tax dollars.

3. Assign $3,000 DEF Life Insurance Company Policy and $75,000 GHI Life Insurance Company Policy to Roberta. This would not effect any tax savings on premiums but would remove the proceeds from James' gross estate. The insurance of which Roberta would become the owner in accordance with this recommendation should have the beneficiary changed to be the Trustee of the Marital Trust created in James' will for her benefit.

Comments:

Your estate is in excellent shape. There appear to be adequate assets to maintain your family in the event of your death. I do suggest considering the above-recommended transfers to minimize income and estate taxes.

James, please call me if you want me to get started on the recommendations I have made. If you think we should get together, let me know.

Very sincerely,

COMMENT:

1. The above letter contains a very thorough review of an estate plan.

2. The lawyer also gives his recommendations for changes in the existing estate.

3. All tax consequences should be reviewed in light of current law.

15.
REVIEW OF ESTATE PLAN FOR CLIENT

Dear Joseph and Elizabeth:

The purpose of this letter is to review your estate plan and to give you a permanent record of your present arrangement.

It appears that in the event of your death, total family assets which would be available to your family would be around $635,000. The total amount of insurance of which you are insured is $400,000. This is outstanding, particularly in view of the fact that your two children, Jimmy and Joan, are getting on up in age, being presently approximately 17 and 15 years old.

The primary vehicle of your estate plan is the will containing trust provisions executed April 12, 19___ . Some of the general terms of your will are as follows:

1. *Marital Deduction Share.* This is given in trust for the benefit of Elizabeth. Elizabeth receives all income from this trust during her lifetime. The Trustee may invade principal for Elizabeth's benefit. Elizabeth has the right to appoint to herself, children, grandchildren or spouses of such descendants any of the property in this trust at any time and from time to time. Elizabeth may dispose of remaining principal by her will; otherwise, the remaining principal goes into the Family Trust.

2. *Family Trust.* The remainder of the estate goes to the Family Trust. Income from this trust is appointed by the Trustee among Elizabeth, Jimmy, and Joan. The Trustee has discretion for tax purposes, but the will states that the preference is to be given to Elizabeth. The Trustee may encroach principal of the trust for Elizabeth and the children in the event of need. After Elizabeth dies and the youngest child is at least twenty-one, this trust is divided into shares. Each child receives one-third of his share at age 21, one-half the balance of his share at age 25, and the balance at age 30.

3. *Household Furniture and Furnishings.* All wearing apparel, jewelry, etc., and other objects of personal use go to Elizabeth if she survives, otherwise to the children. The will recites that the household furniture, furnishings, and automobile used in and about the home are already the property of Elizabeth.

4. *Trustee.* ABC Bank of Garden City is the Trustee.

5. *Executor.* Elizabeth and the ABC Bank of Garden City are the co-executors.

6. *Guardian of Minor Children.* Elizabeth. First alternate is Robert J. Williams and wife, Irene, who are designated to serve as co-guardians, and if one of them does not serve, the other may serve as sole guardian.

The terms of Elizabeth's will are as follows:

1. *Primary Gift.* Entire estate goes to you, Joseph, if you survive by thirty days.

2. *Contingent Gift.* In the event you do not survive by thirty days, the entire estate goes to the Family Trust created in your will dated April 12, 19___ .

3. *Executor.* Joseph. Alternate executor is ABC Bank of Garden City.

One of the principal estate planning assets is a group term policy in the amount of $400,000 maintained under the King Company, Inc., program. I understand the beneficiary on this policy has been changed to be the Trustee named in your Last Will and Testament. This is most important as the scheme of your estate planning will would be largely thwarted if this is not done. In addition to your insurance, you have your account with King Company, Inc., in the approximate amount of $120,000, as well as your U.S. Savings Bonds in the approximate amount of $2,000, your joint accounts at ABC Bank of Garden City and DEF Bank of Newton. There is absolutely no liquidity problem in the event of your death, and practically all the assets of the estate would be cash. This is an enviable position. For example, people whose primary holdings are in real estate, which is not liquid, often run into tremendous liquidity problems on the death of the husband.

General Comments. All in all, your estate is in excellent shape. You have a fine program. I see no liquidity problem. One thing you should jealously guard is the $400,000 term insurance policy with the King Company, Inc. Another tremendous thing you have is the retirement program with the King Company, Inc., under which I understand there is a mandatory retirement at age sixty and under which you would get approximately $2,200 a month.

Joseph, it certainly has been a pleasure getting to know you and Elizabeth. I think having people in Garden City like you is certainly a credit to our community, and I look forward to working with you any time you feel I may be of help. As I stated, I consider it part of preparing your will and your general estate plan setup to answer any questions you may have about it at any time in the future without charge.

Sincerely yours,

COMMENT:

1. Letters such as the above are an excellent way of giving the the client a permanent record of the status of his estate following estate planning services by the lawyer.

2. If desired, the lawyer could suggest that the plan be reviewed annually.

16.
TRANSMITTAL OF ESTATE PLAN SUMMARY AND RECOMMENDATIONS FOR ESTATE PLAN

Dear William and Sharon:

I am enclosing an estate planning summary for your review, information, and any comments you may have. You will note, toward the end of the summary, I have made some recommendations.

I am also enclosing a proposed assignment of your ABC Life Insurance Company Group Policy, held by Drake Furniture Company, Inc., which effects an estate tax savings in the event of William's death. This is in accord with one of the recommendations I have made in the estate planning summary.

After you have reviewed the summary, I would like to get with you to discuss your overall estate plan, together with any additional steps you want me to take.

Very sincerely,

JULY 16, 19___
ESTATE PLAN SUMMARY
William A. Abel
and wife,
Sharon G. Abel

1. Present will of William A. Abel was executed on July 10, 19___ . The first codicil to the will was executed May 12, 19___ ; the second codicil on September 12, 19___ ; and the third codicil on April 15, 19___ .

   (a) Terms of Will as Modified by Codicils:

   (1) Marital Deduction Share. This is given in trust for the benefit of wife. Wife receives all income from this trust during her lifetime. Trustee may invade principal for wife's benefit. Wife has right to appoint to herself up to $5,000 per year. Wife may appoint principal to children, grandchildren, and their spouses. Wife may dispose of remaining principal by her will; otherwise remaining principal goes to Family Trust.

   (2) Family Trust. Remainder of estate goes to Family Trust. Income from this trust is appointed by Trustee among wife, children, grandchildren and their spouses. Trustee may appoint principal to those receiving income. Wife may appoint principal among children, grandchildren and their spouses. Wife has right to appoint to herself each year the greater of $5,000 or five percent (5%) of principal of the Family Trust. Wife may appoint principal in her will to children, grandchildren and their spouses; otherwise to children equally, with share of deceased child going to his children.

   (3) Household Furniture and Furnishings go to wife if she survives, otherwise to children.

   (4) Trustee. ABC National Bank was original Trustee. Change in third codicil to the DEF National Bank of Great Bend, under which DEF National Bank of Great Bend as successor by change of name is presently designated Trustee.

   (5) Executor. Third codicil names wife, Sharon G. Abel, and the DEF Bank of Great Bend as co-executors. DEF National Bank of Great Bend as successor by change of name is a present co-executor to serve with wife.

   (6) Guardian of Minor Children. Wife. First alternate, Roy Mason. Second alternate, Louise Mason. Third alternate, Peter Kennedy.

2. Present will of wife, Sharon G. Abel, was executed July 15, 19___ . The first codicil to this will was executed September 20, 19___ .

(a) Terms of Will as Modified by Codicil:

 (1) Personal Chattels. Jewelry, clothing, household furniture, furnishings, etc., to husband if he survives, otherwise to children.

 (2) Residue. All of remainder of estate to husband if he survives, otherwise to Family Trust created in husband's will.

 (3) Executor. Husband. Alternate executor is by first codicil the ABC Bank of Great Bend, under which the DEF National Bank of Great Bend as successor by change of name is the present alternate executor.

3. The William A. Abel Irrevocable Insurance Trust was created by William A. Abel on March 22, 19___ . ABC Bank was the original Trustee. The DEF National Bank of Great Bend was named successor Trustee by Sharon G. Abel on April 12, 19___ .

 (a) Terms of this Trust:

  (1) During life of wife, income to be distributed among wife, children, grandchildren and their spouses as appointed by Trustee. Trustee may appoint principal to beneficiaries during wife's life. Wife may appoint to children, grandchildren and their spouses during her life and also by her will; otherwise to children and grandchildren after wife's death. Wife may appoint to herself the greater of $5,000 or five percent (5%) of principal each year. Children may receive their shares, after wife's death, when each child is thirty (30) years old.

  (2) Trustee has broad authority to invest and reinvest.

  (3) This trust is irrevocable.

  (4) Wife has right to change Trustee to another bank with trust department, limited in this state to DEF National Bank, GHI National Bank and JKL National Bank.

  (5) By Agreement dated May 20, 19___ , between William A. Abel and DEF National Bank of Great Bend, it is agreed that the life insurance policies insuring William A. Abel, issued by ABC Life Insurance Company, are not a part of this Trust.

4. Clifford Trust No. 1 was created by William A. Abel on March 20, 19___ . Original Trustees are Sharon G. Abel and Joseph B. Jones. By designation dated October 15, 19___ , Gregory J. Summers was named successor independent Trustee to serve with Sharon G. Abel as Co-Trustee.

 (a) Terms of Trust:

  (1) Beneficiaries. Trustee to pay income equally to William A. Abel's four children.

  (2) Trust terminates June 15, 19___ , when principal reverts to William A. Abel.

  (3) William A. Abel may change Trustees provided he appoints independent persons as successor trustees.

5. Clifford Trust No. 2 was created by William A. Abel on March 15, 19___ . R. E. Jones is the Trustee.

 (a) Terms of Trust:

  (1) Children and grandchildren are beneficiaries, and Trustee may pay income to one or more of them within his discretion.

  (2) Principal reverts to William A. Abel March 17, 19___ .

6. Life Insurance. William A. Abel is the insured of the following life insurance:

(a) Total face amount	$1,008,000
(b) Total annual premium	22,884

Effect of minimum deposit is disregarded. Also, ABC Group Life premium paid by Drake Furniture Company, Inc., was not included, but coverage is included.

(c) Ownership of Life Insurance:	
(1) Insured	$50,000
(2) Wife of Insured	500,000
(3) Drake Furniture Company, Inc., Pension Plan	244,000
(4) William A. Abel Insurance Trust	214,000
(d) Beneficiaries of Life Insurance:	
(1) Insured	$50,000
(2) Wife of Insured	500,000
(3) William A. Abel Insurance Trust	214,000
(4) Trustee of Drake Furniture Company, Inc., Pension Trust (this would go to the designated beneficiaries named by William A. Abel)	244,000

(e) The individual policies are as follows:

(1) ABC Life, Policy No. 1000, face amount $50,000; owner Drake Furniture Company, Inc.; beneficiary William A. Abel Insurance Trust. Does not have disability rider.

(2) ABC Life Insurance Company, Policy Numbers 2000, 3000, 4000, face amount (total) $214,000; beneficiary William A. Abel Life Insurance Trust. All policies have waiver of premium for disability.

(3) DEF Life Insurance Company, Policy Numbers 1000, 2000, 3000, face amount (total) $500,000; owner Sharon G. Abel; beneficiary Sharon G. Abel. Policies do not have disability waiver of premium.

(4) GHI Life Insurance Company, Policy No. 1000, face amount $244,000; owner Drake Furniture Company, Inc.; beneficiary Drake Furniture Company, Inc., Pension Plan Trust. Policy does not have disability waiver of premium.

7. Recommendations:

(a) Assign all incidents of ownership in ABC Life Policy No. 1000, face amount $50,000, owned by William A. Abel to wife Sharon G. Abel and have wife named as beneficiary.

(b) Verify that William A. Abel's designated beneficiary for the Drake Furniture Company, Inc., Pension and Profit Sharing Plans and Trust is as follows:

DEF Bank of Great Bend as Trustee of the Family Trust created in the Will of William A. Abel dated July 10, 19___ .

(c) Consider having Sharon G. Abel establish a revocable intervivos trust to be named as beneficiary of the life insurance policies owned by her.

8. Comments: Your estate is in excellent shape. You have minimized both estate taxes and income taxes and have an outstanding estate program for your family.

COMMENT:

1. The above letter is simply a transmittal of the attached estate plan summary.

2. The attached estate plan summary contains recommendations of specific action to be taken in connection with the overall estate plan.

3. The estate plan summary makes a good permanent document which may be referred to in the future in connection with estate planning. Care should be taken that all information contained in the summary is correct so that it can be relied upon with confidence in future reviews of the estate.

4. All tax consequences should be reviewed in light of current law.

17.
TRANSMITTAL OF LETTERS OF ADMINISTRATION

Dear Mrs. Francke:

We have received the Letters of Administration granted to you by Probate Judge Walter Lockhart and enclose the original and five copies for your file and use.

Very sincerely,

COMMENT:

1. The above letter is quite brief. It could be personalized by further information from the lawyer, such as additional steps to be taken in connection with the administration of the estate.

2. The lawyer may desire to send copies of the Letters of Administration to each of the heirs, as well as the administrator.

18.
LEGAL AID SOCIETY'S NOTICE TO CLIENT OF ASSIGNMENT OF ATTORNEY

Dear Mrs. Jones:

The Legal Aid Society has accepted your application for legal services. Your case has been assigned to Dave Wilson for service.

Mr. Wilson will be in contact with you while he is working on your case. All of your future communication with the Legal Aid Society concerning your case should be through Mr. Wilson. Please inform him promptly of any change in your address or telephone number and of any new information you receive concerning your case.

Sincerely,

COMMENT:

1. The lawyer assigned to the case could write to the client promptly, giving her specific thoughts about the case.

19.
TRANSMITTING LETTER FROM ASSOCIATE LAWYER AND REQUEST FOR ADVICE

Dear Mr. Smith:

A copy of a letter is enclosed which we have received from Mr. Clark, the attorney in Rockville.

Please advise us what action you wish to take in this matter. According to Mr. Clark's letter, if we wish to have him file an appearance for us in your behalf, we need to forward him the $200 retainer.

Sincerely yours,

COMMENT:

1. The writer could offer his comments, suggestions, or advice regarding the matter.

20.
TRANSMITTAL OF COPY OF PETITION AND ORDER

Dear Mr. Brown:

We have filed the petition and order in your case and enclose a copy for your records.

We will keep you advised of all developments in your case.

Yours very truly,

COMMENT:

1. The above letter is somewhat brief and impersonal. The lawyer could give the client more information regarding the nature of the petition and order and additional steps or action that will be taken in connection with the matter.

21.
NOTICE OF NEED TO PREPARE ANSWER TO DIVORCE COMPLAINT

> Dear Mrs. Adams:
>
> We understand you are coming in to see us sometime this week and are writing this letter to advise you that, as soon as you do come in, we need to prepare an answer to the complaint previously filed by your husband.
>
> Thank you very much.
>
> Very sincerely,

COMMENT:

1. The letter could outline the information needed to prepare the answer.

2. A status report of the matter could also be given in connection with this letter.

3. Any instructions the lawyer has for the client in connection with the matter should be given with this letter.

22.
NOTICE OF DATE OF TRIAL OF DIVORCE CASE AND REQUEST FOR APPOINTMENT

> Dear Tom:
>
> This is to advise you that the divorce case filed against you by Betty is now set for trial on June 3 at 10:00 a.m. in the Superior Court.
>
> I would appreciate it very much if you would please arrange to see me at your convenience regarding this matter.
>
> Very sincerely,

COMMENT:

1. A date could be set for a conference with the client regarding trial of the case.

2. The lawyer could include a status report of the case.

3. The lawyer could request any suggestions the client may have regarding the trial, such as list of witnesses, documentary evidence, or other matters that may be relevant to the case.

23.
TRANSMITTAL OF DIVORCE DECREE

Dear Mrs. Wilson:

Enclosed is a copy of your final divorce decree. Please note that you may not legally remarry anyone except the person from whom this decree divorces you for a period of sixty (60) days after the date of this decree.

Sincerely,

COMMENT:

1. The letter could also include thoughts on ideas regarding taxes, estate planning, or other problems likely to confront the client following the divorce.

24.
ACCEPTANCE OF POST-DIVORCE MATTER

Dear Mrs. Johnson:

Thank you for your letter dated February 14 in regard to the failure of Mr. Johnson to pay child support in accordance with a previous court decree.

Your original file in connection with this matter is stored in our closed files at another location. We will secure this file, and just as soon as we have had an opportunity to study the matter, we will write you.

We will be happy to do all we can to compel Mr. Johnson to pay support in accordance with the previous court decree.

Sincerely,

COMMENT:

1. Acknowledgment and acceptance of a post-divorce matter received by mail should be made as soon as possible.

2. Additional information required in connection with the matter may be requested in the first letter to the client or in a subsequent letter. Perhaps an information form outlining the detailed information required could be enclosed.

3. It would also be appropriate to describe the fee basis on which the matter is accepted. An estimate of the total fee and other costs involved could also be given and would be helpful to the client. Another approach would be to verify with the client that the fee basis on which the matter is taken is acceptable to him.

4. The original acknowledgment and acceptance of the post-divorce matter could contain a list of the general steps that will be taken in behalf of the client in the matter.

25.
NOTICE TO CLIENT OF INTENTION TO BILL MONTHLY

Dear Frank:

Following our trip to Burlington last Friday, I gave the matter of our billing you for our services in connection with your case some thought.

With this thought in mind, we are sending you a bill covering all of our time down to the present in our files in the amount of $470, and expenses of $130, for a total of $600.

It is my thought that it would be better in the future if I bill you, perhaps, on a monthly basis as time is incurred in the file so you can keep track of exactly where we are.

I am in the process of taking the action which we discussed on the way back from Burlington. We will recall that we need to:

1. Prepare a study guide to errors in the record of your cases.

2. Identify issues in the class action suit in Burlington identical to your claim in U.S. District Court in Boston.

3. Write Leonard Clark what we want him to do.

4. Write the General Accounting Office in connection with your retirement pay problem.

5. Write the Civil Service Commission for a copy of your official records.

We will keep you advised of developments. I also enjoyed very much visiting with you last Friday.

Very sincerely,

COMMENT:

1. Many times lawyers wait in lengthy cases until the trial is over to bill the client. Thought should be given to the matter of the frequency of billing. Often it is better to bill monthly for the purpose of letting the client know the amount of the bill as it accrues, as well as giving him the opportunity to pay it in smaller increments over a period of time.

26.
ACKNOWLEDGING DISCONTINUANCE OF RETAINER

Dear Tom:

I want to thank you for the very kind things you had to say in your letter dated September 12.

In view of the fact that it now appears certain that ABC Corporation will not be able to construct a wood processing plant in Buffalo Falls, we certainly understand the reasons for discontinuing the retainer. We are most grateful for the opportunity of knowing you and representing you in connection with past business in Buffalo Falls, and we will certainly be in a position to represent you should you again have any business there.

I was distressed to learn that Mr. Hunt has been in the hospital undergoing major surgery, but was most pleased to have your report that he is now doing fine, and that you expect him to have a good recovery.

Please give Mr. Hunt our regards and our wishes for a quick and complete recovery.

Also, please express our sincere thanks to Mr. Johnson and the others at ABC Corporation with whom we had the pleasure of working so closely in the past.

Sincerely yours,

COMMENT:

1. Acknowledgment letters such as the above on the occasion of a retainer which was discontinued are important in maintaining warm and friendly lawyer-client relations.

27.
REFUND OF RETAINER FEE

Dear Sarah:

We have received the executed agreement from your ex-husband, Don Jones, his check to you in the sum of $1,240, and his check to us for $850 in payment of our fees. You came by the office and picked up the executed agreement and your check for $1,240.

In accordance with our agreement, we are enclosing a refund of the $100, which you paid us as a retainer.

Best wishes to you and your children.

Very sincerely,

COMMENT:

1. The letter could contain any additional thoughts or ideas the writer has for the client.

28.
ACKNOWLEDGMENT OF PAYMENT OF ACCOUNT

Dear Stanley:

We are glad to acknowledge with many thanks the check for $3,500 in payment of our recent statement. You may be sure it has been a pleasure, as always, to be of service to you and the doctors in these matters. We appreciate, more than we can say, your confidence in us.

Many thanks to you again and with very best personal regards, in which John joins me.

Very sincerely,

COMMENT:

1. The above letter is very thoughtful, warm, and gracious.

2. The lawyer writing this letter has obviously placed the matter of fees on a pleasant and personal basis.

29.
ACKNOWLEDGMENT OF PAYMENT OF ACCOUNT AND SEASON'S GREETINGS

Dear Jimmy:

We want to acknowledge with much appreciation your recent payment of our statement. We are especially grateful for your prompt response.

The end of a year is always a time to reflect upon friendship with your clients and friends. We are pleased that we continue to merit your confidence, and we look forward to being of such further service to you in 19—— as you may deem necessary or desirable.

With best wishes to all our friends at ABC Corporation.

Very sincerely,

COMMENT:

1. The above letter is very thoughtful and personal. Even though the language is general, the message to the client is personalized.

30.
RETAINER AGREEMENT FOR DAMAGE CLAIM

Dear Mr. Adams:

This letter is a written memorandum of the agreement under which we have undertaken to represent you in the prosecution of your claim for damages sustained by you on March 18, 19__ , as the result of an auto accident with Homer Brown in the city of Portland.

We will devote our efforts to this matter for a fee, the amount of which will depend upon the outcome of your claim:

1. If nothing is recovered, you will not be indebted to us for our services.

2. If we are successful, we are to receive 25% of the amount we obtain for you if no suit is filed, and 33⅓% of any amount recovered after suit is filed.

3. Actual costs expended in reaching a settlement, if any, are to be paid by you.

4. Proceeds, if any, coming into our possession by way of settlement or judgment shall be disbursed as follows:
All our costs which have not been reimbursed by you will be deducted; our fees, as set out in the percentage above, will be deducted; and the balance will be paid to you.

5. We may withdraw at any time upon giving reasonable notice.

If this letter correctly states our understanding, will you please so indicate by signing this agreement in the space provided below and return it to us.

Sincerely yours,

Larry Adams

COMMENT:

1. The above letter sets out in detail the exact retainer agreement with the client. Such a letter will often eliminate misunderstanding and controversy.

31.
REJECTION OF PERSONAL INJURY CLAIM

Dear Mrs. Watson:

As I explained in our telephone conversation, we regret very much that it will not be feasible for us to handle your personal injury claim growing out of the injuries sustained by you on November 25 at the Clarkstown Civic Center. We hope that our decision will not discourage you from seeking relief directly from the civic center or its insurer or from contacting other attorneys about this matter.

For your information, we would like to point out that the statute of limitations in our state for filing suit based upon negligence would be one year from the date of your accident. Also, in the event that the civic center is operated directly by the City of Clarkstown rather than by an independent board (a matter that is not within our personal knowledge), then you could be required to file a claim with the Clerk-Treasurer of the City of Clarkstown within six months from the date of the accident. We point out these time limitations for your information because if they are not met, you could be barred from pursuing your claim.

We sincerely appreciate your contacting us about this matter, and we certainly hope that you continue to make progress in recovering from your injuries.

Very truly yours,

COMMENT:

1. The above letter is a good example of combining rejection of a claim with thoughtful comments, advice, and observations regarding the claim.

32.

TRANSMITTAL OF LETTERS AND STATUS REPORT OF EFFORT TO ASCERTAIN WHETHER OPPOSING PARTY OWNS REAL ESTATE

Dear Mr. Wilson:

Enclosed for your records are copies of the response we have received from the probate offices of Madison, Washington, and Jefferson counties regarding a search of their records to determine if Henry Brown owned any land in their respective counties. Apparently Mr. Brown owns approximately 320 acres of land in Washington County, as shown on the enclosed deeds.

I have an appointment to meet with Mr. Don Johnson, the ABC Insurance Company adjustor, on March 12 and will contact you concerning the outcome of that meeting.

Yours truly,

COMMENT:

1. The above letter is an example of a transmittal letter being used to convey a status report of the matter. Status reports are strongly recommended. Clients do not like to be left in the dark. Letters such as this contribute greatly to keeping the client well informed.

33.
NOTICE OF FILING SUIT

Dear Mr. Kirby:

Your suit against Leonard Clark was filed in the Superior Court on April 26 and fell before Judge Adams. In all probability it will be set for trial within six months to one year. Unfortunately, we have no control over the setting of trial dates.

As a reminder, please continue to keep all medical bills, receipts, and an accurate record of all expenses incurred by you as a result of the accident. We can only recover those expenses which we can prove. Be sure to advise us if you have a change of address, for we may have to contact you in the interim.

We will keep you informed of all important matters and advise you of important developments in your case.

Very sincerely,

COMMENT:

1. It is a good idea to notify your client when suit has been filed and keep him advised of the status of the matter until concluded.

2. Anything you want the client to do during the progress of the suit or to assist in connection with the suit should be outlined either in the notice of filing suit or in a subsequent letter.

3. The letter may state that the client is welcome to call at any time regarding the matter.

4. Any other instructions you have for the client during the progress of his suit could be given in this letter.

5. The letter could also outline the various steps that will be taken in the suit, or an information form could be enclosed with it describing the procedure to be followed in the suit filed for the client.

34.
NOTICE OF INTERROGATORIES AND REQUEST TO PREPARE ANSWERS

Dear Mr. Watson:

We have received a set of questions to be answered by you. These questions have been prepared by the defense attorney and constitute what we call discovery interrogatories. These written interrogatories are provided for by state law, and we must answer them within sixty days; therefore, time is a factor since we must abide by this law.

The defense attorneys ask these questions in all cases. This is routine in order that the attorneys may learn something about you and your case. As your counsel, we, of course, prepare similar questions, but of a different nature, to the defendants, and they must answer them in the same manner.

You will note that some of the information called for is of a personal nature, and other questions are directed more specifically to your case. I suggest that you take the time necessary to go through each question and write down the answer on a plain piece of paper. Please write legibly so your answers can be understood by us. When you have answered all of the questions, please forward your answers to us so we can go over them, make necessary deletions or additions, and put the answers in the proper form to be filed with the court.

Every effort should be made to give a full and complete answer to every question. If, upon receipt of your answers, we feel certain information should not be given or should be given in different form, we will make the necessary changes in preparing the final form.

It is vital to your case that each question be answered as completely and as honestly as possible. Be especially careful not to leave out a prior hospitalization, illness, accident, or injury. This is an important part of your lawsuit and will be a matter of record with the court.

Please try to answer all of the questions even though you may have furnished us with information regarding some of the questions previously.

Sincerely yours,

COMMENT:

1. The above letter giving notice of interrogatories and requesting the client to prepare answers could give a date by which the client should prepare the answers and furnish them to the attorney.

2. The letter could also request the client to list any questions he would like his attorneys to ask the opposing parties.

3. In the event the client has any questions or experiences difficulty in answering any of the interrogatories, the letter could state that he should call the lawyer's secretary and discuss the matter. In the event they are unable to resolve the problem, it should be brought to the attention of the lawyer.

35.
NOTICE OF ORDER TO PRODUCE RECORDS

Dear Mrs. Lewis:

This is to advise you the court has entered an order requiring you to produce your income tax returns for the years 19___ and 19___ .

The court has also entered an order requiring you to produce all of the medical bills, hospital bills, receipts for drugs, automobile estimates or repair bills, and any and all other bills, statements, or receipts for money paid out by you or owed by you as a result of your accident.

Please send us your income tax returns and any bills and receipts which you have not already sent as soon as possible since the court has required these documents to be produced within a very limited time.

Very truly yours,

COMMENT:

1. The letter could give a date by which the lawyer wants the client to produce the income tax returns and other records. It could also list the date set by the court for the production of such records or the appropriate time allowed by law.

2. This letter could also request the client's advice whether there are any documents, photographs, statements, or other records in the possession of the opposing party, of which he has knowledge.

36.
NOTICE OF DEPOSITION

Dear Mr. Jones:

This is to advise you that the attorneys for the insurance company have scheduled a deposition for your son, David, in the office of Ford, Lewis, and Adams, P.A., at 3:00 p.m. on December 12.

I would appreciate it very much if you would please have him come by our office at 1:00 p.m. on the same date so we will have an opportunity to go over the matter prior to the taking of the deposition.

Sincerely,

COMMENT:

1. The notice of deposition to a client might also discuss and describe briefly the purpose of a deposition.

2. An information sheet describing the deposition procedure and pointers to the client on how to act at his deposition would be helpful.

3. The client could be invited to call or come in for a conference prior to the deposition to go over the matter well ahead of time.

37.
NOTICE TO CLIENT OF DATE OF DEPOSITION AND ADVICE
FOR PREPARATION FOR DEPOSITION

Dear Alberta:

A deposition has been scheduled in your case for the 30th day of April, 19—, at 10:00 a.m. at the following address:

> Ford, Lewis and Adams, P.A.
> 123 Main Street
> Mason City, Ohio

The defendant has the right to take your deposition, which is your sworn testimony concerning the facts of this case.

It is quite important that you have all background data and wage and medical evidence ready for the deposition. To this effect, you should accumulate your prior income tax returns, employee's earnings records in the form of check stubs or withholding statements, and all paid and unpaid medical bills and expenses including pharmacy expenses, car repair estimates and bills, receipts for car rental, etc.

If this information has not been previously forwarded to this office, you should bring it with you to your predeposition conference.

I will want to go over your testimony with you prior to this proceeding. For this purpose, I have scheduled an appointment for you on the 29th day of April, 19—, at 9:00 a.m., at our office.

Unless I hear from you to the contrary, I shall see you then. At that time, I shall further explain to you the nature of this proceeding.

Very sincerely,

COMMENT:

1. The above letter explains to the client matters the client should consider and review prior to giving his deposition.

2. It is a good idea, as mentioned in the above letter, for the lawyer to review the client's testimony prior to the client's deposition.

38.
NOTICE TO CLIENT OF DATE OF DEPOSITION WITH INSTRUCTIONS FOR DEPOSITION

Dear Stan:

At 3:00 p.m. on September 21 at the offices of Ford, Lewis and Adams, P.A., 123 Main Street, Mason City, Ohio, the opposing attorney will take your deposition.

This is an informal proceeding in the attorney's office where you are questioned under oath in the presence of a court reporter. You will have an opportunity to read the questions and anwers and make any changes that are required before you sign them.

While the deposition is a pretty informal proceeding, it is also a good opportunity to impress the defendants with your personality and potential effectiveness as a witness.

Thus, your attitude and appearance become important.

With this in mind, it becomes very important for you to be *friendly*. If the defense attorney is sarcastic in some of his questions, you must stay friendly. Say everything in a nice way. It's a classic situation of turning the other cheek. It will give you practice in applying a proper approach to testimony in court, assuming the case goes that far.

The most important part of the deposition is to properly answer questions. The most important thing is your answer.

At the trial we may want to add some surrounding facts to some of your answers, but at the deposition we don't want to tell the other side anything more than we must. In other words, be pleasant, answer the questions, but be *brief*.

Remember this principle: There are several ways to get across our message, but every answer puts up a hurdle, an obstacle in our path. Every answer that you give at this deposition is like a building block. It may be helpful, but if it isn't, it's still there for all time. That means that we must take into account every answer that you have given at the deposition. Answers are restrictive. This has nothing to do with truth, honesty, or anything else. At all times, your answers should be truthful, but at the same time, there is no need to volunteer additional embellishments.

It's a very simple rule! Answer *truthfully*, *briefly*, and *pleasantly*. Don't lose your temper. Don't say, "I already answered that thing seven times!" Answer it eight times. Let me do the objecting whenever I feel like objecting, but don't you take it upon yourself to "set that guy straight." We'll let the jury do that, and in the meantime, if he finds that he can't get you to be unpleasant, he will summarize his report on the deposition by summarizing the facts and adding something very helpful, such as this: "This plaintiff makes a very excellent witness. Won't rattle and will make a good impression on the jury."

Just answer the questions truthfully. The attorney has studied them out and knows them, and he knows where he wants you to go. He can't lead an honest person anywhere.

Don't let anybody *shame you* into a different answer than fits your recollection of the facts. Don't let anybody ridicule you into it or bully you into it. What you remember, you remember. What you can't remember, you can't remember.

Your primary obligation is to talk about *what happened* and *how it happened*, not how you related it to the doctor or policeman or how they wrote it down.

Under no circumstances should you attempt to evade what seems to be a harmful question. When in doubt, answer truthfully and honestly. We have nothing to be afraid of in this case and nothing to hide, and so you let *me* worry about what is relevant and what is irrelevant.

Wait until the question has been asked before you answer it. Make sure you understand it before you answer it.

The warmth of your relationship with your attorney will carry favorable connotations throughout the courtroom. This deposition proceeding can be used as a dress rehearsal for an ultimate courtroom appearance.

Within two days of receipt of this letter, will you please contact my secretary for the purpose of determining whether or not I want to schedule an appointment with you before the deposition.

If I don't have some of the records that I've asked for previously, please get them for me. Also obtain for me an up-to-date list of your complaints. Examples speak louder than generalized descriptions. Try to think of some that will illustrate some of your complaints. Things such as "can't sleep so well" are okay, but it would be a much better illustration of the same point to say, "I was always asleep before Johnny Carson came on; now I watch the late show. I have to get up at 4:35 a.m. I couldn't believe that it was that early, so I went in and turned on the light. There was the clock, and it woke up my spouse," etc., etc.

If you have any questions about this procedure, you may ask me or associate counsel in private just before the deposition.

Sincerely yours,

COMMENT:

1. The above letter is thorough and effective in instructing the client regarding his deposition. It is a good idea to give detailed instructions in written form prior to the deposition so the client will have the opportunity to thoroughly familiarize himself with the procedure of a deposition.

39.

NOTICE OF DEPOSITION WITH ENCLOSURE EXPLAINING DEPOSITION

Dear Mrs. Ford:

We have been notified by the attorneys representing the defendant that they wish to take your deposition at 123 Main Street at 10:00 a.m. on January 18.

Upon receipt of this letter, please call my secretary, Joan Adams, so we may be assured of your presence. At that time she will arrange a conference so I can go over with you some of the facts and issues of your case which will be covered on this deposition.

For your convenience and information, I am enclosing a brief explanation of the deposition procedure. Please read this carefully prior to coming to our office for your conference.

Very sincerely,

COMMENT:

1. The lawyer might consider, in this letter, whether he would like to go over the matter with the client on a date prior to the deposition or on the date of the deposition. In involved cases it would be a good idea to go over the matter on a separate date.

2. The client could be requested to prepare answers to questions he thinks will be asked at the deposition, especially questions he anticipates are important.

3. In addition, the client could be asked for the names of any other witnesses or parties whose depositions he feels should be taken in his behalf.

DEPOSITION

A deposition is simply the taking of one's statement under oath when an attorney asks questions and the witness answers them. It is an informal procedure usually taking place either in our office or in the office of the attorney representing the defendant, before a court reporter who takes down the testimony and later transcribes it for the use of the parties and the court. It generally requires approximately one hour to take a deposition such as this. You will be accompanied by an attorney from our office.

Under our court rules, either side has the right to take the testimony of the opposing party by deposition.

There are two extremely important things to remember in connection with the giving of a deposition.

1. TELL THE TRUTH. The one most completely devastating thing that can happen in your case is for you to tell an untruth regarding some element of your case. You may be assured that the defense will investigate you THOROUGHLY and, in fact, probably already knows more about your past than you yourself recall. We, as your attorneys, want you to tell the truth. We cannot be responsible for the outcome of your case if you do not.

2. BE BRIEF. Listen to each question carefully, answer it completely and honestly, but do not overanswer it. That is, do not elaborate unless some elaboration is necessary to clarify your answer. You can hurt your case by being too talkative.

Basically, the questions you will be asked will relate to the following general subjects.

1. THE ACCIDENT. We will go over this with you thoroughly during the conference scheduled in our office before the deposition.

2. INJURIES. Starting at the accident and bringing you up to the present time, the opposing attorney will ask you to tell him all you know about the injuries you received as a result of this accident. He will also want to know your present complaints and what you are unable to do at present because of your injuries, but which you were able to do before the accident.

3. LOSS OF SALARY. We hope you have kept an accurate record of the dates and time, if any, which you have lost from your job. Even if you have been paid by your employer, this information is still important. The defense is entitled to obtain copies of your income tax returns for the past three years. Be sure your testimony regarding lost income will be supported by those returns. You will also be asked about other jobs you have held and any special technical training you have received.

4. PRIOR MEDICAL HISTORY. It is of utmost importance that this information be answered completely and accurately. You will be asked to relate all illnesses, accidents in which you suffered personal injury, diseases, operations, etc., which were of any consequence whatsoever, together with the names of doctors who have treated you in the past and hospitals or clinics where you have received treatment.

5. EXPENSES. You will be asked to relate all additional expense you have incurred as a result of your injuries. This refers, in addition to loss of salary and the expense of doctors and hospital bills, to medicine, extra household help, nursing services, transportation expense incidental to medical treatment, etc. It will be most helpful if you have kept or will prepare an accurate record of these.

In addition to the foregoing, the following information regarding depositions should be of help to you.

1. Do not guess at the answer to any question. It is perfectly proper to answer that you "don't know" or "can't remember" as long as that is the truth. Be especially careful where the question deals with time, speed or distance. You may estimate these if you are able, but do not speculate or guess at the answer.

2. Be courteous and attentive to the opposing attorney. Under no circumstances should you at any time get mad or lose your temper. Your attorney is there to protect you and will not allow you to be mistreated. It is to your best interest to make a good impression on the other attorney.

3. Do not look to your attorney for help in answering the questions. The opposing attorneys are interested only in what you know. Your attorney will object if you are asked an improper question, and then you will follow his instructions. Also, do not testify to what someone has told you unless you are asked specifically about conversations with others.

4. Don't play doctor. Don't use medical terminology in explaining your injuries.

5. Don't be too positive in answering unless you are positive.

6. Listen to each question carefully, and do not answer the question until you are sure it is finished.

7. Voice your answer clearly so the court reporter will have no difficulty in recording it.

8. Do not be afraid to admit that you have discussed your case with your attorney. It is perfectly proper to do so.

After you have read the foregoing carefully, write down any questions you wish to have answered by your attorney, and he will be happy to do so.

40.
NOTICE TO CLIENT OF EXAMINATION BY DOCTOR

Dear Mrs. Hunter:

We have set up an appointment for you to be examined by Dr. Wallace Brown at 11:00 a.m. on August 23, at 224 Second Avenue.

Please make sure that you keep this appointment. Dr. Brown will give you a complete examination and write a report informing us of your condition.

If you cannot keep the appointment, please inform us so that I can make alternative arrangements with the doctor.

Sincerely yours,

COMMENT:

1. If desired, the above letter might contain comments regarding the importance of the examination or suggestions to the client in connection with the examination, such as not exaggerating his injuries and to cooperate fully with the examining doctor.

41.
NOTICE OF EXAMINATION BY COURT-APPOINTED DOCTOR
WITH ENCLOSURE EXPLAINING PROCEDURE

Dear Mr. Wilson:

The defense attorneys have arranged an appointment for you to be examined by the court-appointed physician, Dr. Richard Ford, on May 12 at 3:00 p.m. at his office, which is located at the Medical Arts Building, 224 Spring Street.

I am enclosing a brief explanation of the examination procedure employed by the insurance companies. Please read this carefully before your examination, and call us if you have any questions.

Yours very truly,

COMMENT:

1. The lawyer might consider a conference with the client prior to the examination by the court-appointed physician for the purpose of thoroughly reviewing the matter.

2. The lawyer might, as an alternative, consider asking the client whether he feels a conference would be helpful to him prior to being examined by the court-appointed physician.

3. The letter could also invite the client to advise the lawyer if he feels any particular problems might arise in connection with the examination by the court-appointed physician. Then, if necessary, a conference could be set for further discussion and review prior to the examination.

COURT-APPOINTED DOCTOR EXAMINATION

It is going to be necessary for you to go to a doctor or doctors designated by the court prior to your trial. Under the law the defendant in the lawsuit has the right to ask the court to appoint one or more doctors to examine a person who has claimed he was injured. The judge picks a doctor who he feels is qualified in a particular field and enters an order that you should appear before this doctor and be examined by him. The cost of this examination is paid by the insurance company in the first instance, but later it will be paid by whoever loses the lawsuit. The judge picks a doctor he feels is completely impartial and does not allow the insurance company to name the particular doctor.

After the examination is finished, this doctor will file a written report with the lawyers for the insurance company. We will not get a copy of that report from the doctor. The only way that we will know what this doctor thinks of your condition is to give to the other side all of the medical reports that we had from your treating doctors. This is a decision for your lawyer to make, and the circumstances are different in each case. The court-appointed doctor may testify in the event your case is tried, and we can call him as a witness for our side, or the defendant can call him as a witness for his side.

The usual procedure in the examination is for the nurse or secretary or the doctor himself to take a history from you concerning the accident. You should tell him how the accident happened. His interest in the accident is, or should be, what force or blow or trauma you received and whether or not the accident would justify the injuries that you claim. You should tell him how the accident happened but avoid going into detail with him or anyone else. For instance, there is no reason to discuss the witnesses or distances or time, etc. If any problem arises over this, tell the doctor that you have been instructed by your attorney to discuss the accident with no one, and ask him to get this information from us. By this suggestion we do not mean that you should not tell him briefly how the accident occurred.

You will also be asked at this examination about your present injuries, complaints and aches. Before going to this examination, be sure to spend some time thinking about this so that you can give a complete list of everything that is wrong with you. Take your time and make sure that he is told about everything. Even if he should interrupt you to discuss one particular phase of your injury, be sure to return to your other injuries so that he does know about them. It goes without saying that you should not exaggerate anything, but at the same time be sure that you don't leave out anything. A jury would be at a loss to understand why you did not tell the doctor about a serious complaint.

You should cooperate fully with the doctor and be sure that you are extremely courteous to him. Do not treat him as a person against your side because it may very well be that his opinion will be favorable to you. Be friendly with him but do not volunteer any information that he does not ask you for. Avoid any talk about whether your case will be settled or tried or how much money is involved or anything like that. Merely tell him that your lawyer has not told you.

You should also cooperate with the doctor in the event he wants any x-rays or wants to take your blood pressure or things such as this. You have a right, however, to refrain from any painful procedures such as injecting needles, etc. He, of course, will ask you to go through various motions to see if they are painful, and you should cooperate with him on this.

In the event that the doctor tells you anything about your condition or expresses any opinion whatsoever about the cause of your injury or what the future holds for you, then be certain to sit down and write your attorney a letter in detail about what the doctor said. Don't try to pass this information over the telephone; it is too important, and you should take the time to write a letter immediately about his opinion.

Do not try to tell the doctor about the diagnoses of your treating doctor. He can get this information in other ways.

Be sure to make a full disclosure about any prior accidents or injuries or illnesses that you have had. Do not assume that the doctor will get information from your other medical records. He is starting a complete new file on you, and you must be sure to answer each question as if it is being asked of you for the first time. Do not assume he has any information at all. He will, however, be entitled to check your hospital records and request other information that he might need, such as prior x-rays, etc.

The human equation is important in all our dealings every day. Please do your best to protect your rights, but at the same time be friendly with the doctor.

42.

**NOTICE TO CLIENT OF MEDICAL EXAMINATION REQUESTED
BY OPPOSING PARTY**

Dear Ethel:

The defendant has requested that you submit to an examination by the insurance company's doctor.

The doctor will take a history from you concerning the accident, your injuries and complaints, etc. The history is one of the most significant things in connection with this examination. It is therefore extremely important that you write out that history and submit it to me. Get this to me immediately so that I can review it and make any necessary suggestions.

The defendants have made an appointment for you with the following doctor:

> Dr. Henry Jones
> Medical Arts Building
> 224 Spring Street

The appointment is currently scheduled for 10:00 a.m., June 3.

Please telephone the doctor and confirm this appointment as soon as you receive this letter. If they do not have you scheduled for an appointment, let us know.

Thank you for your cooperation.

Sincerely yours,

COMMENT:

1. The lawyer may prefer to make an appointment with the client to take the history rather than have the client write the history as suggested in the above letter.

43.
NOTICE OF DATE OF PRELIMINARY HEARING AND
STATUS REPORT

Dear Mr. Kirby:

The hearing in your case is set for May 18, at 9:00 a.m. before Judge Watson. Please be in our office at 8:00 a.m. on that date.

Please call me if you have any questions.

Very sincerely,

COMMENT:

1. The writer could make some specific observations or comments regarding the case.

2. The writer could outline additional steps he intends to take in connection with the matter.

44.
NOTICE OF DATE OF TRIAL AND REQUEST FOR APPOINTMENT

Dear Mr. Smith:

This is to advise you the above-referenced case is now set for trial in the District Court on April 26.

There is a good likelihood that it will not be tried at this time since it is pretty far down on the docket.

However, prior to that date I would appreciate it very much if you would please contact me so that we will have an opportunity to prepare the defense and necessary pleadings in the case.

Thanks very much.

Sincerely yours,

COMMENT:

1. The notice of date of trial and request for appointment could suggest the date for appointment or could actually set a date for appointment.

2. The lawyer could include a status report of the case.

3. The lawyer should also review the case to see whether all discovery has been made or scheduled prior to the date of trial.

45.
NOTICE OF DATE OF TRIAL AND REQUEST FOR APPOINTMENT

Dear Mrs. Jones:

This is to advise you that the suit we filed in your behalf against Wallace Ford in connection with the automobile accident is now set for trial on the docket of Judge Hunt for March 5.

However, the case is fairly far down the docket, and there is a chance that it will not be tried. At the same time it is necessary for us to prepare for trial in the event it is tried.

I would appreciate it very much if you will please arrange for us to get together at your earliest convenience to go over the matter and prepare our evidence in connection with the trial of this case.

Thanks very much.

Very sincerely,

COMMENT:

1. The letter could set a specific date for the conference to prepare for trial.

2. The letter could also request the client to give any information or suggestions he has regarding trial of the case, such as list of witnesses, documentary evidence, and specific questions for witnesses.

46.
NOTICE OF DATE OF TRIAL

Dear Frank:

Please be advised that the court, at a recent calling of the docket, set the above-styled case for trial on the date indicated above.

We will be in contact with you shortly to discuss trial preparation in your case. If you have any questions, please contact our office. Meanwhile, if we need any additional information to complete our trial preparation, we will contact you.

Sincerely,

COMMENT:

1. It is important to notify the client of the date of trial as soon as possible.

47.
NOTICE OF DATE OF TRIAL AND INSTRUCTIONS FOR
TRIAL PREPARATION

Dear Richard:

This letter will serve to advise you that your trial has been set for the week of October 12, with a pretrial conference scheduled for September 8.

The pretrial conference is a time set aside by the judge to allow the lawyers for the respective parties to review, with the court, any and all exhibits, witnesses, and issues which may come up at the time of your trial. Although your presence will not be required at the pretrial, please do the following to assist our office in protecting your interests:

1. Check with my secretary at least ten days before the pretrial conference to be sure that we have the correct names and addresses of all the doctors you have seen due to your accident *and* the correct amount of their bills.

2. In the event that you have not been back to your treating doctors within the past several months, please arrange an appointment for an evaluation. At the time you go for the examination, make an appointment for a final evaluation approximately three to four weeks before the trial week. In the event you have any questions regarding this, or which doctors you should see, please call us.

3. Provide our office with any medical appliances you have been required to use, such as neck braces, collars, corsets, etc., since these have to be exhibited to the judge at the pretrial.

4. If you have any items in the form of exhibits, such as photographs you have taken reflecting the damage to your automobile, the injuries you received, or of the scene of the accident, these should also be brought to our office at least ten days prior to the pretrial conference.

5. Please provide my secretary with the names and addresses of at least three persons who will be able to testify at the trial as to the condition of your health before the accident, the effect of the accident upon your health, and the limitations placed on your daily activities by the accident. These persons preferably should not be relatives. Also, the more these people see you, the better it is from the standpoint of their ultimate opinion as to the effect the accident has had upon your health and well-being.

6. Any and all expenses over and above your medical expenses should also be verified with my secretary at least ten days prior to the pretrial. These bills include, but are not limited to, such things as car rental bills, property damage bills, drug bills, medical appliances, transportation costs, domestic help, etc.

7. If you have lost time from your work, under state law, even though you were compensated gratuitously by your employer, we can still claim your lost wages. Therefore, obtain the name and address of the payroll master or some person in authority at your place of business who will testify as to your gross wages at the time of the accident, your time off from work due to the accident, that your status with the company was satisfactory prior to the occurrence of the accident, and that you

would have had a job during this period of time if you had been able to work. This person's name and address should also be supplied to our office prior to the pretrial conference.

Thank you for your cooperation and assistance in providing us with the above items, and we trust that you will give this matter your immediate attention.

Very sincerely,

COMMENT:

1. The above letter could also ask the client for suggestions regarding trial of the case, such as list of witnesses, documentary evidence, or other matters in the case.

2. There should be some positive checks to verify that the client has observed the instructions for trial preparation, such as his advising the lawyer's secretary when the appointment for medical examination and evaluation is made. Also set out a specific date by which photographs, medical bills, and other items need to be taken care of.

48.

NOTICE OF DATE OF TRIAL AND THAT LAWYER WILL NOT APPEAR AT TRIAL

Dear Mr. Adams:

Your case has been set for trial on November 8 at 9:00 a.m. in Circuit Court. This is an earlier trial date than we anticipated.

Please be advised we will not be present at the trial. If you are not represented at this time, the case will be dismissed. Let us know if you want us to appear or help you make other arrangements.

Sincerely yours,

COMMENT:

1. The writer could give his opinion of the course of action the reader should take in connection with the matter. The writer could detail the steps he could take in the client's behalf.

49.

NOTICE OF DATE OF TRIAL AND REQUEST FOR APPOINTMENT

Dear Mrs. Payne:

I am enclosing the latest notice we have received, which sets your case for trial at 9:00 a.m. on January 18.

We need to get together to discuss your case prior to the trial date. Accordingly, I have scheduled an appointment for you on January 14 at 3:00 p.m. If this time is not convenient, please call my secretary, Joan Adams, and reschedule a time mutually convenient.

I look forward to seeing you and going over your case with you.

Sincerely,

COMMENT:

1. The above letter could leave the date of appointment open until the client calls.

2. The writer could make some specific comment regarding the case.

50.
NOTICE OF DATE OF TRIAL AND REQUEST FOR CONFERENCE

Dear Paul:

Your case is set for trial at 9:00 a.m. on May 4 before Judge Kirby. We need to get together before this date to discuss your case. Accordingly, I have scheduled an appointment for you at 3:00 p.m. on April 27. If this time is not convenient, please call my secretary, Joan Adams, and reschedule a time which is mutually convenient.

Also enclosed is a copy of Mr. Johnson's appraisal on the house located at 300 Scenic Drive, Omaha, Nebraska.

Paul, I look forward to seeing you and going over your case with you.

Very sincerely,

COMMENT:

1. The writer could comment on the case or make specific suggestions to the client regarding preparation for trial.

51.
NOTICE OF DATE OF TRIAL AND REQUEST FOR CONFERENCE BEFORE TRIAL

Dear Henry:

Please be advised that your case has been set for March 27, 19___ , at 10:00 a.m.

Please come to our office at 8:30 a.m. so we can discuss your case, and I will accompany you to court.

Thank you very much.

Sincerely,

COMMENT:

1. The writer might include additional comments regarding the case or things the reader should do to prepare for trial.

2. The writer could make some observations regarding the trial.

52.
INFORMATION TO CLIENT OF ATTORNEY'S PROFESSIONAL
RESPONSIBILITY IN RESIDENTIAL REAL ESTATE
TRANSACTION AND POSSIBLE CONFLICT OF INTEREST

Dear Mr. Clark:

I am pleased you have asked me to represent you in connection with the purchase of your new home. Before undertaking to act as your attorney, however, I must ask you to consider the guidelines established by the Supreme Court of Delaware regarding every attorney's professional responsibility in residential real estate transactions.

Before accepting representation of a buyer or mortgagor of residential property (including condominiums under the Unit Property Act of the State of Delaware), upon referral by the seller, lender, real estate agent, or other person having an interest in the transaction, it is the ethical duty of a lawyer to inform the buyer or mortgagor in writing at the earliest practicable time:

> 1. That the buyer or mortgagor has the absolute right (regardless of any preference that the seller, real estate agent, lender, or other person may have and regardless of who is to pay attorney's fees) to retain a lawyer of his own choice to represent him throughout the transaction, including the examination and certification of title, the preparation of documents, and the holding of settlement; and

> 2. As to the identity of any other party having an interest in the transaction whom the lawyer may represent, including a statement that such other representation may be possibly conflicting and may adversely affect the exercise of the lawyer's professional judgment on behalf of the buyer or mortgagor in case of a dispute between the parties. For the purpose of this guideline, a lawyer shall be deemed to have a "possibly conflicting" representation if he represents the seller or has represented the seller on a continuing basis in the past; if he represents the real estate agent or has represented the real estate agent on a continuing basis in the past; or if he represents the lender or has represented the lender on a continuing basis in the past.

By quoting from the Supreme Court's guidelines, I want to make certain you understand that you are free to retain as your attorney whomever you may choose, regardless of any suggestion offered by your real estate agent, lender, or any other interested person. I also want to make certain you understand the significance of the fact that our law firm has represented the ABC Real Estate Agency on a continuing basis in the past. As stated by the Supreme Court, our representation of the real estate agent could possibly conflict with my representation of you, which in turn could adversely affect the exercise of my professional judgment on your behalf.

This means, among other things, that if a dispute were to arise between you and ABC Real Estate Agency or one of its sales representatives (perhaps involving an oral representation about the home which you have purchased), I would not be able to represent you against ABC Real Estate Agency because it has been a client of our firm for many years. At the same time, our loyalty to you would preclude us from defending ABC Real Estate Agency against your complaint.

The foregoing discussion is not intended to imply for a moment that I, or any member of our firm or of ABC Real Estate Agency, would deliberately engage in any unethical conduct. I would decline to act as your attorney if I felt unable to represent you in accordance with the highest standards of professional conduct. But these same standards require me to be certain that you at least know about the existence of the possibilities for a conflict of interest, and that with such awareness you confirm your request that I proceed with the settlement. Your signing and returning the enclosed copy of this letter will give me the assurance which I need.

In the meantime, to avoid delay, and without obligation on your part, I shall assume responsibility for any matter which may require immediate attention. Please let me hear from you promptly.

Very truly yours,

COMMENT:

1. The above letter indicates to the client the high regard the writer has for him and his rights in connection with the real estate transaction.

53.

TRANSMITTAL OF COPY OF SBA LOAN APPLICATION

Dear Mr. Payne:

We are enclosing a copy of your SBA loan application for your file. Also enclosed are the original deeds which you gave to me for our use in preparing the SBA loan application.

We appreciate the opportunity to be of service to you in this matter. We will advise you of all developments.

Very sincerely,

COMMENT:

1. The writer could outline additional steps he will take in connection with the matter.

2. The writer could also outline the expected time for action on the application and additional steps that need to be taken regarding it.

54.
NOTICE TO CLIENT TO ASSESS PROPERTY FOR TAXES

Dear Mr. Jones:

Between October 1 and December 31 of each year, including this year, you must assess the property for taxes. The Tax Assessor's Office is located in the Jefferson County Courthouse.

Your recorded deed will be returned to you by the Probate Office in approximately three weeks, after it has been indexed and microfilmed.

You should take your deed with you when you assess the property during the last three months of this year. If you are living in a house located on the property, you should claim your homestead exemption.

You should also check with the Tax Collector's Office in the Jefferson County Courthouse and pay the ad valorem taxes between October 1 and December 31 of each year. However, if you have a VA or FHA mortgage on your property, no taxes will be due at this time because you will have paid your taxes in the escrow each month through the mortgage company.

If you fail to assess the property between October 1 and December 31, a penalty may be assessed against you, and you will lose your homestead exemption.

Sincerely yours,

COMMENT:

1. The above letter is thoughtful. The attorney is advising the client, who has just purchased real property, of the system of ad valorem taxation prevailing in the local area.

2. The above letter would ordinarily be sent to a client at the closing of a real estate transaction. It is sent for the client's further information regarding real property taxes and also to advise him when the recorded deed will probably be returned to him.

55.
TRANSMITTAL OF RELEASE OF MORTGAGE AFTER
BEING RECORDED

Dear Mr. Hunter:

Enclosed is a Release of Mortgage from Leonard Adams and wife to Frank Johnson, dated September 12, 19___ , recorded on September 13, 19___ , in Book 222 at Page 127 of the Release Records of Lincoln County.

Best wishes to you.

Sincerely yours,

COMMENT:

1. The above letter is a standard letter of transmittal.

56.
LETTER TRANSMITTING TRUST FUNDS TO CLIENT

Dear Sarah:

We are enclosing our check to you in the amount of $3,000 for the month of December.

Sarah, I hope you had a very nice Christmas. Best wishes for the New Year.

Very sincerely,

COMMENT:

1. The above letter could include some specific comment of interest to the reader or observation regarding the matter.

57.
TRANSMITTAL OF DRAFTS OF PROFIT SHARING PLAN, TRUST AND RELATED DOCUMENTS

Dear Mr. Humphrey:

I am enclosing drafts of a proposed Profit Sharing Plan, Trust, and other related documents for ABC Corporation.

I am also sending copies of these documents to Jack Jones and Bill Adams for their review.

Let me know when you've had a chance to review it and get any input from Jack and Bill, and we can make any necessary changes and execute the plan for the corporation. You will note I have made the effective date January 1, 19___ , which I understand is what you want, and I further understand you're on the calendar year basis for accounting purposes.

After the plans are executed and adopted, we will need to prepare and submit an Application for Determination to the District Director of the Internal Revenue Service. In addition, we will prepare an appropriate notice to employees of adoption of the plan and trust.

I look forward to working with you in connection with the Profit Sharing Plan, and I think it is a farsighted move on your part and the part of management of ABC Corporation.

Sincerely,

COMMENT:

1. It is a good idea to send drafts of important documents to clients and other parties for their review and study prior to execution. When a client comes to the lawyer's office without the benefit of studying an important and perhaps lengthy document, there is a danger the client will execute the document without giving it due consideration.

58.
**STATEMENT THAT ACTUARIAL METHODS, FACTORS AND
ASSUMPTIONS ARE UNNECESSARY FOR MONEY PURCHASE
PENSION PLAN**

Dear Mr. Lewis:

Federal Income Tax Regulations 1.404(a)—(a)(7) require submission of a detailed description of all methods, factors and assumptions used in determining costs and in adjusting the costs for actual experience under the plan; an explanation of their source and application in sufficient detail to permit ready analysis and verification; and, in the case of a trust, a detailed description of the basis used in valuing the investments held.

Inasmuch as the ABC Company, Inc. Pension Plan is a Money Purchase Plan and inasmuch as the benefits under said plan are to arrive in the form of an annuity, based upon the vested amount in the particular member's retirement account, there are no methods, factors or assumptions regarding the costs of this plan. Therefore, none are enclosed.

Investments under the trust will be valued in accordance with generally accepted accounting principles. The allocation among the various members' accounts is set out in detail in the pension plan itself. In reference to the valuation of assets, they will be valued at their fair market value.

We trust this information will suffice. However, if further information is needed, kindly address all communications to the undersigned.

Sincerely yours,

COMMENT:

1. The above letter is a letter of explanation to a client made in connection with the client's Money Purchase Pension Plan. Letters such as this are helpful to clients by explaining to them the requirements of pertinent law and regulations.

59.
TRANSMITTAL OF LETTER FROM LABOR DEPARTMENT AND
STATUS REPORT ON COMPLETION OF FORMS

Dear Mr. Clark:

We are enclosing a copy of a letter we received from Mr. Jones, U. S. Department of Labor, in response to our letter of April 21. I note that he indicated a copy was sent to David Kirby, but I wanted to make sure that both of you received a copy.

I am in the process of completing the forms and will keep you advised of all developments.

Sincerely yours,

COMMENT:

1. The writer could make more specific comment regarding the forms or the matter.

60.
STATEMENT TO SUPPORT CASUALTY LOSS DEDUCTION ON
INCOME TAX RETURN

Dear Mr. Brown:

You asked me on the telephone today to write you a letter to the effect that it appears to us that you lost your boat for tax purposes so that it can be recorded as a casualty loss. The circumstance of this loss is that a marine company and boat repair yard took the boat into its possession and performed, without your knowledge or consent, extensive repairs to the boat and claimed in connection with these repairs an aggregate amount which exceeded the value of the boat.

You were not able to regain possession of the boat, and the boat was lost to you as a result of this claim. We made a determination that it would be prohibitively expensive to go to Jackson County and enter a suit and litigate the matter through to a conclusion. Therefore, it appears to us that you have suffered a casualty loss of your boat through no fault of your own.

I hope this will be satisfactory for your purposes in deducting the matter as a loss on your income tax return.

Yours very truly,

COMMENT:

1. The above letter should be helpful to a client in documenting a position to be taken regarding a deduction on his income tax return.

2. Note the letter contains only a recitation of facts and does not contain any expression of opinion by the lawyer regarding the legality of the claimed deduction.

61.
TRANSMITTAL OF LETTER AND ACKNOWLEDGMENT OF APPOINTMENT

Dear Rachel:

Enclosed for your information is a copy of a letter which we received today.

I look forward to seeing you on Friday at 2:00 p.m. and going over your case with you.

Very sincerely,

COMMENT:

1. The above letter is a letter of transmittal and acknowledgment of an appointment.

62.
NOTICE OF COURT ORDER AND REQUEST FOR CONFERENCE

Dear Mrs. Humphrey:

I am enclosing a copy of the order which Judge Smith's secretary sent to us, excluding you from the class action in Houston.

I would like to get together with you one day next week. Please call and let's discuss when is convenient.

Very sincerely,

COMMENT:

1. The writer could state something of interest to the client or make some specific comment regarding the matter.

2. The writer could comment on the significance of the order.

3. The writer could also suggest additional action to be taken by him in connection with the matter.

GROUP B
Reporting Status

63.
STATUS REPORT OF INSURANCE CLAIM AND TRANSMITTAL OF
COPIES OF LETTERS

Dear Mrs. Haley:

We have forwarded the requested information to Mr. John McCampbell of ABC Insurance Company regarding your claim. Enclosed is a copy of our letter to him for your file.

Also enclosed is a copy of our letter to your son, Tom, requesting that he execute the claim form regarding the $10,000 life insurance policy on which he is named as beneficiary. When we receive the executed claim form from him, we will submit your claim, along with those of your daughter and son, to ABC Insurance Company for payment of the proceeds under the policies which Mr. Haley had with the company.

We will keep you advised of all developments regarding these two insurance claims.

Very sincerely,

COMMENT:

1. The writer could state the expected length of time for action on the claims.

2. The writer could state additional action to be taken in connection with the matter.

64.
STATUS REPORT OF INSURANCE COVERAGE MATTER

Dear Mrs. Garber:

I spoke with Ms. Matthews of ABC Insurance Agency, Mason City, phone 232-6884, today regarding the matter of your son, Charles, being covered with insurance under the policy secured through ABC Insurance Company.

I also gave Ms. Matthews, Charles' driver's license number RAD-4487 and advised her it will expire September 12. I called Charles, and he is to mail to ABC Insurance Agency today his driver's training certificate for their use in having him added to the policy.

Ms. Matthews told me since Charles is a licensed driver and resides in the household, in the event he uses the insured auto, which I understand is a 19XX Buick Century, he will be covered by the insurance provided his use of the car is with your consent. I told her the actual physical custody of the car was in your care.

She is going to look into the matter further and recommend to you how best to insure the vehicle to effect the greatest savings in premium to the family.

I know you are vitally concerned about Charles being insured when he uses the car, and I wanted to write you this letter to confirm my discussions with ABC Insurance Agency and advise you of what Ms. Matthews told me.

Very sincerely,

COMMENT:

1. The above letter relates to a matter in which the lawyer is attempting to ascertain that the son is insured under the family automobile insurance policy.

2. The letter indicates that the lawyer has carefully looked into the matter and is diligently attempting to help the client secure the best coverage at the lowest cost.

65.
STATUS REPORT OF SETTLEMENT OF INSURANCE CLAIM

Dear Mr. Hanley:

I talked to you on March 14th about the settlement of the insurance claim, relaying the information I received from Ed Parsons of Brockton. If there are any further developments, I will let you know.

With the thought that you might like to have it for your records, I am enclosing a copy of the statement we took from you, which has been transcribed.

Sincerely yours,

COMMENT:

1. It is a good idea for the lawyer to send a copy of any transcribed conference or written statement taken from the client in connection with his case for review and possible correction and comment by the client.

66.
REPORT OF DENIAL OF CLAIM BY INSURER

Dear Mr. Wheeler:

Eric Schenk of Keystone Insurance Company called on August 12, and said that their adjuster has completed his file in connection with your claim under your homeowner's insurance coverage.

He said they based their position on it primarily on the statements of Norman Wells and Morton Clark, both of whom according to Mr. Schenk, stated you were at fault in starting the fight which resulted in the personal injury.

At any rate, he said they do not intend to honor the claim. I told him I would relay this to you. If you want to do anything further on it, please let me know.

John, I certainly want to wish you a successful year for sales in 19XX, and I feel you will get them.

Yours very sincerely,

COMMENT:

1. The writer could give his opinion regarding the position of the insurance company in not paying the claim. However, it is possible in view of the situation that the writer would prefer not to comment on it.

2. When the facts are unpleasant to the reader, the writer may prefer to simply state the conclusions and offer to discuss the facts in detail at the request of the reader.

67.

REPORT OF COLLECTION EFFORTS AGAINST DEBTOR FOR CLIENT

Dear Dr. Holloway:

Enclosed is a copy of a letter which I sent today to Jean Cunningham in an attempt to collect the debt due you in the sum of $350.

If we have not received payment from her within fifteen (15) days from the date of her receipt of our letter, we will file suit for you for the collection of the debt unless we hear otherwise from you.

It is my suggestion that we bill you straight time for our time involved in this case instead of handling it on a contingency fee basis. We will keep our total time in the case as low as possible. We can try it this way and see how it works out if you like. If this arrangement is not satisfactory to you, please let us know.

I will keep you advised of all developments regarding this matter.

Yours very truly,

COMMENT:

1. The fee basis should be clearly understood by both parties before suit is filed.

68.

STATUS REPORT OF COLLECTION CASE

Dear Mrs. Stowe:

Stanley Garcia, the attorney representing Robert Stowe in the above case, came by my office this morning to discuss this matter. Stanley said he would talk to his client and let us know what they decide to do regarding this case by the 12th of October.

It is my suggestion that we not file suit until this date, in an effort to avoid litigation.

I will keep you advised of all developments of this matter.

Sincerely,

COMMENT:

1. The above status report of a collection case is a good example of keeping the client informed of what the lawyer is doing for the client.

69.
REPORT OF RENT COLLECTED AND DISTRIBUTED

Dear Mr. Trautman:

We are enclosing our check in the amount of $287 in payment of the June rent by Mr. John Stout. We are also enclosing our check in the amount of $300 toward payment of his arrearage. As you know, we communicated with him several times in an effort to get him to pay the rent and finally wrote him a letter giving him five days to pay or we would file an unlawful detainer action against him.

According to our records, Mr. Stout's original arrearage was in the amount of $900 and, in addition to the May and June rent payments, he has paid a total of $887, leaving a balance to be paid in the amount of $600.

We wrote to him today to request that he make his July payment in the amount of $287 as soon as possible.

Should you have any questions or suggestions regarding this matter, please let me know.

Sincerely yours,

COMMENT:

1. The writer might outline proposed additional action in connection with the above matter.

2. The writer might give recommendations for future treatment of the matter to the client for his consideration and decision.

70.
TRANSMITTAL OF CERTIFICATE OF INCORPORATION AND STATUS REPORT OF ORGANIZATION OF CORPORATION

Dear Mr. Dean:

Enclosed is a copy of the Certificate of Incorporation on the above-referenced corporation which was recorded and filed this morning with the Probate Judge of Adams County. Also enclosed is a copy of your Franchise Tax Return and Permit Application, which we have forwarded to the Franchise Tax Division, State Department of Revenue.

We have forwarded your application for a Federal Employer's ID number to the Internal Revenue Service in Chamblee, Georgia, and you should receive your number shortly.

Upon receipt of your corporate kit, which was ordered March 12 from Excelsior-Legal Stationary Company, we will prepare your by-laws and minutes and forward a copy of them to you.

Thank you for letting us handle this matter for you.

Sincerely,

COMMENT:

1. The above is basically a letter of transmittal of documents relating to organization of a corporation. Although brief, it indicates to the client the lawyer is taking care of the various things that should be done.

71.
TRANSMITTAL OF COPY OF CERTIFICATE OF ASSOCIATION AND STATUS REPORT OF ORGANIZATION OF ASSOCIATION

Dear Dr. Whitman:

Enclosed is a copy of the Certificate of Association issued by the Secretary of State's office, effective March 24.

I have ordered a corporate minute book, corporate seal and stock certificate book for the association.

It will be necessary in the very near future for us to have the initial organizational meeting of the association where officers of the association are elected, by-laws are adopted, the seal is adopted, the association is given authority to begin business, depository bank of the association is appointed, a fiscal year is adopted, and share certificates are issued.

It will be necessary for Dr. Fleming to be present for this initial organizational meeting. This could be conducted here at our office or at your office, whichever is more convenient.

Once we have the initial organizational meeting, it will be necessary to have a meeting with you and your accountant as to the mechanical problems involved with the transfer, and further discussion with you insofar as your desires and objectives for the professional association. I am certain you will have many questions, and we can attempt to provide some guidance as to further requirements at such a meeting. It will not be necessary to have Dr. Fleming present, since he is only required for the initial organizational meeting.

However, it may be convenient to combine the two meetings at one time. You might give this some thought and telephone me, and we can discuss this further.

Very sincerely,

COMMENT:

1. The above letter is an excellent example of personalizing a letter of transmittal by including for the client a status report of the matter.

2. In complicated transactions, letters such as this may actually be superior to a detailed explanation to the client during an office conference. In appropriate cases, of course, an office conference explaining the transaction and a follow-up letter giving the status may be desirable.

72.
REPORT OF RECORDS CHECK AND ADVICE THAT NO ARREST WARRANTS ARE OUTSTANDING AGAINST CLIENT'S SON

Dear Mrs. Grace:

Pursuant to your request, I have checked the court records and find no record of any warrant for arrest of your son, Harold.

If we may be of further service to you, please advise.

Very sincerely,

COMMENT:

1. The above letter could be personalized with further comments or details by the writer.

73.
REPORT OF CONFERENCE WITH DISTRICT ATTORNEY AND REQUEST FOR CONFERENCE WITH CLIENT

Dear Mr. Trowbridge:

I had a conference with Mr. George Hamilton, the Assistant District Attorney, who is handling your case.

Mr. Hamilton was very cooperative, and I now have the underlying facts in connection with the charges against you.

I'm asking my secretary to set down on my calendar a convenient time for me to come over to see you and discuss this matter in detail. Just wanted to drop you a note and let you know what is going on.

Very truly yours,

COMMENT:

1. The writer could comment further on the facts of the case.
2. The writer could also state additional action he intends to take in behalf of the client.

74.
REPORT OF DISCUSSION OF CASE WITH DISTRICT ATTORNEY

Dear Mr. Watson:

I have been in touch with Victor Horn, Assistant District Attorney, in connection with your case. I will see him some time in the near future regarding the matter of securing probation for you in connection with the case.

Just as soon as I have additional information for you, I will get in touch with you.

I am most hopeful that we will be able to work this matter out completely to your satisfaction.

Sincerely yours,

COMMENT:

1. The above letter could give more details regarding the conference or telephone conversation with the assistant district attorney.

2. Further details regarding the prospects of securing probation or the status of the matter would be helpful.

3. The lawyer could indicate what additional information he expects to develop or what type of agreement he intends to work out.

4. The lawyer could also request the client to give any thoughts or suggestions he may have regarding the matter.

75.
STATUS REPORT OF CRIMINAL CASE TO CLIENT IN JAIL

Dear Mr. Jones:

I enjoyed talking to you today and want to congratulate you on the fact that your spirits are high and that you have as positive an attitude about your case as you do.

I tried to talk with Mr. Paul Deal but he is unavailable since he is out of town. I have dictated a letter to him and will see him, I hope, next week.

I am most hopeful that we can work out your case along the lines we discussed.

I'll get back in touch with you as soon as I have anything definite.

Very sincerely,

COMMENT:

1. The above letter is a good example of a helpful status report to a client in a criminal case. It shows the lawyer's interest both in the client and his case.

2. If desired, additional detail could be given regarding settlement or a further action to be taken in the case.

76.
STATUS REPORT TO CLIENT OF CONTINUANCE BY
COURT OF CRIMINAL CASE

Dear Mr. Smith:

Last week in court Judge Henry Fleming was somewhat obstinate over the matter of continuing this case. He said that in the event Norman had been present in court, the court could have acted on the matter of his petition to be treated as a youthful offender.

I told him that Paul Sullivan, the Assistant District Attorney handling the matter, had advised me that his chief witness is in the hospital and would ask for a continuance. I also told him I had talked to Mr. Goldstein twice on October 18 before the hearing regarding the case and relayed the matter as best I understood it of Mr. Goldstein's position.

Judge Fleming said he had talked to the victim also and that he wanted to advise us that, just because the District Attorney asked that the case be nolle prossed, the court would not have to accept the motion. I don't know what he had in mind.

Judge Fleming also said he wanted to advise us that, in any event, the next time the case is set for trial, Norman must be here. He said he wasn't angry with me as Norman's attorney, but it seemed we were doing too much talking, and there wasn't enough action going on this case.

I just wanted to pass all this on to you. The thing I can't understand is Mr. Goldstein's position in the matter. This seems to be the hold-up on the whole thing.

Please give me a report from the psychiatrist just as soon as Norman has gotten with one in accordance with our last discussion.

Also, I would appreciate any thoughts you may have.

Hope you're enjoying it in Lansing; I know it will be a beautiful spring there.

Sincerely yours,

COMMENT:

1. The above letter advises the client not only of the status of the case but of the lawyer's observations of the attitude of the judge involved. It is certainly a good idea to keep the client as fully advised as possible during the progress of his case.

77.
REPORT OF NEGOTIATION FOR DIVORCE SETTLEMENT

Dear Mrs. Farr:

Your husband came into the office the other day, and we discussed the matter of the terms of your proposed divorce.

He seemed most cooperative and stated that if you really wanted the divorce, he would certainly accommodate you.

However, he suggested that it would be better for you to come to Brockton one weekend and for both of you to come in at the same time so we will have an opportunity to reach a final agreement as to all terms.

Please let me know what you think about this suggestion.

Thank you very much.

Very sincerely,

COMMENT:

1. The above letter could, if appropriate, state who will pay attorney's fees in the matter.

2. Also, regarding the proposed terms of the divorce, the lawyer could state which terms present the most problems and need further discussion.

78.
STATUS REPORT OF DIVORCE CASE

Dear Mrs. Steele:

I had a conference with Walter Parsons on April 15 regarding your case. He is to get financial data from Albert Rosenberg. I told Walter that I would like to put in the agreement, in the event we are able to reach agreement, that your husband had represented what his income and his finances were so that if it turned out the facts were different, it would lay the predicate for you to do something about it. All in all, I was quite encouraged in talking to Walter that we may be able to work out an agreement.

Walter called me Thursday and stated that your husband's net income last year was $21,600, that his business is not a corporation, and that he is sending us financial data. He said that he is hopeful that we can work things out.

I will be back in touch with you upon receipt of the financial data requested.

Very sincerely,

COMMENT:

1. The above letter is a good example of a personalized status report during a divorce case. The approach could vary depending on the lawyer handling the case. Regardless of style, it is a good idea to keep the client fully informed. Status reports such as the above are most helpful.

79.
**STATUS REPORT OF DIVORCE CASE WITH REQUEST FOR
PAYMENT OF FEES**

Dear Mr. Rust:

This is to advise you that we have received the necessary testimony from your wife, signed by the commissioner appointed by the court, and we are ready to proceed with your final divorce.

As you will recall, on March 12 you paid us $300 and the total remaining to be paid is $200 fee and $40 court costs in connection with this matter.

Also, we need to have some friend come in and give us just a brief statement regarding your residence here in Brunswick.

Thank you very much.

Sincerely yours,

COMMENT:

1. The lawyer could state the additional steps that will be taken to secure the divorce decree.

80.
**TRANSMITTAL OF LETTER FROM OPPOSING ATTORNEY IN
DIVORCE CASE AND STATUS REPORT**

Dear Mrs. Taylor:

Enclosed is a copy of a letter we received today from William Harrison, your husband's attorney.

I have an appointment to meet with Mr. Harrison to discuss this matter next Thursday afternoon and will let you know the results of that conference.

We are in the process of preparing extensive interrogatories to be sent to your husband and will forward a copy of them to you upon our filing the interrogatories in this matter.

I just wanted to keep you advised of the progress of your case. Please come to our office if you would like to discuss it in more detail. Best wishes.

Very sincerely,

COMMENT:

1. The writer could comment in greater detail on the substance of the case.
2. The writer could outline additional action to be taken in the client's behalf.

81.
REPORT OF PROPOSED DIVORCE AGREEMENT

Dear Mrs. Tribble:

We are enclosing a proposed agreement in connection with the divorce proceeding, which was signed by Mr. Tribble.

The agreement is silent as to the terms of sale of the house, and we will make it clear, before delivering the agreement as signed by you, that the house may only be sold on terms that are acceptable to you.

Mr. Donavan did not show us the proposed agreement before it was signed by Mr. Tribble. Indeed, Mr. Donavan, Mr. Tribble's lawyer, stated that he took the original when he left the office, so we are enclosing a duplicate copy which was also signed.

If the agreement is satisfactory to you, with the above condition that a sale must be acceptable to you, please sign and return it to us as soon as possible.

In order to confine the issues and facilitate a divorce without further delay, we propose to amend the original complaint for a divorce to state simple grounds of cruelty.

We understand that Mr. Tribble will then sign the necessary answer and waiver, and it will be submitted to Judge Nicholson as soon as possible.

ABC Mortgage Company called yesterday and said they will have to begin foreclosure soon if the house is not sold.

Mr. Tribble refuses to make any payments. If you want to make a house payment, please let me know.

If it is satisfactory, please return the executed agreement as soon as possible. Please call me in the event you have any questions or suggestions.

Very sincerely,

COMMENT:

1. The above letter outlines the alternatives available to the client.

2. The lawyer could comment on the husband's refusal to make the mortgage payments.

3. The lawyer could also inquire whether the client has any objection to amending the complaint stating grounds of cruelty.

4. In the event a conference with the client is not convenient, as appears to be the case in the above letter, it is a good idea to invite the client to call if there are any questions or suggestions to discuss.

82.
REPORT OF CONFLICT OF INTEREST IN POST-DIVORCE MATTER

Dear Mrs. Watkins:

In accordance with your letter dated March 12, I forwarded the information requested by Thomas Vaughan, attorney of Mr. Watkins.

Please be advised that I have never told anyone, including Mr. Watkins, that he did not have to abide by a decree of court. In the event any party feels aggrieved by changed circumstances, or otherwise by the provisions of any decree, the proper remedy is to make application to the court for a modification of the decree.

I did discuss the matter of a proceeding initiated by you in October against Herbert Gardner. However, I also advised him that since I had previously represented you, I felt that I had a conflict of interest in connection with the matter.

As a result, I do not represent him now in regard to any dispute which he has with you, and I do not feel that I should represent either party since I originally represented you and have done other legal work for Mr. Watkins since the divorce.

I certainly hope that you and Mr. Watkins will be able to work out this matter in a manner that will be agreeable to both of you and will make adequate provision for your children.

Sincerely yours,

COMMENT:

1. The lawyer should be careful to avoid a conflict of interest or even the appearance of a conflict of interest in the representation of clients. The above letter declines the case on these grounds.

2. Where a full disclosure is made to all parties involved, the parties themselves might be asked to decide whether, in their opinion, a conflict of interest exists on the part of the lawyer. The better course of action is to avoid the appearance of a conflict, even at the expense of not handling the matter.

83.
REPORT OF NEGOTIATIONS TO MODIFY DECREE OF CHILD CUSTODY

Dear Mrs. Richmond:

This is to advise you that we reached your ex-husband, Mr. Harvey Richmond, on the telephone the other day and that, pursuant to our request, he came into our office yesterday.

We went over the matter of changed circumstances since the divorce decree regarding the custody arrangement of your daughter, Pamela, and the necessity of modifying the previous decree of divorce.

Mr. Richmond advised us that he would let us know within the next week whether or not he would agree to a change of the custody arrangement, and, if so, what change he would agree to.

Just as soon as we hear further from Mr. Richmond, we will immediately get in touch with you. In the meantime, if you have any questions or suggestions, please let us know.

Very sincerely,

COMMENT:

1. The above letter might give more details regarding change of the custody arrangement.

2. If available, more details could be given regarding the husband's position on various proposed terms of the change of custody arrangement.

84.

REPORT OF FILING PETITION FOR MODIFICATION OF
DIVORCE DECREE WITH DISCUSSION OF ATTORNEY'S FEES

Dear Mrs. Morgan:

We are enclosing the petition for modification of the divorce decree, which we filed in your behalf, together with the order of Judge Gardner setting the matter for a hearing at 2:00 P.M. on Thursday, October 12.

As I told you previously, we will file a motion for attorney's fees in connection with the matter, and we hope to secure an order of Judge Gardner to Mr. Morgan to pay your attorney's fees in this matter.

However, you will recall we previously agreed that in the event this is a contested matter, the fee will be $750 and that it would be paid by you prior to the trial. In the event we are able to get the fee from Mr. Morgan, we will, of course, reimburse you for the amount paid.

We would suggest that you pay $250 per month, and, by so doing, the entire fee would be paid in three months, when it is set for a hearing.

Accordingly, we are enclosing our bill in the amount of $250 for the month of June, and we will send you a bill each month.

We will keep you advised of all future developments. Please let us know if you have any questions or suggestions.

Sincerely yours,

COMMENT:

1. The above letter might elaborate on the prospects of recovering attorney's fees from the husband.

2. The writer could also give more details regarding the petition or modification and the additional steps that will be necessary in connection with it.

85.
LETTER TO INSURANCE COMPANY UPON RECEIPT OF DEFENSE FILE

Dear Mr. Morgenthaler:

This is to acknowledge with appreciation receipt of the summons and complaint and file in the above referenced case for defense. I am entering an appearance on behalf of the insured, as requested.

I am presently reviewing the file and will report to you shortly concerning my recommendations for further handling.

Yours sincerely,

COMMENT:

1. An acknowledgment letter, upon receipt of a file from an insurance company or other client handling a volume of claims or cases, should be sent promptly both for information and record purposes.

86.
STATUS REPORT OF SUIT AND REQUEST FOR APPOINTMENT

Dear Mr. Reddick:

I saw Joseph Gardner in connection with the suit his firm filed against you in behalf of George Roundtree and was advised that, although Mr. Roundtree has moved out of town, the suit will be continued against you.

Therefore, it will be necessary for us to prepare your defense to the suit.

Please arrange to come by my office at your convenience to discuss this matter.

Sincerely,

COMMENT:

1. It is, of course, important to keep your client advised of the status of a suit while it is pending.
2. The letter might suggest a time frame in which the suit will probably come to trial.

87.
STATUS REPORT TO PLAINTIFF WITH INFORMATION AND
INSTRUCTION PAMPHLET ENCLOSED

Dear Miss Greer:

I am pleased to represent you in your case. The investigation of your case has begun. I will continue investigation on the matter until I have obtained all available evidence which may be helpful to me in proving your case.

Enclosed is an Instruction and Information Sheet which I am requesting that you read and follow very carefully.

Thank you again for the opportunity of representing you in this matter.

Very sincerely,

INSTRUCTIONS TO CLIENT AND WHAT YOU,
AS A PERSONAL-INJURY CLIENT, SHOULD KNOW

1. TALK TO NO ONE—Do not talk to anyone about the accident except one of the lawyers or investigators in our office. You should always require identification so that you are sure who you are talking to.

2. YOUR DOCTOR—You should return to each of your doctors as often as necessary and should always tell them about all your complaints. You should not minimize your ailments to your doctors as it is one of his best ways of knowing how to treat you. If you see any additional doctors, be sure we are advised immediately of their names and addresses.

3. HOSPITAL AND DOCTOR BILLS—Have your own auto insurance carrier pay as many hospital and doctor bills under the medical payment provisions of your policy as possible. You should also have your hospitalization insurance pay as much on your bills as possible. Doctors and hospitals are more cooperative when their bills are paid. You should not expect them to wait until your case is tried or settled to receive payment. You should, therefore, pay any balance as soon as possible.

4. RECORD OF COMPLAINTS—Please keep a daily or weekly record of your complaints and progress. This can be very helpful because a year later you will be able to recall your pain and difficulties more vividly.

5. WAGES AND EARNINGS LOST—Please keep an accurate record of all days lost from work because of your injuries.

6. MEDICAL BILLS—Obtain and keep duplicate copies of all medical, hospital and drug bills. You should periodically send these bills to us for our files. Also keep records of any other expenses you may have in connection with your accident, such as the hiring of extra help. All your bills should be paid by check; or you should obtain and keep receipts. You should make and keep a list of all your medical bills.

7. It will help your case to tell me about any PRIOR INJURY OR PRIOR PAIN to any parts of your body. Many good cases are lost by the injured person's concealing or forgetting a previous injury.

8. CAR REPAIR—Do not have your automobile repaired until you are sure that we have obtained pictures of it. After pictures are taken by this office, have your collision insurance carrier repair your car.

9. WITNESSES—Furnish to us immediately the correct names and addresses and telephone numbers of any and all witnesses you may learn of. It may be necessary some day to have friends, neighbors or coworkers testify regarding your disability and pain and suffering; therefore, start thinking about witnesses you may need in the future.

10. *SAVE YOUR CAST, ETC.*—If your injury requires a cast, brace, traction or other appliance, save it for evidence and trial. You should notify us that you are keeping these things, and, when the case is set for hearing, you should bring these items with you.

11. *PHOTOGRAPHS*—Send us the negatives and prints of any photographs pertaining to your case which you or any of your friends have taken. If you are required to be in the hospital and are receiving any type of treatment, such as traction or physical therapy, please notify our office so that we can have our investigator photograph you.

12. *COSTS*—Some of the necessary costs of your injury claim include expenses of the police report, investigation service, filing fee, copying medical and hospital records, depositions, jury fees, transcripts (if required) and witness fees.

13. The amount asked for in your complaint, if and when it becomes necessary for us to file suit, will probably not be the amount for which your case will be settled—it's merely a preliminary figure.

14. It takes many months to settle a claim. In fact, it is dangerous to settle neck or back claims within the first year because it often takes a long time for serious injuries to become evident.

15. *QUESTIONS*—We will probably not contact you until we have something definite to report. If you have any specific questions in regard to these instructions or any other matters in regard to your case, please call or write us.

16. *YOUR ADDRESS*—Be sure to keep us advised of any change in your address or telephone number. Please call our office in advance and set up an appointment before coming in so that you will not have to wait a long time in case I am out of the office. Keep my office advised of any times that you may not be available for a long period of time. An alternate way of reaching you must be in my file at all times.

COMMENT:

1. The above letter is quite thoughtful in advising the client of the status of his case as well as giving the explicit enclosed instructions regarding a personal injury claim.

88.
CASE STATUS REPORT TO CLIENT

Dear Mrs. Skidmore:

We have reviewed your file and are anxious to keep it current in all respects. If you have not seen your doctor regularly, please call this office. Also, if you have had any changes in doctors, condition, treatment or work, call this office immediately. If I am not in, please talk to my secretary or one of my associates.

It is important that we have bills, receipts and any other documents connected with your case.

I repeat my previous admonition to you to NOT DISCUSS THIS CASE WITH ANY-ONE outside this office. If you have any questions about your case or any information for me, please call this office and discuss it with me or one of my associates.

The trial-setting conference will be coming up shortly, and this is the time when we establish our final trial date. I will inform you of the conference date.

In the meantime, if you have changed your address, telephone number, occupation or marital status, or if you have discontinued medical treatment for your injuries, please let my office know immediately.

If you have any current bills, please see that I get copies as quickly as possible.

Very sincerely,

89.
CASE STATUS REPORT TO CLIENT

Dear Miss Spalding:

In order to keep you fully informed of the progress of your case, I am sending this letter to advise you that I have completed a regular review of your case. As you know, I have been negotiating with the defendant's insurance company in an effort to reach a realistic settlement to compensate you.

I am happy to advise you that, following our most recent negotiations, Phillip Hammond has informed me they wish to increase their prior offer as soon as possible and are requesting authority from their home office to make such an increase. I hope to hear from them within 45 days.

In the meantime, I shall continue to keep you informed of all developments and offers as they are made. If you have any questions regarding your case, please do not hesitate to write.

Sincerely yours,

COMMENT:

1. It is certainly a good idea, in a letter such as the above, to completely advise the client of all settlement negotiations as they progress.

90.
NOTICE OF SERVICE OF PROCESS AND STATUS REPORT REGARDING DEFAULT JUDGMENT

Dear Mrs. Spain:

James Henley was personally served with Summons and a copy of the Complaint in Fredericksburg on October 12.

We have drafted a Certificate of Default, Motion for Default Judgment, Order of Default, and Judgment, copies of which are enclosed.

We cannot obtain Judgment until after November 12. We have marked our calendar to apply for the Default Judgment on November 13. We do not anticipate that Mr. Henley will file any answer or other pleading to the Complaint.

Very sincerely,

COMMENT:

1. The above letter, while brief, gives an exact status of the case and fully informs the client about it.

91.
REPORT OF ACCEPTANCE OF SETTLEMENT OFFER

Dear Mr. Stone:

Mr. Grover Hutchinson, the attorney for Lawrence Johnson, called today to advise me that Mr. Johnson is now willing to accept your offer in connection with the leaking roof on the building which Mr. Johnson purchased from your company.

I understand that the manufacturer in Dallas will construct a new roof to be placed over the existing roof and will charge only the cost of the materials, namely $125, and that you have previously offered to pay one-half of this amount.

Mr. Hutchinson tells me that Mr. Johnson is now anxious to have this work done by agreement of the parties as soon as possible.

We are also enclosing our bill for services in connection with this matter in the amount of $175.

Very sincerely,

COMMENT:

1. The writer might conclude the above letter by expressing his opinion regarding settlement.
2. He might also stress the advantage of the settlement to the client.

92.
REPORT OF DISTRIBUTION OF SETTLEMENT PROCEEDS

Dear Mr. Turner:

We settled the case of Lawrence Turner vs. Peter Johnson for the sum of $35,000.

Our fee is one-third of the amount collected, or $11,666. However, we are giving you credit for the $500 previously paid us and are deducting $11,166 from the total proceeds of $35,000.

Accordingly, we are enclosing our check in the amount of $23,834, representing proceeds from this settlement.

I want you to know it was a pleasure handling this matter for you, and I hope we shall have the opportunity of being of service to you in the future when the need arises.

Sincerely yours,

COMMENT:

1. The writer might comment on the advantage of settlement by avoiding further litigation and a possible appeal.

2. The writer might also express his agreement with the client's position regarding settlement if this was, in fact, the case.

93.
REPORT OF DISTRIBUTION OF SETTLEMENT PROCEEDS

Dear Mr. Ward:

As you know, we settled your claims against Edwin Folsom and John Teal in connection with your accident for the total sum of $14,000. Our attorney's fees for services in connection with this matter amount to $4,666. There are also some expenses listed on your account. There is a call to Mr. Frank Turner in Lawrence for $4.80 and a xerox copy charge for $12.50.

Accordingly, we are enclosing our check in the amount of $9,316.70 in payment to you from the settlement proceeds.

In the event you have any questions or suggestions, please let us know. It was a pleasure handling this matter in your behalf.

Very sincerely,

COMMENT:

1. The above letter could be accompanied by a statement of the account reporting all receipts and disbursements.

2. The writer might also comment on the advantages derived from settlement by avoiding protracted litigation and a possible appeal.

94.
REPORT TO CLIENT OF CONCLUSION OF CASE

Dear Mr. Temple:

Thank you for your kind note. I am pleased that we were able to work this matter out without further complications.

I have forwarded copies of the releases to the Department of Public Safety, and this should take care of that problem. If you have any further problems with them, please let us know.

With kindest regards.

Sincerely yours,

COMMENT:

1. The above letter could contain some personal comments of interest to the client.

2. It is a good policy at the conclusion of a case to send the client a wrap-up letter that is perhaps more personal or cordial than the usual transmittal.

95.
STATUS REPORT OF PREPARATION OF TITLE INSURANCE POLICY

Dear Mr. Rawlins:

We are in the process of preparing your title insurance policy on the property you purchased. Just as soon as we get it prepared, we will mail it to you.

Please give my regards to Mrs. Rawlins.

Sincerely yours,

COMMENT:

1. The writer could personalize the letter by congratulating the client on his purchase or by making some general comment about it.

2. The writer could comment on the advisability or advantages of title insurance.

96.
STATUS REPORT OF SBA LOAN APPLICATION AND
REQUEST FOR INFORMATION

Dear Mr. Rayburn:

George Stern and I had what we consider a very successful conference with Henry Fontaine of SBA in Los Angeles yesterday in behalf of your SBA loan application. Henry said your application is in good order and spoke favorably about it. He did say the very earliest we could hear from them would be about four weeks. He said many of the applications are taking eight weeks to three months or longer but indicated that he would attempt to process ours within four weeks.

There are some additional things we need and the purpose of this letter is to outline them. Henry suggested that we tend to all of these matters just as soon as we can, and I certainly concur.

I assume that John Goodson is a member of the board of directors since he is listed as a member of the board on the original incorporation papers. If so, we need to have him prepare a Statement of Personal History, SBA Form 912, which I am going to mail him in a separate letter. I would appreciate it if you would check with him and make sure we get this back as soon as possible. If he is not a member of the board, it is not necessary. We do not need financial data from him, only the Statement of Personal History as a result of his being a member of the board of directors.

Very sincerely,

COMMENT:

1. The writer could outline additional steps to be taken for the client in the matter.

97.
REPORT OF LAND PURCHASED AT TAX SALE

Dear Mr. Seitz:

I am enclosing the tax receipt for 19XX taxes together with the certificate for land sold for taxes which has been assigned to your daughter by Mr. John Singleton and Mr. Anthony Haines. In accordance with our conversation yesterday, I would suggest that you take the certificate to the tax assessor's office and assess the land to your daughter and take it into the tax collector's office and pay all outstanding taxes at the present time.

Just as soon as we get our check from the Probate Judge in the amount of $850, which is the amount required to redeem the property, we will mail you a check in this amount.

Yours very sincerely,

COMMENT:

1. In the event there is an additional action to be taken by the attorney in the above matter, he might state it to the client in this letter.

2. In the event no additional steps need to be taken, the attorney could state that it has been a pleasure handling the matter for the client.

98.
STATUS REPORT OF IRS AUDIT OF FEDERAL ESTATE TAX RETURN

Dear Mr. Singleton:

Please be advised that Mr. Mark Harrison of the Internal Revenue Service in Tulsa, called us today and made an appointment for Thursday, February 14, to come in and go over your estate. He plans to be in Centerville on that date and to come by our office to review and audit our files.

I just wanted to keep you advised of the most recent development in this matter.

Very sincerely,

COMMENT:

1. The writer could outline steps to be taken on behalf of a client in preparation for the audit.

2. The writer could request suggestions from the client regarding the matter.

3. The writer could explain the purpose of the audit.

99.
STATUS REPORT OF UTILITIES PROBLEM

Dear Mr. Stewart:

Bob Henderson, Utilities Director for the city, called me this morning and is trying very hard to alleviate our problem. He realizes your reluctance to petition for water and sewer which might involve assessments against the other owners. However, he must protect himself from the violation of city ordinances. One solution which I believe is reasonable is his suggestion that you sign a petition for utilities but that it not be circulated for additional signatures and that it be held in abeyance by him, possibly and probably for a period of years, until such time as there is other building development in that vicinity which requires water and sewer. In this way, he says that he can allow you to tap on to the existing line. However, he believes that the existing line is only one-half inch, and, if there is not sufficient water for two residences, you may wish to drill a well anyway. In regard to the septic tank, you will need to get the property tested for percolation in accord with county authorities.

However, he has said that he will work with you in any way possible to obtain services, and he has cleared a building permit with the Inspections Department, assuming the land "perks." Please let us know how you wish to proceed.

Very sincerely,

COMMENT:

1. The above letter is a good example of a personalized report letter to the client.

2. The lawyer could, if appropriate, give his recommendations of additional steps to be taken by the client.

100.
TRANSMITTAL OF COPY OF MOTION FOR SUMMARY JUDGMENT
AND RELATED DOCUMENTS AND STATUS REPORT

Dear Mr. Takahashi:

We are enclosing a copy of a Motion for Summary Judgment filed by Mr. Jose Garcia, a copy of a Notice of Setting which we have received from the clerk of the court, a copy of a Motion for Summary Judgment which we have filed for defendants and a copy of a letter which we have written to Judge Towle.

I rather doubt that either of the Motions for Summary Judgment will be granted. However, since Garcia has filed his motion, we may as well file ours too, in case the judge should hold that, as a matter of law, the employer did not have actual knowledge of the accident, and the plaintiff gave no written notice thereof as required by the statute.

Judges do not like to grant summary judgments because, if there is any material issue of fact, summary judgment should not be granted, and the case should go to trial. If summary judgment is granted, it is an appealable order. If summary judgment is not granted, it is not appealable because it is not a final order disposing of the case. Most judges prefer to deny the Motion for Summary Judgment and allow the parties to go to trial. Usually summary judgment is granted only when the facts are very clear.

We will advise you of the outcome.

Sincerely yours,

COMMENT:

1. The above letter is excellent in advising the client of the exact status of the pleadings in his case as the lawyer sees it. The letter not only lets the client know what is going on, it implicitly demonstrates to the client that the lawyer is on top of the matter and thinking ahead.

101.

STATUS REPORT OF APPEAL OF SOCIAL SECURITY DISABILITY CLAIM

Dear Mr. Gonzales:

My legal assistant told me of your call today. I was sorry to learn that your claim for Social Security disability was denied.

Enclosed is an authorization to Release Medical Records which you should execute and forward to Dr. Mason, along with the enclosed cover letter to him.

We are in the process of reviewing and researching the appropriate appeal procedure used in appealing a Social Security claim denial.

Albert, I will keep you advised of all developments.

Sincerely yours,

COMMENT:

1. Status reports, such as the above, are important in keeping the client informed. They also indicate to the client the personal interest of the lawyer in his claim, and that an avenue is still open for further pursuit of the claim.

GROUP C
Explaining Procedure

102.
INSTRUCTIONS FOR ORGANIZATION OF CORPORATION

Dear Mr. LaRue:

The following is a list of items which should be taken care of prior to or immediately after August 17, the date on which your corporation papers will be filed. Some of these items should not be attended to until they come up during the normal course of business.

1. In addition to preparing your Articles of Incorporation, bylaws, organizational minutes, etc., we will prepare for you an employment agreement, bills of sale from you personally to your corporation for major equipment, and an assignment of your lease, if you so desire.

2. You should open and maintain a bank account in the corporate name. Most accountants prefer that this be a new account.

3. All checks should bear your corporate name.

4. All bills and correspondence should be sent out under your corporate name, and letterheads and business cards should bear the corporate name.

5. Listing in the telephone directory should be under your corporate name.

6. All signs on your office door or outside of the office should be changed to reflect your corporate name.

7. All contractual arrangements with hospitals or other organizations should be made in the name of the corporation.

8. Malpractice insurance should cover your corporation in addition to yourself individually.

9. All other insurance policies, including fire, public liability, etc., should be assigned or issued to your corporation.

10. Your regular creditors, such as medical expense insurors, should be notified to change their records into the name of your corporation and to make all checks for services rendered to patients payable to the corporation and not to you.

11. Affairs of your corporation should be run by its officers and board of directors. Information required to keep minutes up to date should be furnished to us. At a minimum, minutes required include minutes of annual meeting of shareholders, organizational and regular meeting of the board and special meetings of the board, to be held near the end of each corporation's fiscal year to authorize payment of bonuses and to fix contribution to deferred compensation plans, if any. You should also have minutes to reflect any major corporate purchase or sale of assets and to document any of your personal financial dealings with the corporation.

12. If you are covered by Workmen's Compensation, the insurance should be assigned to your corporation, and you should list all employees, including yourself, as an employee.

13. At the end of each calendar year you should prepare W-2 forms for all employees including yourself.

14. You should read carefully all of the documents pertaining to your incorporation which I will give you.

15. Before taking any major action, you should contact your accountant or me to be certain that you are satisfying all necessary corporate formalities.

Finally, Pierre you must learn to think of yourself as the agent of your corporation. You are an employee of your corporation as well as its manager. You make business actions on behalf of your corporation. Accordingly, most corporate documents will be signed by you as president of the corporation.

We hope that the foregoing will give you some help in deciding how to conduct yourself in the future. We are sure that you will find that, once you have begun, it is not too difficult to keep up the course. Granted, there are certain inconveniences involved, but we are sure that you will find that the financial advantages far outweigh the inconveniences.

In the event that you have any questions with regard to the foregoing, please let us know.

Very sincerely,

COMMENT:

1. The above letter very thoughfully personalizes and itemizes things the client should do in connection with the organization of his new corporation.

2. The letter is carefully drafted to contain specific things the client should do. Unnecessary technicalities and legalities are omitted.

3. The client would probably preserve the letter for future reference. The letter is a good example of the careful work of a thoughtful attorney.

103.
PROCEDURE FOR ESTABLISHMENT OF
SYNDICATED INVESTMENT GROUP

Dear Mr. Morganthal:

At your request, we have examined several questions pertaining to the establishment of a syndicated investment group for the purpose of dealing in second mortgages on real estate. The following is a summary of our research and discussions:

I. *Selection of Entity Form*.

We believe the first problem to be resolved is that of selecting an entity for transacting the type of business which you propose. We conclude that the most advantageous form of entity is the limited partnership. Other operating forms which we have considered include general partnerships, joint ventures, corporations and "Subchapter S" corporations.

We have ruled out general partnerships and joint ventures because they proffer no advantages which are not obtainable by utilization of the limited partnership vehicle. They pose disadvantages in that:

1. It will be difficult to limit control of the business decisions to a small number of the beneficial owners;

2. The entity's existence will be too easily terminable; and

3. The beneficial owners will not have the advantage of limited liability.

We have eliminated Subchapter S corporations from consideration primarily because of the statutory requirements that they have ten or fewer stockholders and that only natural persons and estates be stockholders. We feel that the Subchapter S corporation does offer certain organizational advantages but that the aforementioned requirements will unduly restrict growth and will make it difficult to obtain the requisite capitalization.

In the organization and operation of a regular corporation, there are no problems except for those dealing with the federal income tax. However, we believe these problems to be prohibitive. Not only would there be the annual corporate tax on earnings and profits, but the corporation would also be subject to a 70% personal holding company tax on undistributed personal holding company income. Since all of the interest income would be personal holding company income, we feel that the tax would render impossible any substantial internally generated growth.

The limited partnership, on the other hand, would not be a taxable entity. It would be required to file informational tax returns to report the income of the partners. The partners would pay their own income taxes on their prorata shares of the partnership's reportable earnings.

The limited partnership will afford the limited partners the limited liability that attaches to a corporation. It will also be a rather simple matter to vest control of the operations in a selected number of persons.

The biggest problem with a limited partnership is organizational in nature. Our state partnership law requires the filing of an amendment to the Certificate of Limited

Partnership upon the addition of new limited partners to an existing limited partnership. Accordingly, you will be required to file an amendment every time a new limited partner is admitted. While this procedural necessity cannot be avoided, it is possible to minimize the inconvenience. Essentially, you could have prospective limited partners sign a subscription agreement which escrows their interest for up to ninety (90) days. Then you only have to file amendments four times a year. Likewise, you would have the initial prospective partners sign only the subscription agreement. In that way, the limited partnership will not even come into existence until you are confident that you have lined up most of your initial capitalization.

II. *Tax Accounting and Tax Effect of Transactions.*

Since you intend to deal in mortgages as your primary business activity, you will not be entitled to take capital gains treatment in the purchase and sale of the mortgages.

If the original mortgagee loaned face value on the mortgage debt, and you purchase the mortgage at a discount, you must realize the discount income as the installments are paid or when you reassign the mortgage.

A cash-basis mortgagee or assignee recognizes the income from a mortgage when it is actually or constructively received. The receipt of promissory notes in payment of interest gives rise to income if the notes are marketable. For example, if the mortgage loan agreement provides that all periodic payments are to be applied exclusively to principal until it is paid in full, the mortgagee recognizes no interest income until the last installments when the interest is paid.

On the other hand, an accrual basis taxpayer must report his interest as it is earned, regardless of the time it is received or payable. So, in the foregoing example, interest would be recognized every month, even though it is not to be paid until the end of the note's term.

Prepayment penalties and premiums are reportable as interest income.

We are not sure whether or not you intend to make mortgage loans yourself, particularly in light of the discussion of the usury and truth-in-lending laws which follow, but in the event that you do so intend, the following is a discussion of the tax implications of such transactions.

In dealing with a noncorporate mortgagor, premiums or discounts paid by the mortgagor in obtaining the mortgage loan are treated as discount income to the mortgagee. For accrual basis mortgagees, the income is recognizable over the period of the loan, like interest, if it is a true discount or premium. However, if the premium or discount is really a fee for services, it is recognized at the time of making the loan. For a cash basis mortgagee, however, the income is recognized as the loan is paid off or disposed of at a gain. Each installment is partially nontaxable principal and partially discount income.

In dealing with a corporate mortgagor, the discount or premium income is realizable prorata as paid.

III. *Usury.*

Usury is defined as an excessive rate of interest. Charging a usurious rate of interest is a misdemeanor giving rise to a fine and is also cause for forfeiture of all interest, usurious and nonusurious.

Corporate borrowers cannot plead usury. This means that there are no applicable maximum interest rates on loans to corporations.

Noncorporate borrowers cannot be required to pay more than twelve percent (12%) per annum on the unpaid balance of unsecured loans. On secured loans, including second mortgages, the maximum rate of interest is ten percent (10%). Premiums and discounts are treated as interest insofar as their treatment under the usury statute is concerned. They must be combined with the interest denominated as such in order to determine whether or not a loan exacts usurious interest.

In buying and selling second mortgages, it will be necessary for you to ascertain the validity of the interest charge on the underlying note. Otherwise, you face the possibility of being the assignee of a non-interest-bearing note. If such a note does not appear to be valid, it may be possible to hedge your bet by having the assignor sign an indemnification agreement as to lost interest.

In lending money for a mortgage, you must be extremely careful not to violate the usury statute, taking the statute into account when you charge points or a premium.

In buying and selling mortgages, the discount or premium involved will usually not be affected by the usury law since there will not be a change in the creditor's status or obligation. The exception comes about when the creditor gives you independent consideration as an incentive for you to purchase his obligation. That incentive will be considered to be additional interest. State Code _____ .

IV. *Truth-In-Lending*.

We are of the opinion that in buying and selling mortgages, you are affected by Title 1 of the Federal Consumer Credit Protection Act, officially known as the Federal Truth-In-Lending Act. Creditors are subject to the act if they in the ordinary course of business regularly extend or arrange for the extension of credit.

The assignee of an original creditor on a secured real estate loan may be sued if the original creditor could have been sued and may be held to the same penalties, including rescission. The assignee may only be sued in such a situation if it had a continuing business relationship with the original creditor at the time the credit was initially extended or at the time of assignment. Even if such a relationship is shown, the assignee can avoid liability by showing that it did not have grounds to believe that the original creditor violated the Truth-In-Lending Act and that it maintained procedures reasonably adapted to apprise it of the existence of any such violations.

The most important exception, however, is the situation where you avoid liability because the original creditor himself was not liable. A large part of your business will undoubtedly arise from the purchase of second mortgages created in the sale of the mortgagee-assignor's residence. The assignor will not be a "creditor" because he is not one who "in the ordinary course of his business regularly extends or arranges for the extension of consumer credit." Accordingly, he will not be within the scope of the act, nor will his assignors.

Of course you will be required to satisfy all of the requirements of the Truth-In-Lending Act when you actually make the second mortgage loan.

V. *Small Loan Business*.

State Code, _____ , are provisions essentially creating an exception to the usury statutes. They allow a licensed business making loans of up to $3,000 to charge significantly more interest than would otherwise be allowable. One may elect not to obtain a license and still make small loans provided that usurious interest is not charged.

VI. *Securities Laws Affecting the Limited Partnership.*

We are of the opinion that all sales of beneficial interests in the business entity which you elect to establish, and all offers of sales, should only be made to bona fide residents of our State. Strict adherence to this program will bring you within an exemption from the Securities Act of 1933, and will obviate any need for filing with the SEC.

We are of the opinion that in its initial status, the enterprise should attempt to avoid registration under the Federal Securities Act of 1933. The most easily available exemption is that under the Securities Act which exempts transactions constituted of an offer or sale of a pre-organization subscription or certificate if no commission is paid for soliciting any prospective subscriber, the number of subscribers does not exceed fifteen, and any subscriber's payments are escrowed.

The procedures for utilizing this exemption will work hand-in-hand with the procedure we have suggested for evading the continual amendment provision in the Limited Partnership Act. Essentially, you will line up a list of subscribers and escrow their funds, probably buying an interesting-bearing certificate of deposit. Then when you have lined up sufficient initial capitalization, you will form the limited partnership.

It appears that it will be necessary, before you can issue limited partnership shares thereafter, to register such shares. Registration will probably be required only one time, but it can be rather expensive and should probably be undertaken on solid ground.

VII. *Securities Laws Affecting the General Partner.*

Assuming that the general partner is a corporation, restriction of sales and offers to sell to state residents will bring offerings of stock within the intrastate offering exemption of The Securities Act of 1933.

Offerings to up to twenty-five (25) stockholders comes with a specific exemption to The Securities Act of 1933. This exemption is only available to corporations. We would anticipate that it would be quite some time before the exemption would be exhausted. Accordingly, we do not anticipate any immediate need for a Blue Sky registration of the corporate securities.

VIII. *Finance Scheme.*

We might suggest that you form the limited partnership as outlined above. The limited partnership shares would be an attractive investment vehicle for the individual who desires a relatively high yielding, safe investment. We feel that there should be a rather high dividend yield on these shares, since the income earned by the limited partners will be taxable to them, whether they receive the income or not.

The corporate general partner can be set up to not only participate in the limited partnership, but to engage in other ventures as well. The general partner may be hired to undertake management of the limited partnership's assets, if you so desire.

Alternately you may wish to act as the manager independently. In any event, the general partner should be geared to provide alternate investment objectives to those offered the holders of limited partnership interests.

We are hopeful that the foregoing will delineate some of the aspects of organizing your business and that it will be helpful to you in focusing your future actions. Naturally, we stand prepared to assist you in the future as you may require. Thank you for allowing us to be of service.

Yours very truly,

COMMENT:

1. The above letter is an example of the effective use of a letter to cover a complicated matter.

2. This letter is far superior to a conference. Of course, conferences are essential in going over matters in detail and discussing them informally. However, a letter such as the one above provides the client with a permanent record, reference and explanation of the matter at hand.

3. All tax and securities law recommendations should be reviewed in light of current law.

104.
LETTER OF INSTRUCTION FOR EXECUTION OF WILL BY CLIENT

Dear Mr. Worthington:

I am enclosing the original and one copy of proposed revised wills for both of you in accordance with Mrs. Worthington's letter.

I decided to dictate new wills since there were several changes, and it was as easy to do new wills as to make codicils to each of them. However, we will bill you only for preparation of codicils, which is the amount of $75 per will.

Please read each will carefully, noting particularly that all names are correctly spelled and that the wills contain every provision you desire. In the event there are corrections to be made or there are portions of the wills that you do not understand, please call me or write me regarding the matter.

In the event the wills are in proper form for execution, please take the following steps to execute them:

1. Get at least three disinterested witnesses who will not receive anything under the will.

2. In the presence of the three witnesses, each of you sign your respective wills on the next to the last page on the line above the point where your name is written out and on the right of which appears the word "(Seal)."

3. Then read aloud to the witnesses the clause just above your name which begins with the words "In Witness Whereof"; read that entire clause and fill in the date of the signing of the will. Then when you have signed the will, filled in the date, and read aloud the clause above described, have one of the witnesses read the language on the last page that begins, "The foregoing was at said date subscribed . . ."

Be sure one of the witnesses reads all that language aloud so everyone can hear it.

4. Then have the three witnesses sign on the last page on the lines provided for their signatures and then put their entire addresses to the right after the words, "residing at."

After this is done, then each of you, as to your respective will, sign each page at the bottom where the long line appears to identify each page as being that of your will.

Then have the three witnesses initial each page of the will on the left hand, bottom side of the page in the place for that purpose.

After everyone has signed as described above, conform the signature and initials on the copy of the will. Do not have each person sign it but just print in their names and initials as signed on the original wills, and return to us for our file, the conformed copy of the wills.

You should retain the original wills either in a bank safety deposit box or where you keep your other valuable papers.

We are also enclosing an information form for the Executor, which you should fill out and give to Mrs. Wright as she is named as Executrix in both of the wills.

In the event you have any questions, please call me.

Very sincerely,

COMMENT:

1. The above letter, of course, will need to be modified to suit the individual procedure customary in your jurisdiction with regard to execution of wills.

2. The better practice, of course, is to execute wills in the lawyer's office, but sometimes this is not convenient, and a letter similar to the above is required.

105.

TRANSMITTAL OF WILLS AND INSTRUCTIONS FOR EXECUTING WILLS

Dear Joseph and Martha:

Enclosed are the originals and two copies of new wills for you and Martha.

The steps which should be followed in executing the wills are as follows:

1. You and three witnesses, together with a notary public, should all be in the same room at the same time.

2. You should tell the three witnesses that you wish them to serve as witnesses of your will.

3. Then you should initial the bottom of each page and then fill in the information called for on page 8 with respect to the date and the names of the three witnesses, and then you should sign on the line provided for your signature on page 7 signing your name just as it is typed on that page.

4. Immediately after you have done this, each witness in turn should sign his or her name and fill in his or her address.

5. Immediately thereafter, and before anyone has left the room, you and each witness should sign at the places designated on page 8.

6. The notary public should then complete the notarization as provided.

The same procedure as outlined above should be followed by Martha in executing her will. You and she can do both wills at the same time.

Only the original of the wills should be signed. The two copies of each which I have furnished, should then be "conformed" to the originals. That is, on the copies someone other than yourself should print or type in exactly what was written by you, Martha and the witnesses on the original wills. Then one conformed copy of each will should be returned to me. The other conformed copies may be kept by you. The originals can be kept by you or by the ABC Bank, as you wish. If you want the bank to keep the originals, they will give you a receipt. They do not charge for keeping the originals in their vault.

If there is something in the wills that you or Martha particularly want to change at the last minute, you can strike through and write in the change, but be sure to initial the page opposite whatever change you make and have Martha initial whatever change she makes in her will.

If you have any further questions before you proceed with the execution of the wills, you might call me.

Best personal regards.

Sincerely,

COMMENT:

1. The above letter simplifies what is actually a complicated transaction, namely the execution of a will outside the lawyer's office by his client.

2. Although it is preferable for the client to execute his will in the lawyer's office, many times this is impractical or impossible.

106.
LETTER ADVISING CLIENT WHO WILL HANDLE
PERSONAL INJURY CASE

Dear Lois:

Your case is presently being handled in our office by Tom Drake.

Please call him about any problem concerning your case.

Whenever it is necessary for us to contact you, we will do so. If you do not hear from us, please rest assured that we are continuing to work on your case.

We suggest that you talk only to personnel of our office about your case. If someone desires information, we suggest that you refer them to our office.

Sincerely yours,

COMMENT:

1. The writer could also add a brief description of additional things that will be done in behalf of the client in connection with the case.

2. The writer might request that the client keep him advised of his address and telephone number in the event of any change.

3. Some additional comment regarding the substance of the case would be helpful.

107.
LETTER TO CLIENT EXPLAINING PROCEDURE IN HANDLING CLAIM
WITH MEMORANDUM FOR PERSONAL INJURY CLIENT

Dear Mr. Smith:

We will continue working on your case until we have obtained all available evidence.

The next step is usually the filing of the written complaint on your behalf. This is normally followed by the filing of a written answer by the defendant in the action. After all preparation is completed by both sides, including depositions and interrogatories, a memorandum will be filed for a trial date. Your case then goes on a trial calendar to await its turn for a trial-setting conference. The waiting period is normally about three months from the date of the filing of the memorandum.

At the time of the trial-setting conference, a trial date will be assigned, which will be about one month to two months after the trial-setting conference. For any number of reasons this date may not be as certain as we would like it to be, and it may be continued once or twice. You will be informed of such continuance if it occurs.

Pending the trial date, doctors and nurses will be interviewed; medical reports, medical bills, etc., will be accumulated; and the preparation for trial will continue. Within six months, oral statements before a court reporter will probably be required of the parties and witnesses. If necessary, we will make an appointment with you in preparation for your deposition.

Do not, under any circumstances, discuss your case with anyone, except members of this office.

Please inform this office immediately of any change of address or telephone number. Inform this office immediately of any change in your physical condition.

Notify this office immediately should your doctor stop giving you treatment.

Be sure to send all receipts, cancelled checks, bills, and other papers pertaining to medical treatment; automobile repairs; loss of earnings; damage to personal property; and papers showing any expense connected with your case. I must have all of these things either for settlement or for evidence in the case if it is necessary to go to trial.

If you have any other accident, injury, or illness, notify me at once. You will be informed of any reasonable offer that is made to settle your case.

I am enclosing a memorandum and medical sheet. Please make proper entries on the enclosed medical sheet.

Very sincerely,

COMMENT:

1. The above letter and enclosed memorandum is an excellent way of explaining the procedure involved in handling the clients personal injury claim.

MEMORANDUM

WHAT YOU, AS A PERSONAL INJURY CLIENT, SHOULD KNOW:

1. Insurance companies do not pay money willingly. The insurance company can be expected to thoroughly investigate the facts of the accident, the claim for medical treatment, and any past injuries or claims. The insurance company will obtain copies of all past medical records.

2. The insurance company may hire a private investigator to take movies of any physical activity that you may engage in. The insurance company may even lay a trap for you, such as attempting to hire you to do physical activity, causing a flat tire, or placing something in the yard that will need to be lifted, etc.

3. The insurance company may hire a private investigator who may carry a concealed tape recorder in talking to you or to your friends. You should not discuss your case with anyone, including friends.

4. It will help your case to tell me about any PRIOR INJURY or PRIOR PAIN to any parts of your body. Many good cases are lost by the injured person's concealing or forgetting a previous injury.

5. You should be sure to furnish me with the names and addresses of all doctors who have treated you. Particular attention should be given to all doctors in the local area, where it will be easy for the defense to obtain full copies of the medical records. I do not expect you to remember everything in your medical history; therefore, it is advisable to have copies made of all medical records of the family doctor, etc., so that you may review your own previous complaints to refresh your memory.

6. Insurance companies keep a record of any and all claims against any insurance company. The insurance company is sure to find out if you have ever made a previous claim.

7. Tell your local doctor all of your complaints. The doctor's records can only be as complete as what you have told the doctor.

8. Keep track of all prescriptions and medicines taken, preferably saving all bottles or containers of medicine.

9. Keep a diary of all of your complaints. This will help you remember many months later.

10. It may be necessary some day to have friends, neighbors or co-workers testify regarding your disability and pain and suffering; therefore, start thinking about the witnesses you may need in the future.

11. Keep me informed of anything that in any way might affect your case. Certainly nothing should be signed without first consulting me. Applications for insurance benefits, reports to the State, any change in doctors, returning to work, any change in treatment, etc., should be reported to my office promptly. Disability or unemployment applications should first be checked by me.

12. Keep my office advised of any vacation times when you may not be available. An emergency telephone number and an alternative way of reaching you must be in my file at all times.

13. Some of the necessary costs of your injury claim include expenses of the police report, investigation service, filing fee, copying medical records and medical reports that the doctors submit, depositions, jury fees, transcripts (if required), and witness fees.

14. If you have other insurance and need help, our office will submit your claims, particularly medical payment claims.

15. It sometimes takes many months to settle a claim. In fact, it is dangerous to settle certain types of claims too soon because it often takes a long time for serious injuries to become evident. The amount asked for in the complaint is, of course, merely a figure and will be adjusted up or down (usually down) depending upon the future development of your case.

108.
TRANSMITTAL OF INTERROGATORIES TO CLIENT WITH INSTRUCTIONS

Dear Carolyn:

Enclosed is a list of questions called interrogatories which have been submitted to you under our state Rules of Civil Procedure, Rule 87. This rule requires you to answer each of these questions separately and fully in writing.

Please review each of these questions and then write your answers using the same numbering sequence. Then forward the questions and answers to us for review. We will review your answers extensively and have them typed in proper form. We will call you to come to our office to sign your answers, and your signature will be notarized at our office. The final typed answers will be filed with the court in your case.

If you have any difficulty answering any questions, please call and discuss the matter with me over the telephone. During the discussion, we can determine whether or not it will be necessary for you to come to our office to discuss the matter further.

Please have your written answers mailed or delivered to our office within fourteen days.

Very sincerely,

COMMENT:

1. The above letter could include some thoughts or comments regarding the preparation of answers to the interrogatories.

GROUP D
Giving Advice

109.
TRANSMITTAL OF LIMITED PARTNERSHIP DOCUMENTS AND
ADVICE FOR GENERAL AND LIMITED PARTNERS

Dear Ms. Mason:

You have requested our law firm to prepare the legal instruments necessary for the formation of a limited partnership under the State Limited Partnership Act contained in Title _____ Section _____ , state code, as last amended.

Copies of the necessary documents are enclosed for your review. Please review these documents, and, if you have any questions, please contact me for further discussion.

If the documents meet your needs, please contact me, and we will deliver the final documents for signatures.

We would like to inform you that there are different classes of partners in a limited partnership, consisting of general partners and limited partners. The contributions and liabilities of these different classes of partners vary. The general partner makes a contribution, is liable for partnership obligations to an unlimited degree, and actively engages in the management and business of the partnership. The limited partner contributes his capital primarily as a financial investment, his liability is generally limited to his investment, and he generally is not an active participant in the partnership management or business.

We would like to point out to you several requirements under state law for your general information. These requirements pertain to limited partnerships and are as follows:

1. A limited partnership must have one or more general partners.

2. A limited partnership must have one or more limited partners.

3. A certificate must be signed by the partners (similar to the certificate enclosed for your review).

4. The certificate must be filed in the office of the Probate Judge in the county in which the principal place of business is designated.

5. A limited partnership may carry on any business which a partnership without limited partners may carry on, except banking or insurance.

6. The contributions of a limited partner may be cash or other property but may not consist of services.

7. The surname of a limited partner shall not appear in the partnership name unless it is also the surname of a general partner. If the surname of a limited partner is used with knowledge of the limited partner, then the limited partner becomes liable as a general partner to partnership creditors who extend credit to the partnership without actual knowledge that he is not a general partner.

8. The name of every limited partnership shall contain the word "limited" or its abbreviation "ltd," and such designation shall be used in every instance in which the partnership name is used.

9. A limited partner must not act as an agent for the partnership for any purpose,

and, if he acts contrary to this provision, he is liable as a general partner to any partnership creditor who extends credit to the partnership in the good faith and belief that he was dealing with a general partner.

10. Additional limited partners may be admitted upon filing an amendment to the original certificate in accordance with state law.

11. Where there are several limited partners, the members may agree that one or more of the limited partners shall have a priority over the other limited partners, but, in the absence of such a statement in the original certificate, all the limited partners shall stand upon equal footing.

12. A limited partner's interest in the partnership is considered personal property; therefore, we are of the opinion the general partners would have the right to convey real estate owned by the limited partnership. It would be advisable for the respective spouses of the general partners to join in the execution of a deed of conveyance to the partnership property. There is no specific provision in state law pertaining to the conveyancing of real estate by a limited partnership; however, this opinion is based upon a previous research of the law and extensive discussions with other attorneys in this regard.

If you have any questions about this matter, please call me.

Yours truly,

COMMENT:

1. The above letter is thoughtful and raises a number of matters which should be considered by the client.

110.
INFORMATION FOR FORMING ONE-BANK HOLDING COMPANY

Dear Mr. Brown:

At your request, we have examined the possibilities of forming a one-bank holding company under state law. We understand that you are interested in transfering ownership of your corporation to a holding company which would be owned by the present stockholders of ABC Corporation.

The general scheme for turning a publicly owned corporation into a wholly owned subsidiary of another company is relatively simple. The first step is to create two new corporations, one of which owns 100% of the common stock of the other. The subsidiary corporation holds stock of its parent as an asset. In the second step, the subsidiary corporation and the existing publicly held corporation enter into a merger, wherein the old corporation survives, but the shares of stock of the old corporation are converted into shares of the new parent corporation. When the second step is completed, the former shareholders of the old corporation are the owners of the new parent corporation, and the new parent corporation is in the position of being a holding company for the old corporation. The new subsidiary corporation which was created in the first stages disappears with the merger.

If possible, it will be desirable for a general business corporation formed under the Business Corporation Act to serve as the subsidiary corporation created to merge into the existing bank. This would eliminate the requirement of establishing a second state bank for the sole purpose of being able to effectuate the transaction. However, this is not possible in our state.

Our state, _____ , has a specific statute, Code _____ , Section _____ , which specifically disallows the merger of a state bank and a general business corporation. That statute does allow, however, for a "shadow state bank" to be created for various purposes, the formation of one-bank holding companies included. Essentially, there is a shortened procedure for obtaining a bank charter for a corporation whose only function will be to act as a party to a merger with an existing bank.

Your state, _____ , does not have an equivalent statute or procedure. Your Code, Section _____ , of the State Statutes Annotated, sets forth the procedure for merger and consolidation of two state banks or a state bank and a national bank. However, it is completely silent on the question of whether a state banking corporation and a general business corporation may merge and neither approves nor disallows such a transaction.

The provision of the Banking Act respecting powers of state banking corporations provides that "State banks shall have: (a) All the powers provided and conferred on them in the Banking Act *and such general corporate powers as are appropriate to its purpose.* . . ." (Emphasis added). We have been unable to find any cases or other material construing this provision. However, we believe that the reference to purpose was probably intended to mean the purpose of conducting a banking business on a day-to-day basis rather than to allow a banking corporation to have all of the powers of any other corporation. If the broader definition of purpose were allowed, then banks would not only be allowed to conduct their businesses, but also to merge, sell assets, liquidate and so forth under either the Business Corporation Act or the Banking Act.

We have spoken with Tom Joyce, _____ State Banking Examiner, on the telephone, and his interpretation agrees with ours. It is the position of the State Banking Department that state banks may only be merged with other state banks or with national banks. However, your state, _____ , does not have a holding company statute and will follow the federal government's lead in approving bank mergers for the purpose of forming bank holding companies. This will include the approval of bank mergers involving phantom banks.

The Federal Deposit Insurance Corporation and the Federal Reserve Bank are charged, by the Bank Holding Company Act of 1970 and the regulations thereunder, with approving the creation and operation of bank holding companies. They expressly recognize the use of phantom banks in their procedures but also require compliance with applicable state statutes. The following is an explanation of the procedure that will be required to form a bank holding company through the merger approach. Of course, it does not apply to the situation where a holding company is formed and then makes a tender offer to the stockholders of an existing bank.

The first step in the procedure is to undertake to form the shadow state bank. Under our state statute, five or more individuals, a majority of whom are residents of the state, may act as incorporators. They must each subscribe to and pay in full for, in cash, at least one percent (1%) of the authorized capital stock. The organizers then file with the Banking Commissioner a Notice of Intent to organize a state bank and pay an investigation fee equal to one-half percent (.5%) of the capital structure.

Simultaneously, the organizers should form a corporation under the Business Corporation Act. The corporation should be organized for the purpose of becoming a holding company. This corporation should then immediately enter into a contract with the organizers of the proposed state bank to acquire all of the otherwise unsubscribed stock of the proposed new bank, subject to the approval of it as a holding company by the Federal Reserve and the FDIC.

At the time of subscribing to the stock of the proposed bank, each subscriber must pay, in addition to his subscription, in cash, an amount which will be used to defray organization expenses. When the bank opens, unexpended funds are transferred to undivided profit. If the bank's application is denied, the unexpended funds are returned pro rata to the subscribers.

The Commissioner of Banking will automatically approve the Notice of Intent as soon as the statutory requirements as to its contents are satisfied. The organizers must then, prior to filing an application for permission to file a corporate charter with the Corporation Commission, satisfy the requirements of the Securities act of 1933; issue a receipt to each subscriber and file a duplicate receipt with the Banking Commission providing that all subscribers' funds, except for those used for organizational expenses, will be returned to the subscribers; and file an escrow agreement whereby another bank will receive subscribers' funds and hold the same until such time as their release is authorized by the State Securities Commissioner or the State Banking Department. The subscribers, other than the five organizers, are not required, however, to pay for their stock until after the Articles of Incorporation are filed with the State Corporation Commission.

The proposed holding company must subscribe to all of the stock not subscribed for by the organizers, and the requirements set forth in the preceding paragraph must be completed within sixty (60) days of the filing of the Notice of Intent to organize the state bank or within whatever extensions of time are granted by the Banking Commissioner. As soon as those requirements are completed, and within the sixty days, the organizers of the proposed state bank must apply to the commissioner for permission to file Articles of Incorporation with the State Corporation Commission. The application contains certain general information and must be accompanied by the proposed Articles of Incorporation and by-laws of the banking corporation.

Our statute requires the commissioner, upon receipt of the application, to make a careful investigation relative to:

(1) the character, reputation, and financial standing of the organizers or incorporators;

(2) the character, financial responsibility of proposed directors and banking or trust experience and business qualifications of those proposed as officers;

(3) the ability of the community to support the proposed bank, giving consideration to:

(a) the services offered by existing banks and other financial institutions;

(b) the banking history of the community; and

(c) the opportunities for profitable employment of bank funds as indicated by the demand for credit, the number of potential depositors, the volume of bank transactions, and the business and industries of the community, with particular regard to their stability, diversification and size; and

(4) whether or not the full amount of the authorized capital structure has been subscribed;

(5) whether or not the proposed capital structure is adequate in the light of current and prospective banking conditions;

(6) whether or not the name of the proposed bank resembles so closely as to be likely to cause confusion the name of any other bank transacting business in this state; and

(7) such other facts and circumstances bearing on the proposed bank and its relation to the community as in the opinion of the commissioner may be relevant.

Upon the completion of his investigation, the Banking Commissioner either rejects the application or endorses his approval on the proposed Articles of Incorporation, at which time the Articles of Incorporation may be filed with the Corporation Commission, and the banking corporation is created.

The Banking Holding Company Act, 12 FCA S1841 et. seq. (1973 Supp) makes it illegal for any corporation to hold twenty-five percent (25%) of the stock of any banking corporation without first having obtained the approval of the Federal Reserve Board as a bank holding company. Since the proposed holding company will subscribe to a large portion of the stock of the phantom bank and the stock subscriptions must be paid in full within sixty days of the filing of the Articles of Incorporation of the proposed state bank, and Application for Permission to Become a Holding Company should be filed with the Federal Reserve Board immediately after the proposed holding company has subscribed to the stock of the phantom bank.

When the application is received by the Federal Reserve Board and involves a state bank, the board notifies the State Banking Commissioner and requests that his views be submitted within thirty (30) days. If the commissioner disapproves the application, the board must set up a hearing on the application at which all interested parties may testify. Following the hearing, the board will either approve or disapprove the application. If the State Banking Commissioner approves the application, the board must either disapprove the application within ninety-one days of its filing, or it is automatically approved. In making its determination, the board is charged with considering the financial and managerial resources and future prospects of the company and the banks concerned, and the convenience and needs of the community to be served.

Within thirty days of the filing of the Articles of Incorporation, the proposed directors must call for the payment of stock subscriptions in full to the escrow agent. Within thirty days after the call, the incorporators must deliver a statement of the escrow agent to the Banking Commissioner setting forth the amount paid into escrow by the subscribers, stating that the entire authorized capital has been paid into escrow and that the corporation will be prepared to transact business within one hundred eighty (180) days. As soon as the full subscription has been paid, a meeting of stockholders shall be held for the purpose of electing directors, adopting bylaws, and calling the first meeting of directors for the purpose of electing officer.

The only remaining requirement prior to beginning the merger procedure of the phantom bank into the existing bank is that of obtaining a Certificate of Authority for the phantom bank. It is unlawful for the phantom bank to conduct any business, other than perfecting its organization, without first having a Certificate of Authority. The Certificate of Authority must be requested within one hundred eighty (180) days of the filing of the Application for Permission to file Articles of Incorporation and must contain the following:

(1) the address at which the bank will operate;

(2) a statement that all of the by-laws adopted have been attached as an exhibit to the request;

(3) a statement that the full amount of the authorized capital structure has been paid to the escrow agent;

(4) the signed oaths of the directors; and

(5) such other information as the commissioner may require to enable him to determine whether a Certificate of Authority should be issued.

If the Certificate of Authority is issued, the phantom bank may begin the merger process. If the Certificate of Authority is denied, the subscribers' money is liquidated by the commissioner.

It will be necessary for the phantom bank to obtain FDIC approval since it will never engage in the banking business or accept deposits. However, as will be shown later, the holding company and the resulting bank growing out of the merger must obtain such insurance.

By the time that the Certificate of Authority is issued, the holding company will have been approved and will own up to ninety-five percent (95%) of the stock of the phantom bank. Thus, the situation will be such that it will be possible to begin merging the old bank and the phantom bank.

As the first step in merging two banks, the board of directors of each merging bank must, by a majority of the entire board of directors, approve a merger agreement containing the following items:

(1) A statement that the merger agreement is subject to approval by the State Bank Examiner and by the stockholders of each bank;

(2) The name and address of each bank;

(3) The name and location of the principal office and other offices of the resulting bank;

(4) The name and residence of each proposed director of the resulting bank;

(5) The name and residence of each proposed officer of the resulting bank;

(6) The amount of capital, number of shares and par value of each share of the resulting bank;

(7) The nature of any preferred stock of the resulting bank;

(8) Any amendments to the charter and by-laws of the resulting bank;

(9) The manner of converting shares of the merging banks into shares of the resulting bank;

(10) The manner of disposing of the shares of the resulting bank which are not taken by the dissenting stockholders of each merging bank; and

(11) Such other provisions which the State Bank Examiner may require.

Our statute does not expressly recognize three-party mergers, i.e., where the stockholders of the two merged banks receive stock in a third corporation rather than in the surviving bank. Requirements (9) and (10) above reflect this gap in the statute. Accordingly, to be safe in even beginning the entire process of forming and then merging a phantom bank, it will be necessary to obtain an advance ruling from the Banking Commission as to the possibility of conducting a three-party merger.

After approval by the board of directors, the merger agreement shall be submitted to the State Bank Examiner for approval, together with certified copies of the resolutions of each of the board of directors approving the merger agreement. The State Bank Examiner shall approve or disapprove the merger agreement. He must approve the merger if he finds that:

(1) The resulting bank meets the requirements for formation of a new state bank;

(2) There is adequate capital structure including surplus, in relation to the deposit liabilities of the resulting bank and in relation to its other activities;

(3) The agreement is fair; and

(4) The merger is not contrary to the public interest.

If the State Bank Examiner disapproves the agreement, he shall do so in writing, and the merging bank shall be given the opportunity to amend the merger agreement.

The merger as revised and amended must then be approved by two-thirds of the outstanding voting stock of each class of each of the merging banks. That vote shall constitute the adoption of the charter and by-laws of the resulting bank. The notice requirements of our statute regarding the meeting of stockholders must be satisfied.

The merger, unless a later date is specified in the merger agreement, is effective upon filing with the State Bank Examiner signed copies of the merger agreement along with copies of the resolutions of the stockholders of each bank and a list of the shareholders who voted against the transaction. The charters of the merging banks immediately terminate. The State Bank Examiner issues a certificate of merger, and, insofar as state law is concerned, the transaction is closed except for the settlement of the interests of dissenting shareholders.

However, the Bank Holding Company act of 1970 makes it illegal for a bank to take any action that causes the bank to become a subsidiary of a bank holding company. Accordingly, it will be necessary to condition the merger agreement upon approval of the Federal Reserve Board. It will also be necessary for the merger agreement to be conditioned upon the holding company and the resulting bank being insured by the FDIC.

Essentially, the Federal Reserve Board requirements and the FDIC requirements will be substantially satisfied at the time that the application to become a bank holding company is approved, inasmuch as that application will set forth the details of the entire proposed transaction.

The foregoing is an outline of the procedure in our state for forming a bank holding company through the merger process. It contains a summary of every step in the procedure. It is conceivable that some of the procedures may be shortened once the Banking Commissioner is made cognizant of the fact that we are dealing only with a shadow state bank and that it will never be a competitive or operating force in the local banking community. However, since our statutes do not contemplate shadow banks, we believe it desirable to set forth the maximum burden which can be required of you.

After you have had the opportunity to review these matters, we shall be pleased to discuss them with you.

Very sincerely,

COMMENT:

1. The above letter explains in a straightforward way the detailed information required to form a one-bank holding company.

2. The lawyer, by reducing a complicated matter to writing in the above letter, has performed an invaluable service for the client by explaining in plain language the information required. The client has the advantage of being able to study the letter at his leisure and fully absorb the multitude of matters covered in the letter.

3. Substantive legal matters should be checked against current law.

111.
REPLY TO LETTER REGARDING NONSUPPORT CASE

Dear Linda:

This will acknowledge receipt of your letter regarding the failure of your ex-husband to make support payments in accordance with the decree granted you on June 12, case number 3304, which was granted here in Lincoln County.

I would suggest that your best means of enforcing the decree for support would be by securing a lawyer in Texas, where your husband is presently living.

Of course, the decree rendered here in Lincoln County would be entitled to full faith and credit in Texas and would be enforceable there as to all payments which are in arrears.

You may try the nearest bar association office to secure the name of an attorney in Houston or, in the event you do not have any success there, we will recommend a lawyer to you.

If we can be of any further assistance in this matter, please let us know.

Very sincerely,

COMMENT:

1. In the event the writer desires to handle the matter in behalf of the prospective client, he may outline the terms and suggest a course of action to the client in lieu of the language above.

112.
TRANSMITTAL OF COPY OF ORDER AND ADVICE REGARDING CHILD

Dear Mr. Carpenter:

I am enclosing a copy of an order by Judge Murphy dated September 16, but which I only received today. Unless you have a definite commitment from Jane that she will voluntarily go to high school as a student, it is very important that you file a petition against her as an undisciplined child, and in that way the court can force her to go somewhere. Otherwise, there will only be a charge against you for neglect, and the court will be helpless to do anything with Jane and can impose some kind of restrictions or punishment upon you.

Please call me and let me know what decision Jane has made, and I shall be glad to advice you accordingly.

Sincerely,

COMMENT:

1. Letters such as the above touch upon very emotional matters for the client. For this reason, the lawyer may desire to conclude or enlarge the letter by stating or commenting upon some more positive, pleasing or satisfying aspect of the matter for the client.

113.
RECOMMENDATION FOR DISPOSITION OF JUVENILE CASE

Dear Ronald:

I talked at length with Joseph Johnson, the Juvenile Probation Officer in connection with your case, as well as with Roy Miller, the Assistant District Attorney who will be handling your case.

I have worked out what I consider the best agreement we can make with them. This is that you will admit the juvenile offense and will be placed on probation until you reach age 18, which will be next May, and, in addition, will be required to serve one week in the Juvenile Detention Home. You will have to pay court costs, but there will not be any fine in connection with the case.

Ronald, I think this is the best possible arrangement we could make in view of the fact that there were six bags of marijuana involved. Due to this quantity, Mr. Johnson and Mr. Miller stated that they were convinced that you were in the business of selling marijuana. Also, they suggested that I pass on to you the fact that Max Taylor and the other officers in the Narcotics Squad of our Police Department are well aware of your activities and will be watching out for anything you do. My very strong advice is for you to completely avoid anything to do with any type of controlled substance.

I consider that you are coming out lucky in this case, and I hope you will let it serve a constructive purpose.

In the event you take exception to my recommendation that we accept the arrangement I have described in this letter, let me know. Otherwise, just come to my office thirty minutes before the time set for trial, and we'll go over and get it disposed of. Also, Ronald, your father must come with you.

Thank you very much.

Sincerely yours,

COMMENT:

1. The above letter is an example of a status report and recommendation by the lawyer for disposition of a juvenile case.

2. Letters such as this are helpful in keeping the client informed and advising the client in advance of the lawyer's recommended course of action.

114.

RECOMMENDATION THAT CLAIM SHOULD NOT BE PURSUED

Dear Louise:

I think your letter to me of August 27 is very well written, and each of the points you have made is well taken. However, I do not feel there is any substantial basis for a lawsuit against the insurance company in connection with the matter for reasons that I will set forth in this letter.

First, I would like to comment on the various paragraphs of your letter. The third paragraph, in which you mention the actions of Mr. Powell in connection with your claim, indicates, of course, that the adjuster has done a commendable job in assisting you to collect on your claim pursuant to your homeowner's insurance policy. This, of course, was his job, but it does seem that he did it well and took an interest in doing all he could, especially in view of the tragic circumstances involved. I would have thought that his report to the insurance company which prompted the payment of the claim in the amount of $1,280 would have given sufficient information to the insurance company to indicate that the matter should be closed at that point.

I am also surprised that Ralph's contacts with the home office in Omaha did not immediately terminate the investigation.

It is clear to me, with regard to your telephone conversation on July 2 with the claims supervisor, that he was completely off base and handled the matter in an unprofessional manner, to say the least. I would think that his conduct in connection with this transaction and your telephone conversation with him on July 2 should be reported to his superiors at the home office.

In addition, I think that Mr. Bowen, who identified himself as the regional manager, handled the matter in a very loose manner. I would further think that his activities should be reported to his superiors at the home office.

However, Louise, I simply don't see that we have a sufficient claim for a lawsuit. Section 1681 (b) of the Fair Credit Reporting Act provides that one of the permissible purposes of reports is that the person securing it intends to use the information in connection with the underwriting of insurance involving the consumer. In your case, I suppose it would be the continued underwriting of insurance.

Louise, I hate to keep saying I don't think we have a claim, but this has been my candid opinion and advice to help guide you in your course of action. If you would like to discuss it in more detail and have me explain my reasons in more depth, I suggest you come back to the office.

I think you would have made an excellent lawyer, and, as I said, I think your letter is extremely well written, and your points are well taken but it is my judgment that the claim is not substantial enough to warrant litigation in your behalf.

Please give my best to your husband.

Very sincerely,

COMMENT:

1. In rejecting a claim, it is a good idea to emphasize to the client the principal reasons the claim is rejected and perhaps suggest an alternative course of action.

115.
LETTER TO CLIENT EVALUATING CLAIM AND
RECOMMENDING AGAINST FILING SUIT

Dear Mr. Williams:

Thank you very much for letting me have a complete file in the case of Ralph Mason, who was separated from service with the federal agency after 19 years of honorable service. The file is quite complete, and I have reviewed it in its entirety.

I certainly agree with you and John Richardson, who handled the administrative appeal to the Civil Service Commission, that the agency should not have separated Ralph after his 19 years of honorable service, during which time he never received any adverse performance ratings until the matter which led to his separation, all of which occurred well within his last year of service.

You asked me specifically for my opinion of our chances of success in reversing this action through filing suit in the United States District Court, for the Southern District of our state. In the event we filed an appeal for Ralph in the U.S. District Court, it would be pursuant to the Administrative Procedure Act. We would be limited to the record which has been produced in his case. The court would not grant relief unless it made a finding that the action of the Civil Service Commission was arbitrary, capricious, an abuse of discretion, or otherwise not in accordance with law. The burden would be on Ralph to prove that the Civil Service Commission acted arbitrarily, capriciously or abused its discretion. The court would not allow a trial de novo of the matter, in which we could produce witnesses and so forth to attempt to prove Ralph's case, but would restrict its review to the record. While I disagree with the action of the agency and of the Civil Service Commission, I do not feel, after reviewing the record, there is sufficient chance of success in the case to warrant an appeal to the U.S. District Court.

I would appreciate it if you would please give Ralph a copy of this letter, and, in the event he would like to discuss the matter in greater detail, you might suggest that he come down to visit with me at his convenience.

I know that Ralph appreciates your interest in his case. I regret that my opinion is what it is, but I have found from experience it is better to be realistic about the chances of success before you begin one of these cases than it is to be disappointed with the results of an appeal. It is really difficult to overturn these administrative decisions unless you can point to some glaring procedural errors. While there appear to be procedural errors early in the proceeding, Ralph was eventually afforded the right to a full hearing, to be heard and so forth, and I have not discovered any substantial errors in the record on which to base the appeal.

Sincerely yours,

COMMENT:

1. The above letter evaluating the client's claim and recommending against suit has been strengthened by the writer's going into detail and giving specific reasons to support the recommendation against filing suit.

116.
RECOMMENDATION TO USE EXPERT WITNESS

Dear Mr. Murphy:

Thank you for your letter dated November 17, in which you enclosed a copy of the letter contract you have with ABC Company.

Frankly, if we had an expert witness available to us in Johnson City who had no previous contact with ABC Company, and we were trying to decide between him and another expert witness who did have previous contact with ABC Company, I would suggest that we take the one who had no previous contact, assuming all other factors were equal.

However, in this particular situation, Dr. Paul is the only local expert witness who is available. To me it is much more important that he is local than the fact that he is doing and has done previous consulting work for ABC Company.

Therefore, it is my recommendation that we plan to use Dr. Paul as our expert witness in connection with the case against DEF Corporation.

I would appreciate it very much if you would please contact Dr. Paul and ask him to get in touch with me at his earliest convenience.

Please let me know if you have any questions or suggestions regarding the matter.

Sincerely yours,

COMMENT:

1. The writer could outline the matter he expects the expert witness to cover.

2. The writer could outline the manner in which he intends to prepare the expert witness for trial and coordinate the matter with the client.

117.

REPORT OF SURPLUS IN HOME MORTGAGE ESCROW ACCOUNT
WITH SUGGESTION FOR ADJUSTMENT BETWEEN BUYERS AND SELLERS

Dear Mr. Brown:

We are enclosing a report from ABC Mortgage Company, Inc., regarding the status of the escrow account in connection with the sale of your equity.

You will note that there is an excess of $85 in the account, which may be utilized by applying the excess to the next mortgage payment.

Therefore, we suggest that the buyers, Mr. and Mrs. Johnson, apply the excess to the next mortgage payment and forward you a check in the amount of $85.

Thanks very much.

Very sincerely,

COMMENT:

1. The above letter could state that the suggestion is in accord with the usual practice or custom in connection with the transaction.

2. The writer could state that he would like to be advised in the event the buyers do not forward a check as suggested.

118.
ADVICE TO CLIENT REGARDING SPONSORSHIP OF GOSPEL SINGERS

Dear Mrs. Murphy:

I enjoyed very much meeting you and talking with you on May 3 when you were in the office. After you left I did get a chance to talk to Jim Powell in Memphis. He told me the $5,000 payment was not in connection with the proposed record but was for advertising materials.

He gave me the following breakdown of the items that would be purchased with the $5,000.

1. 1,500 8 × 10 glossy prints
2. 3,000 copies of resumes
3. 10,000 soft paper pictures
4. manila folder
5. demonstration tape on cassette tape

He also told me that he would get a commission on the $5,000, which I understood would be approximately 25%. However, I did not cross-examine him on this as to his full participation in connection with the advertising materials.

The other charge of $1,750 was in connection with the records.

Later in the day yesterday, I had a chance to talk to William Burgess, a friend and client of mine who manages Burgess Music Company in Nashville. He didn't like the sound of the business proposition and said that Tom Miller of Johnson City lost about $18,000 on a group similar to this.

His thought was that the group should get on a circuit for gospel music, and in this regard they might contact Foster Douglas of ABC Music Company for information. His further thought was they were not ready for a record.

I thought I would pass this information on to you, and I suggest we hold up on both the advertising materials and the proposed records until we have had a chance to get together and discuss it more fully. I would think the next time we get together, you should bring or arrange to have the boys come in at the same time, and I can meet them.

My overall impression that it would be very, very difficult for you to make any money out of this venture and very, very easy for you to lose money is still with me. Of course, as I told you, I have no particular experience in this field and am relying on my general knowledge and experience as a lawyer.

I know the boys are very appreciative of everything you have done for them. I would also think there are plenty of ways you could help them without, at the same time, running too large a risk of loss yourself. In the long run their success must depend on their own ability and reception and not upon financial banking from you.

Very sincerely,

COMMENT:

1. Specific details, as enumerated above, add strength and depth to a letter of advice to the client.

119.

CERTIFICATION UNDER RULE 144 OF SECURITIES ACT OF 1933 IN CONNECTION WITH SALE OF STOCK

Dear Mr. Bowden:

We have previously advised you that ABC Securities Company, our New York stock transfer agent, has requested your opinion to the effect that the sale on November 20 of 14,000 shares of DEF Corporation common stock (the "Stock") by you and your mother does not violate Rule 144 under the Securities Act of 1933, as amended. In connection with such request, we certify as follows:

1. ABC Securities Company has filed all reports required to be filed by Section 13 of the Securities Exchange Act of 1934 during the 12 months immediately preceding the sale of the stock.

2. The sale of 14,000 shares of DEF Corporation common stock is less than one percent of the common shares outstanding and also less than the average weekly reported volume of trading in such securities on all securities' exchanges during the four calendar weeks preceding the filing of the Form 144 pertaining to the Stock with the SEC.

3. ABC Securities Company is not aware of any circumstances that would lead it to believe that the sale of Stock is in violation of Rule 144.

Yours very truly,

COMMENT:

1. If desired, the lawyer could further explain Rule 144 to the client. In addition, the lawyer could include his recommendation regarding the opinion which has been requested from the client.

GROUP E
Giving Opinion

120.
TITLE OPINION ON REAL ESTATE

Dear Mr. and Mrs. Powell:

Pursuant to your request, we have examined title to the above-described property through April 16, 19XX from the Probate Records of Lincoln County.

It is our opinion, after examination of the aforesaid records, that good and merchantable title to said property is vested in Daniel Schmidt and wife, Margarita, subject to the following exceptions:

1. 19XX ad valorem taxes which become due and payable on October 1.

2. Easements and restrictions of record regarding said property.

3. Such state of facts as would be disclosed by an accurate engineering survey and inspection of the premises, including rights of parties in possession which are not a matter of record.

This opinion is submitted to you in connection with the purchase of real estate, and our liability is limited to $8,000.

Sincerely yours,

COMMENT:

1. The title opinion letter is generally used in connection with real estate transactions in which title insurance is not obtained.

2. It would be a good idea for the lawyer to discuss with the client the advantages and expenses of title insurance.

3. The above opinion is based upon a search of title directly in the land records of the county. In many cases the search would be made on the basis of an abstract of title provided by an abstract company. In many localities abstract companies issue title insurance without the assistance of local attorneys.

121.
TITLE OPINION FOR EQUITY SALE

Dear Mr. and Mrs. Alvarez:

Pursuant to your request, we have examined title to the following described property from October 12, 19XX, through June 27, 19XX:

Lot 3, Block 4, according to the plat of Shady Acres, Second Addition, as recorded in Plat Book 27, page 84, Probate Records of Lincoln County.

Assuming as of October 12, 19XX, that Thomas McCampbell and wife, Jennifer, had a good and merchantable title to the above-described property, it is our opinion, after an examination of the records on file in the Office of the Probate Judge of Lincoln County, from October 12, 19XX, that good and merchantable title to said property is vested in Randolph Perkins and wife, Lucille, subject to the following exceptions:

1. Mortgage from Thomas McCampbell and wife, Jennifer, to ABC Mortgage Company, dated October 12, 19XX, recorded October 12, 19XX, in Mortgage Book 364, Page 796, in the office aforesaid.

2. Easements and restrictions pertaining to said subdivision, recorded in the Probate Records of Lincoln County.

3. Ad valorem taxes for the year 19XX, which are not due and payable until December 31, 19XX.

4. Such state of facts as would be disclosed by an accurate survey and inspection of the premises.

Yours sincerely,

COMMENT:

1. The original principal amount of the mortgage could be listed in Exception 1.
2. The writer may wish to state the limit of liability for rendering the above opinion.

122.
REAL ESTATE TITLE OPINION LETTER

Dear Mrs. McIntyre:

We have examined the records in the Register of Deed's of Henry County, according to the indices therein contained, from September 14, 19XX, to and including February 18, 19XX, to the following described real estate located in the County of Henry, State of Tennessee, to-wit:

(DESCRIPTION)

From such examination we are pleased to advise we are of the opinion a good and merchantable title in fee simple is vested in James Jordan and wife, Lucille Jones Jordan, subject to the following exceptions and objections.:

1. Ad valorem taxes for the current year, which constitute a lien upon the property beginning last January 1 and which will be due and payable next December 31. At the present time these ad valorem taxes are in the amount of $870.

2. The mortgage executed in favor of ABC Mortgage Company in the original principal amount of $18,000, which mortgage was duly recorded in Mortgage Book 326, page 408, on September 14, 19XX, in the Register of Deeds Records of Henry County.

3. Subject to utility and drainage easements and minimum building lines as indicated on the plat.

4. Subject to restrictive covenants recorded in the Register of Deed's Office of Lincoln County, in Deed Book 313, page 495.

5. The City of Chesterton public improvement assessments are paid.

This opinion does not reflect a search or review of any zoning regulations.

You should also satisfy yourselves in respect to the rights, if any, of any person in possession of the above-described real estate or any part of it.

This opinion does not cover unrecorded easements, if any, above or below the surface, nor does it cover any discrepancies or conflicts in boundary lines, shortages in area or encroachments which a correct survey or inspection of the premises would disclose.

This opinion does not cover possible liens which might arise from unpaid labor or material in connection with recent improvements on said premises or improvements now in process on same, which liens have not been filed for record in the office of Register of Deeds of Henry County.

This opinion is furnished on the basis of a purchase price, loan value or equity value of $12,000, and our liability is expressly limited thereto.

Yours very truly,

COMMENT:

1. Title opinion letters are generally written to clients for whom an examination of title is made in connection with a real estate transaction. For example, the letter may be rendered to a client who is purchasing real property. On the other hand, the letter may be rendered to a bank or other lending institution which is making a mortgage loan secured by the property.

123.
TITLE OPINION FOR PURCHASE OF REAL PROPERTY

Dear Mr. and Mrs. Smith:

Pursuant to your request, we have examined title to the above-described property located in Adams County.

From our examination of an abstract of title prepared by ABC Company, abstractors, covering a period from August 12, 19XX, to April 15, 19XX, and our examination of the records on file in the office of the Probate Judge of Adams County, we are of the opinion that the title to said lands is good and merchantable and at this time rests in Tom Jones and his wife, Laura Fields Jones subject to the following liens:

1. Ad valorem taxes due and payable on October 1, 19XX.

2. Mortgage from Ralph Blakefield and wife, Alberta Blakefield, to DEF Mortgage Company dated February 27, 19XX and recorded in Mortgage Book 414, Page 312, Probate Records of Adams County, which said mortgage has a balance due of $43,000 as of April 19, 19XX.

3. Restrictions pertaining to all lots and blocks in May Fair Subdivision as the same are recorded in the Probate Office of Adams County, in Deed Book 176, Page 428.

4. Zoning ordinances and laws pertaining to said property.

5. Conditions, limitations, easements and rights-of-way of record.

6. Such state of facts as would be disclosed by an accurate engineering survey and inspection of the premises, including rights of parties in possession, which are not a matter of record.

Sincerely yours,

COMMENT:

1. The writer could limit his liability in connection with the above opinion by stating that the liability is limited to the consideration paid for the real property subject to the title examination.

124.
TITLE OPINION OF REAL ESTATE

Dear Mr. Gordon:

As requested by you, we have examined the indices to the records in the office of the Judge of Probate of Lincoln County, for instruments filed for record which might affect the title to property recently conveyed to you, the same being described as:

Lot 15, Block 7, Mountain Heights Subdivision, 12th Addition, according to the plat of said Subdivision recorded in the Office of the Judge of Probate of Lincoln County, in Plat Book 3 Page 48.

As the result of our examination, we are pleased to advise that as of this date, in our opinion good and merchantable title to said property is now vested in William Tinsley and wife, Rose Jones Tinsley, subject to:

1. Restrictions recorded in Deed Book 312, page 187, Probate Records of Lincoln County, filed August 13, 19XX.

2. Mortgage executed by you in favor of ABC Mortgage Company, a corporation, dated August 18, 19XX, recorded in Mortgage Book 297, page 305, securing an original principal indebtedness of $85,000.

3. Lien for ad valorem taxes due October 1, 19XX.

4. Forty-five foot minimum building setback line and drainage and utility easements as shown on recorded plat.

This opinion of title does not purport to cover those matters which an accurate survey of the premises would show, nor does it cover matters which are not of record in the office of the Judge of Probate of Lincoln County.

Sincerely yours,

COMMENT:

1. The above opinion expressly sets forth all restrictions and easements relating to the property. In many cases the client desires specific information regarding all restrictions and easements and an opinion setting forth each in detail. In other cases such particularity is not required, and general language excepting restrictions and easements of record would be sufficient.

2. Obviously, greater care must be exercised in detailing each restriction and easement than would be required when the opinion simply excepts restrictions and easements of record.

GROUP F
Requesting Information

125.
REQUEST FOR INFORMATION TO PREPARE SUIT

Dear Mr. Haley:

In connection with the dealership contract, we need the following information:

1. Was the letter mailed to ABC Company dated March 3, 19XX, from your company stating that account is to be carried full recourse actually mailed? A copy of the letter is attached for your information.

2. We need the fully executed and dated original of the application and agreement between your company and ABC Company. A copy of this agreement is attached for your information.

We need to know the present amount and status of the reserve account which you hold in behalf of ABC Company.

We are also enclosing a draft copy of the complaint to be filed against ABC Company. Any comments or suggestions you have will be appreciated.

Sincerely yours,

COMMENT:

1. The above letter could describe the draft complaint in more detail.

2. The letter could also request more specific comments or suggestions from the client with regard to important facts involved in the litigation and other documents of importance in the litigation.

126.
REQUEST FOR INFORMATION TO PREPARE SUIT

Dear Mr. Murphy:

Mr. Joseph Johnson of ABC Company Claims Department in Topeka forwarded us the file in connection with the above-referenced matter and instructed us to file suit in Federal Court since the defendant has denied liability.

As you know, Grant Sales Company has refused to repurchase three farm equipment conditional sales contracts with Homer Jacobs and Horace Williams.

In connection with the assignment contract, we need the following information:

1. Was letter from ABC Company dated January 2, 19XX, accepted by Grant Sales Company and copy returned? A copy of the letter is attached for your information.

2. Did ABC Company send demand by certified mail to Grant Sales Company to purchase the conditional sales contracts? If not, we recommend that you send via certified mail a demand to Grant Sales Company to purchase the contracts.

3. The original Conditional Sale Contract between Grant Sales Company and Homer Jacobs should be secured.

The original contract is attached.

Very sincerely,

COMMENT:

1. The above letter might give the client more details regarding the proposed suit.

2. The above letter might request specific suggestions or comments from the client regarding the proposed suit.

127.
REPORT OF RECEIPT OF TRUST AGREEMENT, POSSESSION OF
INSURANCE POLICY, AND REQUEST FOR ADVICE.

Dear Paul:

As I stated to you earlier, we have now received the signed trust agreement.

We also have in our files here a $15,000 ABC Life Insurance policy. However, I do not see in the file your DEF Life Insurance policy with the face value of $125,000. I am wondering if, by chance, you have this policy.

Also, as I recall, you may want to change or cash surrender one of these policies and take out additional insurance under your group program at GHI Corporation.

Therefore, please let me know whether or not you want me to hold the trust agreement to make this change or whether you want me to deliver what I have to the JKL Bank.

Thanks very much.

Sincerely yours,

COMMENT:

1. The writer may want to include his advice or thoughts regarding the proposal to change or cash surrender one of the insurance policies and take out additional insurance under the group program.

128.
REQUEST FOR INFORMATION FOR PETITION TO
MODIFY DIVORCE DECREE

Dear Linda:

I understood you were going to check with Larry to see if he would voluntarily agree to a petition to modify the divorce decree along the lines we discussed when you were last in my office.

I would appreciate it very much if you would let me know whether or not you have done this.

Also, I do not see his address in the file and would appreciate it if you would please let me have his address.

Very sincerely,

COMMENT:

1. The above letter is a personalized request for information from the client regarding a postdivorce matter. The lawyer could, if desired, comment further on the proposed modification of the divorce decree as discussed in the office conference.

129.
TRANSMITTAL OF INTERROGATORIES TO CLIENT WITH INSTRUCTIONS FOR ANSWERS

Dear Mrs. Campbell:

Enclosed are some "Written Interrogatories" from the attorneys representing the defendant. They have a legal right to have these questions answered within fifteen (15) days after they were received by this office.

Therefore, will you please answer them as quickly as possible, and in no event later than seven (7) days from the date of this letter. Return the questions and answers within that time.

You should answer them in your own language in as detailed form as possible, denoting the number of the question alongside your answer. Make the answer as complete as you can. Before the answers are sent to the opposing attorneys, we will edit any unnecessary statements. We will then request that you sign them.

Answer them to the best of your ability. If any questions arise, we can discuss them at a later date.

Very sincerely,

COMMENT:

1. Whenever interrogatories are transmitted to a client for answers, it is a good idea to give instructions to the client for use in preparing the answers.

130.
REPORT AND REQUEST FOR ADVICE REGARDING REAL ESTATE MATTER

Dear Mr. Brown:

I am enclosing the letter I received from Jack Jones regarding the property on 3rd Avenue in Jefferson City.

Would you please let me know who the buyer is? If you want me to take additional steps to try to get the records cleared up, I will be happy to do so.

Also I am wondering, in the event you do want me to try to clear it up, whether you or the buyer would be paying the legal fee to Johnson, James & King.

Sincerely yours,

COMMENT:

1. The writer could give more details regarding the additional steps required to clear the records.

131.
**REQUEST FOR OPINION FOR RESPONSE TO LETTER AND
REGRETS FOR SHORT CONFERENCE**

Dear Edith:

I would appreciate it if you would let me know how you want me to respond to this letter that I just received from Edward Powell.

Also, Edith, I am sorry that our conference was cut a little short the last time you were in the office. At any rate it is always a pleasure to see you, and I enjoyed talking to you.

Thank you very much.

Very sincerely,

COMMENT:

1. The above is a personalized transmittal letter combined with a request for advice from the client.

Requesting Action

132.
REQUEST FOR VERIFICATION OF ACCOUNT

Dear Mr. Taylor:

I am enclosing a copy of the Summons and Complaint on Joseph Johnson for your records. Also enclosed is a Verification of Account form. Please sign and return this to us as it must be attached to the Summons and Complaint when we file it.

We would also like you to send us a bill addressed to Mr. Johnson, written on your regular stationery for that purpose.

Sincerely yours,

133.
STATUS REPORT OF INSURANCE CLAIM AND REQUEST FOR
SIGNATURE ON CLAIM FORM

Dear Miss Morganthal:

We are in the process of filing our claim for the proceeds under the life insurance policies held by your father. You are named as the beneficiary on one of his ABC Life Insurance policies. We enclose their claim form, which is to be signed by you at the place indicated with a check mark. Please be sure to complete your date of birth and have your signature witnessed.

After you have executed the form, please return it to us in the self-addressed envelope enclosed so we may forward your claim form, along with those of your mother and sister, to the ABC Life Insurance Company.

Very truly yours,

COMMENT:

1. The above letter could give an estimate of the time required to secure the insurance proceeds.
2. The letter could also give other details regarding the administration of the estate.

134.
TRANSMITTAL OF ARTICLES OF ASSOCIATION AND
INSTRUCTION FOR EXECUTION

Dear Dr. Simpson:

Enclosed are four copies of the Articles of Association for Paul R. Simpson, M.D., and Associates. If these articles are satisfactory to you, please sign all copies on page 16 and have your signature notarized on page 17 thereof. Three copies of the articles should be returned to us, and one copy may be retained by you for your records.

We have mailed a copy of the Articles of Association to Dr. Albert for his review.

Please also mail me a check payable to the Secretary of State in the amount of $65, in payment of the filing fee.

If you have any questions with regard to the enclosures, please telephone me or my legal assistant, Mrs. Haley.

Very sincerely,

COMMENT:

1. If desired, the lawyer could comment further on the documents in a general or nontechnical way as they relate particularly to the client.

135.
TRANSMITTAL OF BUY-SELL AGREEMENT AND
REQUEST TO RETURN EXECUTED COPY

Dear Mrs. LaRue:

I am enclosing the original plus copies of your Buy-Sell Agreement with Max Taylor and Marie Henderson and your Indemnity Agreement. Please execute these and return to our office one signed copy of each agreement.

Very sincerely,

COMMENT:

1. If desired, the letter could include the lawyer's comments on the agreement and a request for any suggestions or changes the client may desire incorporated into the agreement.

136.

NOTICE OF FAILURE TO EXECUTE WILL AND
REQUEST FOR APPOINTMENT TO EXECUTE WILL

Dear Mrs. Gonzales:

In reviewing your file, I notice you have not executed your will. I have made an appointment on March 3 at 4:00 P.M. for you to come in and do so. If this time is not convenient with you, please call my secretary and schedule another appointment that is convenient for you.

I look forward to seeing you and your taking care of this important matter.

Sincerely yours,

COMMENT:

1. The above letter could state that, in the event the reader wants any changes made in the will, to let him know or, if the reader wants to discuss it further prior to execution, to advise him.

137.

NOTICE OF PREPARATION OF DOCUMENTS AND
REQUEST FOR APPOINTMENT

Dear Tom:

We have prepared for your signature a Certificate of Mailing concerning the Notice of Appointment and an Inventory of the McCampbell property. Please come in at your convenience to sign these instruments. No appointment will be necessary.

Very sincerely,

COMMENT:

1. The lawyer could give detailed information to the client regarding the documents.

138.

TRANSMITTAL OF STATEMENT FOR EXPENSES OF DEPOSITION AND
REQUEST FOR PAYMENT

Dear Mr. Abernathy:

Enclosed is a statement from Mary Carpenter, deposition reporter, for expenses incurred in your case. Please forward us a check for $126.

Best wishes to you.

Very sincerely,

139.
REQUEST TO CLIENT TO PAY FEE OF SPECIAL CONSULTANT OF COURT

Dear Mr. and Mrs. Haley:

I am preparing a Motion to Dismiss, an order dismissing the suit we filed in behalf of your daughter, Julia Haley, versus ABC Company, et al, Civil Action Number 16513 in the Circuit Court.

The bill incurred for the services of Dr. Carpenter as special consultant to the court is the sum of $900. Judge Morgan had indicated earlier that the party not prevailing would be required to pay this fee.

Accordingly, I would appreciate it very much if you would please let us have a check in the amount of $900 made payable to Dr. Carpenter for services rendered as special consultant to the Circuit Court in connection with this case.

Thank you very much.

Very sincerely,

COMMENT:

1. It is generally better, as is done above, to write the client and transmit a bill for expenses such as the expense for the special consultant involved above. The client may not understand the necessity of the expense or the fact that the lawyer approves of his paying the expense if the bill is simply transmitted to the client.

140.
NOTICE OF CHECK RETURNED FOR INSUFFICIENT FUNDS AND REQUEST FOR PAYMENT

Dear Mrs. Mitchell:

Your check to us in the sum of $319 was returned to us marked, "Insufficient Funds." We would appreciate it if you would take care of this as soon as possible.

Sincerely yours,

COMMENT:

1. The above letter deals with an unpleasant subject in a pleasant but firm way.

141.
REQUEST FOR PAYMENT OF ATTORNEY'S FEE

Dear Mr. Parks:

We have a tickler system, and your file came to my attention today.

I tried to call you on the telephone inasmuch as we can't understand why you haven't taken care of our bill dated November 17, 19XX.

There has been only one payment of $35 on January 24, and I would appreciate it if you would please take care of this as soon as possible.

Our fees from services rendered which are regularly billed, such as yours, are the only way we have of paying our expenses and making a living. Your immediate attention will be appreciated.

Sincerely yours,

COMMENT:

1. The lawyer could have a check system by which subsequent stronger letters are sent if there is no response within a week or two.

142.
REQUEST FOR PAYMENT OF FEE

Dear Mrs. Ford:

We understood that you were to pay $10 every week toward the total fee of $225 in connection with this case.

According to our records, you paid $10 on April 6, and we have not received any payments since that date.

We would appreciate it very much if you would please make arrangements to make these payments.

Thank you very much.

Very sincerely,

143.
REQUEST TO PAY ACCOUNT

Dear Mr. Willis:

The enclosed statement has been outstanding now for almost a year, and we certainly would appreciate your taking steps to arrange for its payment.

Sincerely yours,

COMMENT:

1. The lawyer could also state that in the event the client is not in a position to pay the statement on a current basis, he is requested to contact the writer and discuss the matter.

144.
TRANSMITTAL OF PAST DUE STATEMENT AND
REQUEST FOR PAYMENT

Dear Mr. Mason:

Enclosed is a copy of our statement to you in the sum of $260, which has been due and payable since October 1, 19XX.

Mr. Mason, as you will recall, you employed me to represent you in the above-referenced matter in response to a garnishment on judgment which ABC Company served on you. On your behalf, I made numerous telephone calls to ABC Company and had several discussions with you. I also filed an Answer of Garnishee in your behalf before the arrangement to settle the judgment, as per my letter of September 13 to ABC Company.

Mr. Mason, I acted in good faith in my representation of you in this matter and would appreciate your immediate payment for my services in this regard. If you are having financial problems and cannot pay the balance due in full, please make monthly payments to me until it is paid in full.

Thank you.

Sincerely,

145.
REQUEST TO CLIENT TO PAY LONG OVERDUE ACCOUNT

Dear Mr. O'Reilly:

We make it a policy not to sue our clients. However, we do expect our clients to make every effort to pay our bills.

We have been billing you for over a year, and you have made no effort to contact us regarding payment. I would appreciate your taking care of this bill.

Very sincerely,

146.
REQUEST FOR ASSISTANCE IN SECURING MEDICAL REPORT

Dear Mr. Field:

We still have not received a medical report from Dr. Carlson of Radiology Associates of Johnson City.

We would appreciate it very much if you would please assist us in securing this report from Dr. Carlson since we need it to evaluate the case.

Very sincerely,

COMMENT:

1. The writer might mention when or the number of times he has written for the medical report.

147.
REQUEST FOR ASSISTANCE IN SECURING MEDICAL REPORT AND RECOMMENDATION TO FILE SUIT

Dear Mr. Burns:

I would appreciate it very much if you would please contact Dr. Brown and Dr. Talwell and ask them to send us an interim report of your injuries and treatment.

It is our opinion that we should go ahead and file suit rather than wait until you have been discharged by your doctor since it will take at least a year for your case to come up for trial after it is filed, and I am sure you are interested in having the matter either settled or tried at the earliest possible date.

We can, of course, amend the complaint and add new matters or information regarding your injuries in accordance with all future developments.

Therefore, we will appreciate it if you would please contact Dr. Brown and Dr. Talwell and ask them to send us interim reports, together with their bills for the reports.

Thank you very much.

Sincerely yours,

COMMENT:

1. It is not clear from the letter whether the lawyer has written the doctors directly to request reports. This is usually done first, after the proper authorization by the client has been signed.

148.

REQUEST TO CLIENT TO EXECUTE RELEASE FOR SETTLEMENT

Dear Joe:

Enclosed is an original release from the defendant's insurance carrier for settlement of the above referenced case in the amount of $4,000.

It is necessary to date and sign your name on the lines indicated and return the signed release to this office. Upon its return, I will process it with the insurance carrier and obtain a draft in that amount for your endorsement.

Please give this matter your immediate attention.

Very sincerely,

COMMENT:

1. The lawyer may wish to give his express opinion regarding the proposed settlement.

149.

REQUEST TO BOARD MEMBER TO PREPARE FORM FOR SBA LOAN APPLICATION

Dear Mr. Caldwell:

I am representing ABC Corporation in connection with securing an SBA loan. I assume that you are a member of the board of directors of ABC Corporation, since your name is listed as a member of the board on the original incorporation papers. If this is the case, we need you to prepare a Statement of Personal History, SBA Form 912, which is enclosed. You will note this particular form requires your social security number in block 4. I call this particular blank to your attention because it is easily overlooked.

Mr. Caldwell, please complete the enclosed form and return it to us as soon as possible so that we may complete the application.

Sincerely yours,

COMMENT:

1. The writer could comment generally on the loan or the importance of the loan.

2. The writer could express appreciation on behalf of the client for the assistance requested in the letter of the board member in connection with the loan application.

150.
REQUEST TO SIGN FORM FOR MORTGAGE COMPANY

Dear Mr. and Mrs. Barlow:

Enclosed is a copy of a letter dated August 16 from ABC Mortgage Company with an enclosed form which they desire for their files. I will appreciate your signing the form and returning it to me for forwarding to them.

The transfer of escrow funds will not prevent any reimbursement for any unpaid premium already in the hands of the insurance company.

Very sincerely,

151.
REQUEST FOR RELEASE OF LAND FROM EXISTING MORTGAGE

Dear Mr. Miller:

This is to advise you we have examined title to the 75 acre tract of land which you plan to mortgage to ABC Bank in connection with your $95,000 loan, and we find you have good title to the land with the exception of the encumbrance of the mortgage made by your father, John W. Miller, to Federal Land Bank, dated March 14, 19XX, and covering a loan of $35,000.

We would appreciate it very much if you would have your father contact the Federal Land Bank and arrange to have a release prepared, releasing your 75 acres from the coverage of this mortgage.

Thank you very much. If you have any questions, please call me.

Sincerely yours,

COMMENT:

1. The writer could suggest, in the alternative, his willingness to prepare the necessary release if desired by the client.

2. The letter could include the book and page number of the mortgage encumbering the property.

152.
ACKNOWLEDGEMENT OF CLIENT'S LETTER AND REQUEST FOR CONFERENCE

Dear Mr. Miller:

Thanks very much for your letter of October 12, regarding your desire to further pursue your claim under the Workmens Compensation Law and specifically to secure a review of the substance of your case.

I am interested in your claim and would like to set up a meeting with you to discuss it. I am leaving tomorrow to go to Los Angeles and try a case. I expect to be gone all next week and would like for us to get together just as soon as I get back, which would be any date the week of February 18.

I look forward to seeing you.

Very sincerely,

COMMENT:

1. The writer could, if appropriate, comment more specifically about the case.

153.
TRANSMITTAL OF LETTER FROM U.S. SENATOR AND REQUEST TO SEND PERMISSION LETTER TO U.S. SENATOR

Dear Mr. Paul:

Enclosed is a copy of a letter I received from Senator Williams.

We have prepared the enclosed letter for your signature regarding your permission for Senator William's office to obtain all necessary information regarding your claim. If it is agreeable with you, please forward it directly to Senator Williams in the self-addressed envelope enclosed.

Sincerely yours,

COMMENT:

1. The writer could make some comment regarding the subject matter.

2. The writer could outline additional steps to be taken in behalf of the client in connection with the matter.

3. The writer could request any suggestions the client may have.

154.
REQUEST TO SEND NEWS ARTICLE TO INTERESTED PERSON

Dear Mr. Taylor:

Mrs. Hobson, the wife of another oil company employee we are representing in a case very similar to yours, called the other day regarding the article about you in the Wall Street Journal.

I checked in our folder and for some reason cannot find the article. I will appreciate it very much if you will please make a copy of this article and mail it to her.

Her name and address are: Mrs. Hubert M. Hobson, Route 5, Box 415, Johnson City, Iowa.

Thank you very much.

Sincerely yours,

COMMENT:

1. The writer could comment on the article in a way that would be pleasing to the reader.

GROUP H
Requesting Review or Decision

155.
REQUEST TO REVIEW AND SIGN LEASE

Dear Mr. Paul:

Mr. Roy Miller contacted me last week regarding your building. Mr. Miller is from Jefferson City and gives the appearance he would be a good tenant. He plans to use the building in his produce business.

I have prepared a lease for your property on South Market Street, leasing the premises to Mr. Miller for one year for the monthly rent of $650.

If you approve this lease, please sign it and return it to me in the self-addressed envelope enclosed.

Thank you very much.

Sincerely yours,

COMMENT:

1. The writer could include a statement that the reader should call in the event he feels any changes should be made in the lease. In the alternative, he could suggest that it be returned for change or correction.

156.
TRANSMITTAL OF INCORPORATION PAPERS FOR SIGNATURE

Dear Mr. LaRue:

Additional papers in connection with the incorporation of ABC Corporation have been completed and are ready for your signature.

Please sign all indicated spaces on the Domestic Corporation Franchise Return and the Application for Employer Identification Number. The Consent to Action and common stock forms must be signed by you and your wife.

We are enclosing a copy of each of these forms for your personal files and ask that you return the executed originals to our office. We are enclosing a self-addressed envelope for your convenience.

Thank you very much.

Very sincerely,

COMMENT:

1. The lawyer may wish to invite the client to call him or arrange an appointment in the event he has any questions regarding the documents he is being requested to sign.

157.

TRANSMITTAL TO CLIENT OF CERTIFICATE OF INCORPORATION FOR SIGNATURE

Dear Mr. Gonzales:

Enclosed are the original and a copy of your Certificate of Incorporation. Please date and sign the original and return it to us. Signatures are required on pages 8, 9, and 10.

Thank you very much.

Sincerely yours,

158.

TRANSMITTAL OF CORPORATION FRANCHISE TAX RETURN FOR SIGNATURE AND FILING

Dear Mr. Jones:

Please sign the enclosed Domestic Corporation Franchise Tax Return and send it with your check for $45 to:

Franchise Tax Division
Department of Revenue
Montgomery, Alabama

Thanks very much.

Sincerely yours,

COMMENT:

1. The above letter could be further personalized by the lawyer commenting on the transaction or stating additional steps that will be taken in connection with the matter.

159.
TRANSMITTAL OF BUY AND SELL AGREEMENT TO PARTNERS FOR REVIEW AND SIGNATURE

Dear Mr. Christopher:

I am enclosing the original and three copies of the Buy and Sell Agreement between the partners of ABC Leasing Company. The agreement has been revised in accordance with your instructions to reflect the fact that the insurance is to be purchased from DEF Insurance Company and there will be three life insurance policies.

If the agreement appears to be in order, I would appreciate it if all of you would execute it, the original as well as all three copies. Each of you retain a copy for your records and return the original to us for your permanent files.

I am enclosing a copy of a financial statement and other data on DEF Insurance Company, which I secured from Best's Insurance Reports. The company appears to be reliable although it is quite small.

Please call me if you have any questions.

Yours very sincerely,

COMMENT:

1. The writer could state to the client the additional problems or questions that may arise from time to time regarding the buy-sell agreement and the importance of reviewing it at least annually.

160.
REQUEST FOR REVIEW AND EXECUTION OF CORPORATE MINUTES AND STOCK CERTIFICATES

Dear Mr. Abernathy:

We are enclosing the minutes of the incorporators and the first meeting of the board of directors for your examination and for the signatures of all the stockholders if these appear to be in order.

We are also enclosing the stock certificates to be signed by the president and the secretary. You may either retain the certificates or return them to us, and we will put them in your corporate kit. Also, if the minutes are in order and are signed by all of the proper parties, please return them to us, and we will put them in your corporate kit for your permanent record.

Again, I want you to know how much we appreciate the opportunity of handling this matter for you. Please let us know if you have any questions or suggestions.

Very sincerely,

COMMENT:

1. The writer could offer suggestions or comments regarding additional action that should be taken from time to time by the corporation.

161.
TRANSMITTAL OF CORPORATE MINUTES AND STOCK CERTIFICATES WITH REQUEST FOR SIGNATURE

Dear Mr. Tanaka:

We are enclosing the following documents relating to the transfer of 1,000 shares of stock to Mr. Sumato and his election as director of Mitsui Corporation.

1. The original and one copy of the Minutes of Special Meeting of Directors of Mitsui Corporation, to be signed by you and Mr. Park. The original should be returned to us to be filed in your corporate kit. The copy is for your records.

2. The original and one copy of your sale, assignment and transfer of 1,000 shares of your stock to Mr. Sumato to be signed by you. The original of this document should be returned to us to be filed in your corporate kit. The copy is for your records.

3. The original and one copy of Mr. Sumato's consent to the corporation remaining a small business corporation. Mr. Sumato should sign this, and the original should be returned to us to be filed in your corporate kit. The copy is for your records.

4. Stock Certificate No. 890, to you as the owner of 115,000 shares of stock, dated the date of the incorporation of Mitsui Corporation, June 27, 19XX, to be signed by you as president of the corporation and by Mr. Park as secretary of the corporation. After execution of this certificate, the same should be returned to us to be marked "VOID" and placed in your corporate kit.

5. Stock Certificate No. 891 to Mr. Park as the owner of 10,000 shares of stock dated the date of the incorporation of Mitsui Corporation, June 27, 19XX, to be signed by you as president of the corporation and by Mr. Park as secretary of the corporation. You may keep the original of this certificate in your records.

6. Stock Certificate No. 1102 to you as the owner of 110,000 shares of stock dated September 14, 19XX, the date of the assignment of 5,000 shares of stock in your name to Mr. Chung Lee, to be signed by you as president of the corporation and by Mr. Park as secretary of the corporation. You may keep the original of this certificate in your records.

7. Stock Certificate No. 1105 to William Androtti as the owner of 8,000 shares of stock dated August 24, 19XX, the date of the transfer of 3,000 shares of stock from you to him, to be signed by you as president of the corporation and by Mr. Park as secretary of the corporation. You may keep the original of this certificate in your records.

Please date the minutes, your transfer document, Mr. Sumato's consent document, and stock certificate number 1105 and 1102 the same date in August.

If you have any questions, please let us know.

Sincerely yours,

162.
REQUEST FOR REVIEW AND EXECUTION OF CERTIFICATE OF DISSOLUTION OF CORPORATION

Dear Mr. Worthington:

We have prepared, as you requested, the Certificate of Dissolution of ABC Distributing Company, Inc., dissolving the corporation.

You and Mr. Williams should have your signatures witnessed and, in addition, should have his second signature notarized where he signs as president of the corporation.

After execution of the certificate, please return it to us.

Thank you very much.

Very sincerely,

COMMENT:

1. The above letter could state what will be done with the certificate after it is executed and returned.

2. The letter could give more information regarding any additional matters that need to be attended to in connection with the dissolution of the corporation.

163.
REQUEST FOR REVIEW OF WILL DRAFTS AND FOR APPOINTMENT TO EXECUTE WILLS

Dear Mr. and Mrs. Smith:

I am enclosing drafts of your wills which we have prepared in accordance with your instructions. Please read each will carefully, noting particularly that all names are correctly spelled and that the wills contain every provision you desire. In the event there are corrections to be made or there are portions of the wills you do not understand, please call me or come to the office to discuss the matter.

In the event the wills are in proper form for execution, please call our office and arrange an appointment at your convenience to execute them.

Thank you very much.

Very sincerely,

164.
**REQUEST TO REVIEW WILL DRAFT AND
FOR APPOINTMENT TO EXECUTE WILL**

Dear Mr. Mitchell:

I have attached a draft will for each of you. Please review them to determine if they satisfy your desires. Please call me after you have read them and I can complete them with whatever corrections you may have.

I will need to know your brother Wilson's home town.

Sincerely yours,

COMMENT:

1. The above letter transmits will drafts and requests appointment for execution. This is a good practice as it gives the client an opportunity to review the proposed will at home prior to execution.

165.
**TRANSMITTAL OF PETITION FOR LETTERS OF ADMINISTRATION AND
GUARDIANSHIP FOR SIGNATURE**

Dear Mrs. Johnson:

Enclosed are the papers necessary so that you may administer Mr. Johnson's estate and be appointed guardian of your children's estate.

Please sign the petition for Letters of Administration and Petition for Guardianship of your children's estate on the lines beside the penciled "X's" and have these notarized.

There are two bonds: one for the Letters of Administration and one for the Petition for Guardianship. These should be signed by you, your husband, and, if possible, any other adults who may wish to sign for you. It is best to have several signatures besides those of you and your husband. The bonds do not have to be notarized.

Then return all papers to us so we may proceed. If you have any questions, please call me.

Very sincerely,

COMMENT:

1. The lawyer could, if desired, describe to the client the purpose of the enclosed petition for Letters of Administration and Petition for Guardianship. He could also state the additional action that will be taken following the filing of the petitions.

166.
**TRANSMITTAL TO EXECUTORS OF DECLARATION OF
PARTIAL DISTRIBUTION FOR SIGNATURE**

Dear Mrs. Johnson and Mrs. Mitchell:

I am enclosing the original and two copies of a Declaration of Partial Distribution covering the $50,000 distributed on June 18, 19XX.

I would appreciate it very much if you would both please sign the original and return it to us. You may retain the copies for your records.

Thank you very much.

Sincerely yours,

COMMENT:

1. The above letter could be further personalized by specific comment on the status of the estate or a description of additional steps to be taken in connection with administration of the estate.

167.
**TRANSMITTAL OF ESTATE DOCUMENTS WITH REQUEST FOR
SIGNATURE AND RETURN**

Dear Mr. Carter:

I enclose the following instruments:

1. Petition for Probate of Will. Please sign at both places checked on page 2. Please note that this must be signed before a Notary Public.

2. Acceptance of Service. Please sign but do not date it.

3. Letters Testamentary. Please sign at the bottom of the page where I have placed a check mark. Please note that this form must also be signed before a Notary Public.

4. Notice of Appointment of Executrix. Please sign but do not date it.

5. Consent. Please sign at page 3 before a Notary Public.

As soon as you have done the above, return the forms to me, and I will file them with the court. Copies of the Petition for Probate, Acceptance of Service, and Notice of Probate will be mailed to you after the petition has been filed and a date has been set for the hearing. A Renunciation has been prepared for your mother's signature wherein she renounces her right to act as Executrix.

If you have any questions, please let me know.

Yours very sincerely,

P.S. I enclose a stamped, self-addressed envelope for your convenience in returning the enclosed instruments to me.

168.
REQUEST TO REVIEW DRAFT OF ESTATE INVENTORY

Dear Mr. Williams:

Enclosed is a rough draft of the inventory of Mrs. Williams' estate, which we have prepared. Please review it very carefully and let us know if there should be any changes made. If there are corrections to be made, please make them on the draft and return it to us.

If it is satisfactory, please call me and let me know, and I will have the inventory prepared in final form for your signature.

Very sincerely,

COMMENT:

1. The lawyer, if desired, could comment upon additional steps which will be taken in connection with the administration of the estate following preparation of the inventory.

169.
REQUEST TO REVIEW DIVORCE AGREEMENT

Dear Mrs. Carpenter:

We have prepared the agreement in your case and enclose two copies of it. Please give one copy of the agreement to Mr. Carpenter. After you have both reviewed the agreement, please call me and we will discuss any changes or suggestions you have regarding the agreement and preparation of the remainder of the divorce documents.

Thank you very much.

Sincerely yours,

COMMENT:

1. The writer might offer some observations regarding the agreement or his recommendation about it.

170.
REQUEST FOR REVIEW OF DRAFT OF COMPLAINT

Dear Mr. Mason:

A draft of the complaint is enclosed, which I have prepared in the above case. Please review the complaint and have all of the other plaintiffs review it to be sure it correctly states the claim. If you have any questions or suggestions, please let me know.

If the complaint is satisfactory, please call my secretary, Mrs. Jones, and make arrangements for all of the plaintiffs to come in and sign the complaint before it is filed.

I am sorry for the delay in the preparation of this complaint, but I have been out of town and behind in my work. Thank you for your patience in this matter.

Sincerely yours,

COMMENT:

1. Sometimes it may be best not to apologize for delay since it may simply serve to emphasize a negative aspect to the matter.

2. The writer could conclude with some comment or observation on a more positive matter, such as additional steps that will be taken by him in connection with the case.

171.

AUTHORIZATION FROM CLIENT FOR MEDICAL INFORMATION

Please take notice that Epworth, Smith & Howard has been retained by me to prosecute a claim for personal injuries sustained. Your full cooperation with my attorneys is requested.

You are hereby authorized and requested to furnish Epworth, Smith & Howard, or any representative of said law firm, with any and all information or opinions that they may request regarding my present or past physical condition and treatment and to allow them to see or copy any X-rays, records, or other documents or instruments that you may have regarding my past or present condition or treatment.

You are further requested not to disclose any information concerning my past or present condition or treatment, or the record thereof, to any insurance adjuster or other persons other than my attorney without written authority from me to do so (pursuant to privilege and confidential communication laws).

ALL PRIOR AUTHORIZATION OF DISCLOSURE IS HEREBY CANCELLED. I hereby waive any privilege I have to said information to my attorneys and to no one else except their representative.

This the 12th day of April 19XX.

Joseph Mahew

COMMENT:

1. The authorization from client for medical information should be signed by the client during the first conference after a decision has been made by the lawyer to take the case. In the event the client is not available to sign the authorization in the attorney's office, it may be forwarded to him by letter with a request that the client sign it.

2. All physicians and hospitals will require authorization prior to divulging confidential medical information regarding a patient.

172.
REQUEST TO REVIEW AND SIGN ANSWERS TO INTERROGATORIES

Dear Mrs. Brown:

We are enclosing answers to the interrogatories which we previously forwarded to you and which were returned by Ralph Gibson, together with the additional information for answer to interrogatory number 12 which was supplied to us by Roger Williams, manager of Townhouse Apartments.

If the answers to the interrogatories are correct, I would appreciate it if you would please sign them and return to us, and we will prepare the notary acknowledgment for you.

Thanks very much for your cooperation.

Very sincerely,

COMMENT:

1. The writer may make some general statement regarding the answers to the interrogatories which have been prepared.

173.
REQUEST TO REVIEW AND SIGN ANSWERS TO INTERROGATORIES

Dear Mr. Kaufman:

We are enclosing answers to interrogatories, together with a copy of the interrogatories, which we have prepared in accordance with the information supplied to us by you.

We would appreciate it very much if you would please check the answers, and, if they appear to be satisfactory to you and correct, please sign them at the end, and we will sign as notary.

We would appreciate your doing this as soon as possible and returning them to us.

If you have any questions or suggestions, please let us know.

Sincerely yours,

174.
REQUEST TO SIGN AND RETURN REAL ESTATE SALES CONTRACT

Dear Mr. & Mrs. Abernathy:

We are enclosing an original and one copy of the contract signed by Mr. and Mrs. Carpenter to purchase your house in Bellows Falls. Mr. Carpenter has given us his check in the amount of $1,000 as earnest money to be delivered to you upon your signing the contract along with your wife.

We will appreciate it very much if you will please sign the original and copy of the contract and return them to us as soon as possible. You will note that Mr. Carpenter requested that we write in the provision that this contract is to be signed by all parties within ten days from the date of the contract, which was October 6, 19XX.

Should you have any questions regarding the contract, please call me.

Thank you very much.

Sincerely yours,

COMMENT:

1. The writer might comment on the advantage of the contract to the reader.

2. The writer could also explain details regarding the closing, which will occur after the contract is signed by all the parties.

175.

TRANSMITTAL OF REAL ESTATE SALES CONTRACT
FOR REVIEW AND SIGNATURE

Dear Mr. Nussbaum:

I am enclosing the real estate sales contract prepared in accordance with our telephone conversation. If everything looks all right, please send it to Mrs. Fanning in Lexington and ask her to sign it before a Notary Public and have him take her acknowledgment.

After you and your wife have signed it and Mrs. Fanning has signed it, please return it to me and I will advise Mr. Brown, at which time we will secure from him his check for $1,500 in payment of the earnest money. The contract will not be delivered to him except upon payment by him of the full amount of earnest money. In the event Mr. Brown fails for any reason to fully perform the contract by purchasing the property and paying the balance of $35,000 plus closing costs, less the preparation of the warranty deed, then Mr. Brown under the contract will have forfeited the earnest money paid to you.

Please call me if you have any questions.

Very sincerely,

COMMENT:

1. The above letter is a good example of an effective transmittal letter for a document to be reviewed and executed by the client.

SECTION 2
LETTERS TO OPPOSING AND OTHER PARTIES

Letters to opposing and other parties in connection with a case or matter are helpful in expediting various legal transactions such as real estate transactions, contracts, leases, etc. In addition, letters to opposing parties help resolve disputes without litigation. Letters to opposing parties should always be in a friendly tone and simply state the position of the client regarding the matter. For example, the position may well be that unless the opposing party pays a certain sum, the client has authorized and instructed the lawyer to file suit in his behalf. It is not necessary to use threatening or abusive language. Such language only escalates the underlying dispute which already exists. A friendly letter, warm in tone, stating a firm demand or position is more effective.

It is a good idea to send copies of all the letters written to opposing and other parties to your client. After a matter has reached the state of litigation and there is an opposing attorney involved, ordinarily correspondence would be directly to the opposing attorney. In the event letters are written to the opposing party, the lawyer should send a copy of such letter to the opposing attorney. It is not considered ethical, of course, for a lawyer to speak to the opposing party who is represented by an attorney unless the attorney is present or has given his permission for the conversation.

GROUP A
Giving Notice or Information

176.
STATEMENT THAT CLIENT DISPUTES ACCOUNT AND INTEREST CHARGES

Dear Mr. Miller:

We wrote you on May 6, 19XX, regarding your alleged account with Edward Brown, our client. We would appreciate it if you would please refer to our original letter.

Mr. Brown has forwarded to us a copy of your recent statement to him and which includes interest charges on the alleged account. Mr. Brown has authorized us to advise you that he has no intention of paying the interest or the bill until the matter of the doors discussed in our letter to you is taken care of.

In the event you would like to get together to discuss this or call me, please let us know. Otherwise, we can see no resolution of this matter unless, of course, you want to go ahead and file suit and resolve it in court.

Sincerely yours,

COMMENT:

1. The above letter is appropriate when the lawyer's client disputes an account claimed by the adverse party.

2. It is recommended that letters such as the above always contain a friendly offer to negotiate or discuss the matter in dispute.

177.
STATING POSITION OF CLIENT ON INSTALLMENT PAYMENTS FOR EDUCATIONAL COURSE

Dear Mr. Lynch:

Mrs. Carolyn Reed has explained to us a problem she has encountered with you regarding the tuition assistance plan.

Mrs. Reed gave us copies of the tuition assistance plan dated June 7, 19XX, regarding herself, and her two children Allison, age 16, and Brian, age 13.

The total amount listed on each plan is identical, and Mrs. Reed tells us that she understood the total deferred price of $250 covered the tuition charge for herself and her two children. She says that she has now learned this is not correct.

We understand she is willing for you to retain the $50 cash down payment she made for each child, namely a total cash down payment for the two children of $100. However, now that she has learned that the total amount of deferred payment price is three times $250 instead of the simple $250 she says she is not willing or in a position to have her children continue with the plan.

Our conversations with her reveal that it was truly a mistake on her part when she executed the original plan thinking that it was one price for all three rather than three times the one price listed. Accordingly, this is to advise you that her two children will discontinue the course; she is willing for you to retain their cash down payments; and she will refuse to pay anything further in connection with any tuition which may be claimed from them.

I understand Mrs. Reed is going to continue the course herself, and she will, of course, pay the remainder of her contract in accordance with its terms. I might mention, in passing, although I have not researched the matter, it appears that the annual percentage rate charged on your contract would be usurious under our state law.

Please let us hear from you in the event you take issue with the position taken by our client in accordance with this letter.

Very sincerely,

COMMENT:

1. The above letter is a good example of the advantage of going into detail to the opposing party when a strong position is taken by the client regarding an account or claim. The opposing party is given not only the position of the client but implicit in the recitation of the facts is the defense intended to be used to the claim. Letters such as this are effective in discouraging litigation.

178.
TRANSMITTAL OF SETTLEMENT CHECK FOR SMALL CLAIM

Dear Mr. Gonzales:

Mr. Roy Miller, who kindly volunteered to mediate in the above matter, informed me that you would settle your claim against Mrs. Wanda Carter for $200. Pursuant to this information, I enclose herewith Mrs. Carter's check to your order for $200 in full settlement, and I will ask you to notify the clerk of the county court of this settlement.

In passing, I wish to mention again that I still consider the legal action a gratuitous insult to Mrs. Carter and premature while alternative settlement offers were pending. Your contention that Mrs. Carter was aware of your charges because you had previously done some work for her at an agreed figure could not have been binding on her in this case. In the former work you did for her, some skilled labor and considerable equipment were involved in what amounted to tree surgery; whereas, in this case only a rake and shears were involved in what almost any unskilled laborer could do. Mrs. Carter has paid for her mistake of not having ascertained your charges before commissioning the work.

Sincerely,

179.
NOTICE TO DEFENDANT OF REPRESENTING PLAINTIFF IN
ACCIDENT CASE

Dear Mr. Schmidt:

This letter is to inform you that this office represents Miss Allison Burns for injuries sustained in the accident which occurred on September 5, 19XX.

If you are insured, please notify and turn this letter over to your insurance carrier immediately.

Sincerely yours,

COMMENT:

1. The above letter could include the action requested by the writer in the event the defendant does not have liability insurance.

180.
NOTICE OF REPRESENTING ESTATE IN AUTO ACCIDENT CASE

Dear Mrs. Blair:

This letter is to advise you that I have been retained to represent the estate of Ray Brandon in a cause of action brought against you as the result of an automobile-truck accident which occurred on April 18, 19XX. My investigation indicates that this is a case of liability on your part.

You should immediately turn a copy of this letter over to your liability insurance carrier so that they may properly look after your interest in this matter.

Sincerely,

COMMENT:

1. It appears obvious in the above letter that the writer is aware of the fact that the defendant does have liability insurance. In the event the defendant does not have liability insurance, the writer should state the action requested or information desired.

181.

ADVISING INSURANCE COMPANY OF FILING SUIT AGAINST UNINSURED MOTORIST AND ASSERTING CLAIM UNDER UNINSURED MOTORIST COVERAGE

Gentlemen:

This is to advise you that we are representing Henrietta Johnson and Alberta Johnson in connection with their claims against Mr. Roy McCampbell, an uninsured motorist, for injuries and damages sustained by them in the automobile accident which occurred on Murphy Road, on U.S. Route 20 near Hale City.

Henrietta Johnson is a named insured stated in the above policy and was occupying your insured automobile under the above policy. Alberta Johnson was also occupying your insured automobile under the above policy at the time of the accident.

We are also representing Henrietta Johnson and Alberta Johnson in connection with their claims against your company under the provisions of the uninsured motorists' protection afforded by your above-referenced policy.

As you know, Mr. Johnson, husband of Mrs. Henrietta Johnson, and relative of the other claimant, Alberta Johnson, has negotiated for several months with your adjusters, and particularly with Joseph Murphy of ABC Adjusters. Mr. Johnson and your representatives were never able to reach any agreement with regard to liability and the amount of damages pursuant to the uninsured motorists' provisions of the policy. The parties were able to reach an agreement, I understand, whereby your company has paid medical expenses under the medical payments provisions of the policy in the amount of $4,700 for Henrietta Johnson. She has a claim for unpaid medical expenses at the present time of some $1,100, I understand.

I further understand that your company has paid medical expenses for Alberta Johnson in the amount of $320 and that at the present time she has unpaid medical expenses growing out of the accident in the amount of approximately $180.

Also, as you know, since the parties were unable to reach a firm agreement regarding the amount to be paid pursuant to the uninsured motorists' provisions of the policy, the claimants were forced to file suits against the uninsured motorist to keep the Statute of Limitations from running in our state. These suits were filed in the Superior Court of Lincoln County, early in August, 19XX, since the Statute of Limitations would run on September 12, 19XX. Henrietta's suit is styled Henrietta Johnson vs. Roy McCampbell, et al, in the Superior Court for Lincoln County, Case No. 76,129 and Alberta's suit is styled Alberta Johnson vs. Roy McCampbell, et al, in the Superior Court for Lincoln County, Case No. 76,130.

We are enclosing copies of the complaints for your records. We understand that Mr. Johnson advised your adjusters, ABC Adjusters, of the fact that he would be required to file suit to prevent the Statute of Limitations from running.

The purpose of this letter is to advise you of our representation of the claimants, of the status of the suits, and to request your written permission to prosecute said actions against the uninsured motorist to judgment.

The defendant, Roy McCampbell, in both of the above-described suits, was served, we understand, on August 21, 19XX. As of the date of this writing, we are advised that he has not entered an appearance or filed any pleading, answer or demurrer to either of the suits.

We understand that your company will be represented generally in connection with the matter by King, Jones and Smith, Attorneys, in Hale City. We will keep you advised of the progress of the two suits described above. Unless we hear from you to the contrary, we will have all of our dealings with Rubin Jones, as your attorney in connection with the claims of Henrietta and Alberta.

Sincerely,

COMMENT:

1. The above letter is a detailed letter advising an insurance company of a suit which the lawyer has filed for his client against an uninsured motorist and asserting the client's claim pursuant to his uninsured motorist coverage.

2. The letter complies with notice requirements under the uninsured motorist coverage.

182.
LETTER TO INSURED IN DEFENSE CASE

Dear Mr. Abernathy:

We have been retained by ABC Insurance Company to defend you in the suit brought against you by Wilson Jennings in the Circuit Court arising out of your automobile accident on December 29, 19XX. We have entered an appearance in this case in your behalf and shall take all necessary steps for your defense.

We shall keep you advised of any significant developments in the case and shall inform you as far in advance as possible when the case is to be tried, and when other proceedings in the case which will require your presence are set. We do not always have the opportunity to give substantial notice, and, consequently, we ask that you inform us should you move from your present address or be absent therefrom for any period in excess of one week.

Enclosed is a copy of this letter upon which we request that you insert the name, address and telephone number of your employer and your current residence address and telephone number. We would appreciate your keeping us advised of any changes in these addresses or telephone numbers. A self-addressed envelope is enclosed for your convenience in furnishing us with this information.

Very sincerely,

COMMENT:

1. The above letter is written to the insured at the time the lawyer undertakes the representation of the insurance carrier in a case in which the insured is involved. The usual case, as above, involves an automobile accident.

183.
NOTICE OF BEING RETAINED BY INSURER TO DEFEND INSURED IN
SUIT IN WHICH CLAIM EXCEEDS POLICY LIMITS

Dear Mr. Gonzales:

This law firm has been retained by ABC Insurance Company to defend you in the suits brought against you and your employer, DEF Company, by Max Taylor.

(Case No. 19436, Linda Taylor
(Case No. 19437, Mark Taylor
(Case No. 19438, Liza Taylor
(and Case No. 19439, in the Superior Court of Haley County, arising out of the accident of January 2, 19XX, on Golf Road. This defense of these suits is afforded you under the liability insurance coverage provided by the policy which you carry with the company.

I invite your attention to the provisions of the insurance policy requiring that you cooperate with the attorneys employed by the company in the defense of any action covered by the policy. I am sure you will understand the importance of such cooperation, which is in your own interests, and will give it. This law firm will take all required steps in the defense of these suits and will notify you as far in advance as possible each time that it may be necessary for you to appear in court or to take any other steps in connection with the defense of the suits. However, it might sometimes happen that we would be compelled to contact you on very short notice, and, consequently, we request your immediate advice of any change in your address or your place of business.

We invite your attention to the fact that the claim of damages made by Linda Taylor, combined with that made by her husband, Max Taylor, and the total of claims for personal injuries made by the four plaintiffs together exceed the limits of the coverage afforded to you under the insurance policy referred to. It is your privilege to employ additional counsel to represent and defend your interests in the defense of these suits, in event you see fit to do so, at your own expense.

Should you elect to employ additional counsel, this law firm will be delighted to cooperate in every way with such counsel and to have the cooperation and assistance of such counsel.

The file on the investigation of this accident made by adjusters employed by ABC Insurance Company has been made available to us for study and preparation of the defense of these suits. We will want to talk with you about these cases before they are tried, however. We would be most grateful if you would call our office to arrange an appointment at your convenience for that purpose.

Sincerely yours,

COMMENT:

1. The above letter is known as an excess letter and is written when the claim made by plaintiff exceeds the policy limits.

184.
LETTER TO INSURED RE TRIAL DATE

Dear Mr. Cornwall:

The suit of Mrs. Carlton against you has been set for trial on October 2, 19XX at 9:00 A.M. The trial is to be held in the Lincoln County Courthouse in Johnson City.

It will be essential that you be present for the trial of the case unless we advise you to the contrary. Please be in our offices at 8:00 A.M., on October 2, 19XX.

If for any reason you cannot be present for this trial on the date stated, it is imperative that you advise us immediately.

Yours truly,

COMMENT:

1. The lawyer should keep the insured fully advised of the status of the case at all times as the insured's cooperation is essential to the representation of the insurance carrier.

185.
NOTICE OF DEPOSITION TO INSURED

Dear Miss Martin:

The attorney for the plaintiff in this case has set your deposition for Friday, April 3 at 2:00 P.M. I request that you be in my office by 1:00 P.M. on that date so that we will have an opportunity to go over some of the aspects of your case which will be covered on this deposition.

For your information, a deposition is simply the taking of one's statement under oath where an attorney asks questions and the witness answers them. It is an informal procedure, usually taking place either in our office or in the office of the attorney representing the other party, before a court reporter who takes down the testimony in shorthand. Of course, I will be present to represent you at the taking of this deposition.

Under our court rules, either side has the right to take the testimony of the opposing party by deposition prior to trial for discovery purposes.

At this deposition, you will be asked questions relating to the accident. The two most important things to remember in connection with the giving of a deposition are to tell the truth and be brief. You should listen to each question carefully, answer it completely and honestly but do not overanswer it. That is, do not elaborate unless some elaboration is necessary to clarify your answer and do not answer questions which are not asked.

If you have any questions concerning this, please feel free to call me and discuss it. Otherwise, I will expect to see you at 1:00 P.M. on April 3, and I can answer any questions you may have at that time.

Sincerely yours,

COMMENT:

1. Alternative language for the above letter, when appropriate, may be added as follows:
   (a) "Upon receipt of this letter, please call my secretary and confirm that you will be present at that time."
   (b) "Upon receipt of this letter, please call me to arrange an appointment to visit the scene of the accident with me and discuss the facts surrounding it. This should be done before your deposition."

2. The following language may be used when the lawyer intends to set an additional deposition following the original deposition:
   (a) "Immediately following your deposition, I will take the deposition of Mr. Fanning. You are welcome to sit in the deposition of Mr. Fanning if you desire, but this is not necessary and is entirely up to you."

186.

TRANSMITTAL OF REAL ESTATE SALES CONTRACT TO BUYER

Dear Mr. Campbell:

I am enclosing a copy of the real estate sales contract which we have prepared for William Mitchell, his wife, and Ray Morganthal.

Please let me know if you have any objections to the form of the contract as written.

I have forwarded it to Mr. Mitchell and his wife with the request that they sign it and send it to Ray Morganthal for signature. We will advise you as soon as we have the signed contract in hand.

Thank you very much.

Sincerely yours,

COMMENT:

1. The writer could, if desired, add additional details regarding the transaction or state the action that will be taken subsequent to the execution of the contract.

187.
NOTICE TO EMPLOYER OF WORKMEN'S COMPENSATION CLAIM

Dear Mr. Fanning:

Our firm represents Mr. Max Taylor who was injured in the course of employment by your company while engaged in the duties of employment.

We are sending you herewith formal notice of said claim as required by the State Workmen's Compensation Act.

Sincerely yours,

COMMENT:

1. The above letter, if desired, could include the nature of the injuries or the accident resulting in the injuries to the employee.

NOTICE OF WORKMEN'S COMPENSATION CLAIM

You are hereby notified that an injury was received by the above-referenced employee who was employed by you at the time of said personal injuries, and these injuries were received in the course of employment on June 18, 19XX. The injuries sustained came about as a result of lifting a heavy tool chest. As a result of such injury, said employee received medical and surgical attention from physicians. Said employee is now residing at the above-referenced address. Said personal injuries consisted of a ruptured disc in the lower back.

You are further notified that said employee claims compensation of you for said injuries arising from said accident pursuant to the state Workmen's Compensation Laws.

188.
TRANSMITTAL TO TRUSTEE IN BANKRUPTCY OF SUMMONS AND
NOTICE OF TRIAL ISSUED BY BANKRUPTCY CLERK

Dear Mr. Murphy:

In order to effectuate service of summons pursuant to Rule 704 of the Bankruptcy Rules, I enclose with this letter the original of a summons and Notice of Trial issued by the Bankruptcy Clerk under date of June 18, 19XX, together with a copy of the Complaint therein.

Should you have any questions concerning this matter, please call me.

Sincerely yours,

COMMENT:

1. The above letter is written pursuant to the Federal bankruptcy rules of practice.

Requesting Information

189.
REQUEST FOR INFORMATION FROM BANK ABOUT
GUARANTY AGREEMENT CLAIM AGAINST CLIENT

Dear Mr. Miller:

Mr. Ralph Johnson has been out of town, and today I had an opportunity for the first time to discuss with him your letter of September 14, 19XX. Ralph tells me that the "two" guaranty agreements, dated October 15, 19XX, which you enclosed were two copies of one guaranty in the amount of $20,000. We would appreciate it if you would please double check on the matter of the second guaranty. After you have had a chance to check it out, we would appreciate your statement of whether you have it or not. Also, if you do not have it, we would like to know if you ever had it. If you do have it, we would like to have a copy.

In connection with each of the guarantees, we would appreciate your advice as to when and how the guaranty agreements were delivered to the bank and in what manner our client was advised of acceptance of the instruments by the bank. We would also like to know what consideration was given to our client for the guaranties. If the consideration was corporate stock, were the state blue sky laws complied with in connection with the transaction.

We would like your statement in writing as to whether a total line of credit of at least $300,000 was obtained by ABC Corporation from your bank. We would like to have complete details of establishment of the $300,000 line of credit and utilization made of it. Please include the dates and amounts of all advances made pursuant to it as well as your efforts to collect it. The names, addresses and amounts of other guarantors together with the amounts paid by them to the bank pursuant to their individual guaranties would be helpful.

Would you please let us know, if you know, what was the date on which ABC Corporation first began serving ten or more customers. This event is referred to in the agreement attached to the guaranty.

You sent two agreements dated October 15, 19XX which presumably were attached to the guaranty agreements. One was signed by our client and the bank, and one was not. Why was one of the agreements not executed? Do you have two executed agreements? We would like to have copies of both as signed.

Mr. Miller, I have told our client that I need this information in order to evaluate the bank's claim. Your cooperation will be appreciated.

Yours very truly,

COMMENT:

1. The above letter is an example of a subsequent letter sent to an opposing party requesting additional information following a reply to an original letter requesting information. It is a good idea in connection with a claim by an opposing party to secure all of the details possible about the claim as well as the opposing party's interpretation of any documents involved and the opposing party's position relating to the law involved.

190.
REQUEST TO BANK FOR INFORMATION OF CLAIM AGAINST CLIENT UNDER GUARANTY AGREEMENT

Dear Mr. Miller:

Mr. Ralph Johnson has given us your letter of June 12, 19XX, regarding a guaranty agreement, in which you state a claim against Ralph as guarantor.

Ralph has given us a copy of a document entitled "Guaranty Agreement" dated October 15, 19XX, relating to the extension of credit from time to time to ABC Corporation in the limited amount of $300,000. We would appreciate your advice as to when and how this instrument was delivered to the bank and in what manner Ralph was advised of acceptance of the instrument by the bank.

We do not have a copy of a second unit valued at $20,000 as stated in your letter of June 12, 19XX, and we would appreciate it if you would please send us a copy of it.

Assuming the Guaranty Agreement is valid and Ralph is liable to the bank, I do not see, upon first reading, how the bank could claim any more than the stated amount regardless of whether it is principal, interest, or what have you.

In addition, we will appreciate your advice regarding the underlying credit debt extended by the bank to ABC Corporation, when it was extended, what efforts have been made to collect, what amounts have been paid by guarantors, and in short, complete and full details relating to the transaction.

Sincerely yours,

COMMENT:

1. The above is an example of a letter requesting information of an opposing party who is asserting a claim against the writer's client. Such a letter indicates to the opposing party that the claim is being given serious consideration.

191.
REQUEST TO CORPORATION FOR FINANCIAL STATEMENT

Dear Mr. Cornwall:

This is to advise you that we are representing Mr. William Carpenter in connection with his ownership of 1000 shares of stock in ABC Corporation. We are enclosing copies of letters from Mr. Carpenter mailed to your attention dated September 24, 19XX, and October 18, 19XX, wherein Mr. Carpenter requested current financial information regarding the company as well as other information.

Mr. Carpenter tells us that he has not heard from you, and he has been unable to reach you on the telephone although he has tried frequently.

This is to request, in behalf of our client, that you supply to us the corporation's most recent financial statements showing in reasonable detail its assets and liabilities and the results of its operations. Mr. Carpenter, as a stockholder has this right pursuant to the state code, Title _____ , Sec. _____ .

I would like to state that Mr. Carpenter is somewhat exasperated over the matter at this point and has instructed us to take all steps which are reasonably necessary to protect his rights as a stock owner of your corporation.

We would like to hear from you at the earliest date.

Yours very truly,

COMMENT:

1. Under the corporation code or law in most states, stockholders are entitled to current financial information. The above letter is sent to a corporation to request such information when it has failed to forward it to the stockholder.

192.
REQUEST TO OPPOSING PARTY FOR DETAILS OF ACCIDENT

Dear Mr. Wilson:

Mrs. Margaret Jones has consulted our law firm in regard to an accident. We are now in the process of investigating the matter.

Sometimes there are several versions as to what occurred at an accident, and, before proceeding further, I would like to know your account of what occurred at this accident; i.e., whether you feel the accident was your fault or another party's fault, the reasons for your belief, and also the names and addresses of any other witnesses.

If you are covered by liability insurance, please be certain to indicate the name of your insurance company so that we can deal directly with them and minimize further inconvenience to you.

Thank you for your cooperation and the courtesy of your prompt attention to this matter.

Sincerely yours,

COMMENT:

1. It is very helpful as well as thoughtful to invite the opposing party to give his account of the accident at the beginning of the case. Of course, after the matter is placed in the hands of an opposing attorney, such information would have to be acquired by deposition or interrogatories.

193.
**REQUEST TO INSURANCE COMPANY FOR COPY OF
STATEMENT OF CLIENT**

Dear Mr. Brown:

Please forward to this office a copy of any statement you or your principals have obtained from my above-named client.

In addition, please advise us the names and addresses of any witnesses known to you or your principals.

Both of the above requests are in order under our state rules of discovery, and I hope it will not be necessary to utilize formal procedures for this information. We will cooperate in making all similar information, including authorizations, available to you as requested.

Thank you for your courtesy and cooperation in this matter.

Sincerely yours,

COMMENT:

1. Letters such as the above, in which the parties cooperate on matters of discovery, avoid expensive formal discovery procedure.

Requesting or Demanding Action

194.
REQUEST FOR PAYMENT OF ACCOUNT

Dear Mr. Patterson:

Mr. Harold Brown of Culver City, has turned over to us for handling his claim against you in the amount of $19,820 on account dated August 18, 19XX plus interest.

Perhaps you are interested in paying this account. If you are, please let us know, and we will work with you on it. In the event we do not hear from you within ten days or satisfactory arrangements are not made for the payment of this account in full within ten days, we intend to file suit against you in behalf of Mr. Brown on the account.

I want to assure you that we would much rather work with you on the matter than file suit and cause you the additional expense of defending this suit. Please let us hear from you.

Yours very truly,

COMMENT:

1. The above is an example of a friendly but firm request for payment of an account.

195.
REQUEST FOR PAYMENT OF ACCOUNT OR SUIT TO BE FILED

Dear Mr. Fanning:

We represent Dr. Joseph Murphy in his claim against you for $125. This claim arises out of his examination and treatment of you in June, July and August, 19XX.

Though the amount owed is not large, Dr. Murphy has authorized us to file suit to collect the full amount. If that is necessary, and we obtain a judgment, you will become liable for court costs and attorneys' fees, in addition to the amount you already owe. This will more than double your bill and is a needless waste of your money, not to mention the inconvenience and aggravation.

Therefore, we urge you to make payment in full to this office within ten (10) days. Otherwise we shall be forced to take this matter to court.

Yours truly,

COMMENT:

1. The tone of a collection letter such as the above should be tailored to fit the exact situation. Care should be taken to avoid unintended rudeness.

2. The statement regarding attorneys' fees should only be made if they are allowed in your jurisdiction.

196.
REQUEST FOR PAYMENT OF DEBT WITHIN FIFTEEN DAYS OR
SUIT TO BE FILED

Dear Mr. Miller:

Please be advised that Dr. Richard Wilson has retained our firm to collect the debt you owe him in the sum of $780 for dental work completed last September. The total amount due for the dental work performed was $830, of which you have paid $50.

Dr. Wilson advises us that the ABC Credit Union has approved your credit application under their Dental Budget Plan and that you could obtain the funds with which to pay him through the ABC Credit Union.

Dr. Wilson has authorized us to file suit against you if we have not heard from you within fifteen (15) days from the date you receive this letter.

Please advise our office if you wish to make satisfactory arrangements with Dr. Wilson regarding the payment of your account without the necessity of a lawsuit. If a lawsuit is required to collect this indebtedness, you will, in all probability, be required to pay the court costs and your attorney's fee in this regard.

Yours truly,

COMMENT:

1. The above collection letter points out to the adverse party that unless he pays the debt, suit will be filed, resulting in the expense of defense of the suit.

197.
NOTICE OF SUIT TO BE FILED IF ACCOUNT NOT PAID WITHIN TEN DAYS

Dear Mrs. Brownell:

Our firm has been retained by ABC Bank in connection with your debt to the bank which has been past due since October 18, 19XX. The amount due as of this date is $3,876, and interest is accruing at the rate of $1.15 per day.

It is our understanding that all efforts by the bank to obtain payment on a voluntary basis have proved unsuccessful, and the matter has therefore been turned over to us for whatever action may be necessary. If this obligation has not been satisfied within ten days from the date of this letter, we shall recommend to the bank that suit be filed without further notice to you to recover the full amount due plus court costs and attorney's fees. Your immediate response is essential if that step is to be avoided.

Yours very truly,

COMMENT:

1. The above letter in a firm way advises the adverse party of additional action to be taken in the event of further default in paying an account.

198.
REQUEST TO PAY PROMISSORY NOTE OR SUIT TO BE FILED

Dear Mr. Barrow:

We represent Mr. and Mrs. George Johnson. Our clients advise us that on or about April 17, 19XX you delivered to them your promissory note in the original principal amount of $7,500, payable in full on or before April 17, 19XX and bearing interest at the annual rate of 8% per annum. Our client further advises that this promissory note provides that, in the event of your default, you promise to pay reasonable attorneys' fees in addition to the amount due thereon.

Our clients advise us that you are in default in said note by your failure to pay any part of said note and that there is now due and owing $6,400, constituting principal and interest and attorneys' fees for services to date of $185.

This letter is final notice to you that unless $1,000 or more is paid to this office on behalf of Mr. and Mrs. Johnson on or before September 15, 19XX, legal action will be taken against you to collect said note. This will result in substantial additional expense to you for court costs and attorneys' fees. If you wish to avoid this, please pay $1,000 or more on or before September 15, 19XX.

Very sincerely,

COMMENT:

1. The above letter could be changed in the event the lawyer wished to hold open the possibility of further negotiations for terms of payment prior to beginning the suit.

199.
REQUESTING PAYMENT IN ACCORDANCE WITH AGREEMENT

Dear Mr. Mitchell:

We will appreciate receiving your payment to ABC Corporation in accordance with our previous agreement.

Sincerely yours,

COMMENT:

1. The above letter is brief but explicit.

2. The letter could be personalized with a friendly closing paragraph.

200.
REQUEST TO PAY OR ARRANGE TO PAY ACCOUNT WITHIN
TEN DAYS OR SUIT TO BE FILED

Dear Mr. Bell:

Our client, ABC Corporation of Boston has given us their claim on account against you in the amount of $34,685.

We understand that repeated demands have been made of you to pay this amount, and you have steadfastly refused.

We will appreciate your making firm arrangements with us, satisfactory to our client, for the payment of this account within ten (10) days. In the event this account is not paid in full or satisfactory arrangements are not made for the full payment of this account within ten days, we will prepare and file a suit against you on the account.

In the event you feel a conference on this matter will be helpful, I assure you that we will be happy to meet with you or your attorney.

Yours very truly,

COMMENT:

1. The above is a collection letter. It is suggested that when a letter containing a demand to pay within ten days is sent, in the event of default for ten days, a suit should be promptly filed on the matter.

2. The letter contains a friendly closing paragraph offering to work out the matter without litigation.

201.
REQUEST FOR FURTHER PAYMENT ON ACCOUNT OR SUIT TO BE FILED

Dear Mr. Miller:

Please let us have a further payment on your account. I am sure you realize that when no payment is made, we get a letter from our client asking what the situation is, and we are unable to explain it.

In the event no payment is received within five days, we will have no alternative but to put this matter before the court.

In the event a payment has been made, please disregard this notice and accept our thanks for your attention.

In order to ensure proper credit to your account, be certain to state the name of our client on all payments.

Sincerely yours,

COMMENT:

1. In the event there may be any doubt regarding the amount of payment due, the letter should state the amount due, as well as the minimum amount of payment expected.

202.
REQUEST TO PAY ACCOUNT DIRECT TO CLIENT WITHIN FIVE DAYS OR
SUIT TO BE FILED

Dear Mr. Halstead:

Amount Due: $385.

I have been retained by ABC Finance Company to represent them in action against you for default in payment on your account.

You are now past due in the payments in the above amount, plus late charges and interest. If you have not contacted ABC Finance Company within five (5) days from the date of this letter, we shall proceed with whatever legal action is necessary to obtain this amount.

If such action is necessary, you will be responsible for court costs and attorneys' fees. By contacting ABC Finance Company directly and bringing your account up to date, you will save yourself unnecessary expense and embarrassment.

Yours sincerely,

COMMENT:

1. The statement contained above regarding attorneys' fees should not be made unless attorney's fees may be legally claimed.

2. The above letter could be altered, if desired, by inviting negotiation or explanation.

203.
SECOND REQUEST TO PAY ACCOUNT WITHIN FIVE DAYS OR
SUIT TO BE FILED

Dear Mr. Epworth:

This is to advise you that, due to your failure to respond to our first letter, our client has asked us to give the account mentioned above our immediate legal attention.

This is a serious matter and deserves your prompt attention. Your cooperation at this point will save all concerned the trouble and expense of a lawsuit and will, of course, be in your best interest.

We are giving you the opportunity to come by this office within five days and make satisfactory arrangements for the payment of this account. If we fail to hear from you within that time, we shall take immediate legal action to protect the interest of our client.

You should understand that if, by your failure to contact this office within five days, we are compelled to bring suit against you, you may be held liable for not only the amount you owe our client, but also for our attorney's fees, court costs, and additional expenses — most of which can be avoided if you will act now.

Yours truly,

COMMENT:

1. The language in the above letter regarding attorney's fees should be deleted unless there is a legal basis for such fees. In the event a promissory note is involved, such note generally contains a provision regarding attorney's fees. However, in the event an account only is involved, in many jurisdictions there is no right to claim attorney's fees. However, in all jurisdictions, court costs would be allowed to the prevailing party, and in many jurisdictions other expenses of trial may be allowed.

204.
FINAL NOTICE FOR PAYMENT OF ACCOUNT OR SUIT TO BE FILED

Dear Mr. Brownell:

Suit will be filed within forty-eight hours if you have not taken care of this account.

This is our final notice and demand.

Yours truly,

COMMENT:

1. Suit should be filed promptly as stated in the above letter in the event payment is not made as demanded.

205.
DEMANDING PERFORMANCE OF CONTRACT

Dear Mr. Carter:

This is to advise you that we are representing ABC Acceptance Corporation in connection with its claim against you resulting from your failure to repurchase the above-referenced conditional sale contract in accordance with your previous agreement.

Demand is hereby made upon you to repurchase this contract in accordance with said agreement forthwith.

Your continued failure to repurchase in accordance with the agreement will result in an immediate suit against you.

Yours sincerely,

COMMENT:

1. The above letter is a formal demand for the adverse party to repurchase a conditional sales contract in accordance with a previous agreement.

2. The adverse party is advised in a friendly but firm way that failure to repurchase in accordance with the prior agreement will cause the matter to be litigated.

206.
REQUEST TO OPPOSING PARTY TO PAY ATTORNEY FEE
AS PROVIDED IN JUDGMENT

Dear Mr. Bell:

We previously sent you a statement on May 12, 19XX for our fees in connection with your recent family law problems. Judge Wilson entered the decree whereby you were directed to pay us part of our fee for services rendered to Mrs. Bell in this regard.

I would appreciate it very much if you would please take care of this bill as soon as you can. I saw your attorney, Mr. Joel Miller, the other day, and I mentioned it to him. He said he would talk with you.

I suppose if we have a dispute regarding the matter and you fail to pay us, the proper procedure would be for us to file a petition in this case. I would much prefer not to do this and would be grateful if you would take care of it. In the event you have any financial hardship, I would appreciate your coming in, and let's discuss this matter.

Thank you very much.

Sincerely,

COMMENT:

1. The above letter is a good example of being firm in a friendly way. Such a letter should, of course, be tailored to fit the situation.

207.
REQUESTING APPOINTMENT WITH DEFENDANT IN DIVORCE CASE

Dear Jake:

This is to advise you that we have again been in touch with your wife in connection with the proposed divorce.

We would appreciate it very much if you would please arrange to come by our office to discuss this matter at your earliest convenience.

Very sincerely,

COMMENT:

1. The above letter could be further personalized by indicating to the client what the lawyer has learned from the client's wife regarding the proposed divorce.

2. The lawyer might also mention in the letter the specific matters to be discussed or decided at the requested conference.

208.
REQUESTING DEFENDANT TO SIGN DIVORCE PAPERS

Dear Mr. Brownell:

We are enclosing a copy of a proposed complaint against you by Mrs. Brownell for a divorce on the grounds of abandonment. We are also enclosing the original and one copy of the proposed agreement between you and Mrs. Brownell regarding the support and custody of the children, a copy of the complaint, the original and one copy of an answer and waiver, and the original and one copy of a bill of sale from you to Mrs. Brownell for the 19XX Ford automobile.

We understand from Mrs. Brownell that these papers have been agreed to by you.

In the event you want us to proceed with the divorce, please sign the original and copy of the agreement, the original of the answer and waiver and the original bill of sale and return them to us as soon as possible via air mail.

In the event you have any questions regarding this matter, you may call me at the number listed above.

Yours truly,

COMMENT:

1. The above letter is an example of a letter used in connection with a proposed divorce to find out whether the adverse party is agreeable to the terms of the divorce proposed by the lawyer's client.

2. In the event the adverse party is agreeable, instructions are contained in the letter for execution of necessary documents to facilitate a noncontested divorce.

209.
REQUEST TO SPOUSE OF CLIENT IN DIVORCE CASE TO
SIGN DIVORCE PAPERS

Dear Mr. Bell:

Our office is representing your wife in legal proceedings to obtain a divorce. Enclosed is a copy of the complaint we plan to file with the Family Court.

Also enclosed is an answer and waiver form. If you agree to this divorce on the terms indicated in the enclosed complaint, please sign the answer IN INK and have someone sign, ALSO IN INK, as a witness. Then return the answer to us in the envelope provided. You may keep the copy of the complaint, and we will send you a certified copy of the final divorce decree when signed by the judge.

If you have any questions concerning these papers, please contact a lawyer of your choice, or call or come by our office. Thank you.

Sincerely yours,

COMMENT:

1. In the above letter it appears that the terms of divorce are covered in the complaint. In the event a separate agreement is prepared, the proposed agreement should be enclosed with the letter.

210.
REQUESTING DEFENDANT TO SIGN DIVORCE PAPERS

Dear Mr. Parker:

Your wife, Louise, called and requested that we forward the enclosed proposed divorce papers to you.

I presume the two of you have discussed terms in an effort to reach an agreement regarding the divorce. Therefore, we are enclosing a copy of the proposed complaint to be filed by Louise for a divorce on the grounds of incompatibility under our state law. We are also enclosing the original and one copy of the proposed agreement between you and Louise regarding the support of Jeffrey and an answer and waiver to be signed by you in the event you approve of the agreement and would like to cooperate in connection with the proposed divorce.

In the event you want us to proceed with the divorce, please sign the original and one copy of the agreement and return the original to us. Also sign the original and copy of the answer and waiver and return the original to us. You will note that no provision is made in the agreement regarding payment of attorneys' fees. The total cost for the divorce is $300 attorneys' fees and $36 court costs. I suggest that you and Mrs. Parker discuss the matter and decide between yourselves who is to bear this expense and in what proportion. Ordinarily, as you know, the husband pays all expenses in connection with a divorce. It is considered one of the husband's responsibilities in connection with a marriage. Under our local rules, none of the divorce papers may be submitted to the judge for the signing of a divorce decree until all court costs and fees are paid.

In the event you have any questions regarding this matter, you may call me on the telephone at the number listed above.

Sincerely yours,

COMMENT:

1. The above letter is an example of a letter used in connection with a proposed divorce to find out whether the adverse party is agreeable to the terms of the divorce proposed by the lawyer's client.

2. In the event the adverse party is agreeable, instructions are contained in the letter for execution of necessary documents to facilitate a noncontested divorce.

211.
REQUEST TO SIGN DIVORCE PAPERS

Dear Mr. McIntyre:

Your wife has been in to see me about a divorce which she said has been mutually agreed upon between yourselves.

According to the information your wife gave me: you were married on the 14th day of June, 19XX, in Memphis, Tennessee; you separated on or about the 6th day of October, 19XX; as a result of your union, one child was born, Linda Kay; and the child is now in Spring Valley with her mother. Mrs. McIntyre indicated to me that you and she agreed that the primary custody would be placed in her which is as usual in these cases. She also said you agreed that the furniture accumulated during your marriage would go to her and that no child support or alimony would be requested in the divorce.

Accordingly, I have prepared a bill of divorce and an answer and waiver, and I am enclosing a copy of the bill of divorce together with an original and one copy of the answer and waiver. First examine the bill for divorce and note that her petition comes under our state's incompatibility law, wherein there is no plaintiff or defendant and no finding of fault by or against either party. There is a simple averment that incompatibility does exist between the parties, and for that reason the bonds of matrimony should be dissolved. Examine, if you will, the bill of divorce, numbered paragraph by numbered paragraph. In the numbered paragraphs of the answer you admit each numbered paragraph of the bill of divorce. The unnumbered paragraph in the answer we term as "Waiver," and by this waiver you simply waive your right to a trial, which, of course, is unnecessary should you consent.

If, in fact, you do agree on a divorce based on incompatibility, sign the original answer and waiver, have a witness sign it and return it to me in the enclosed, self-addressed stamped envelope. You may retain the copies of the bill of divorce and answer and waiver for your records. Upon receipt of the answer and waiver, Mrs. McIntyre will secure a divorce, and I will send a copy of the divorce decree to you.

If you have any questions, please write or call. If I do not hear from you in a few days, I will assume that my information was not correct and that you do not want a divorce based on the incompatibility law.

Yours truly,

COMMENT:

1. The above letter should be tailored to fit all procedural requirements of your jurisdiction. In the event a written agreement is desired, the agreement should be included with the letter.

212.
REQUESTING DEFENDANT TO AGREE TO CHANGE IN CHILD CUSTODY AGREEMENT

Dear Mr. Hallman:

This is to advise you that I talked to Mrs. Hallman in connection with the matter of revising the custody arrangement for Jennifer following my telephone conversation with you yesterday.

I do not feel that there is any question but that Judge Campbell would grant a change in the custody arrangement upon this matter being taken to court in view of the matters which we discussed in my office the Saturday you were kind enough to come in and see us.

Therefore, this is to advise you that, in the event you would like to discuss further the proposed change in the custody arrangement within the next five days we will be pleased to discuss the matter with you. However, in the event you do not, please be advised that we will file a proceeding against you in the Circuit Court of Lincoln county, thereby causing you, and our client, both the inconvenience and expense of a court proceeding.

Very sincerely,

COMMENT:

1. The above letter states the position of the lawyer's client regarding a change desired by the client in the child custody arrangement made in a prior court decree.

2. The lawyer obviously has discussed the matter with the adverse party and has formed an opinion that the facts warrant a change in the custody arrangement.

3. The letter further states in a friendly but firm way that unless an agreement is reached regarding the matter, an action will be filed in court for its resolution.

213.
DEMANDING RESUMPTION OF SUPPORT PAYMENTS

Dear Mr. Morris:

We understand from your former wife, Mrs. Mary Morris, that you have not been making payments of $350 per month in accordance with the decree of the Washington County Superior Court.

Needless to say, we would prefer to save you the expense and inconvenience of a contempt proceeding regarding this matter, and to this end we will appreciate it if you will please resume your payments and make an arrangement with Mrs. Morris regarding the payments which are in arrears.

In the event we are unable to resolve this matter by agreement, we hope you understand that a contempt proceeding will become necessary.

Sincerely yours,

COMMENT:

1. The above letter points out in detail the default made by the adverse party in connection with support payments required by the court decree.

2. The adverse party is firmly advised to resume current payments and arrange for the payment of arrears.

3. He is further advised that the matter will be taken to court for resolution in the event of his continued default.

214.
PROPOSED AGREEMENT FOR LUMP SUM TO BE PAID IN LIEU OF SUPPORT PAYMENTS TO FORMER WIFE

Dear Mr. Smith:

Your former wife, Joyce Barnes Smith came to our office today, and we discussed at some length the matter of a proposed agreement between the two of you relating to future support payments for your two minor children, namely: Mark and David. I understand they are respectively 7 and 9 years old at the present time.

Joyce told me that you and she have discussed the matter of your paying her a lump sum of $10,000 which amount would discharge you from further obligation to pay the $100 per week child support for the two children. Actually, this proposed arrangement does not meet with our approval, and we advised Joyce that we did not think it was in her best interest to do it. However, in spite of our advice, she states that she wants to enter such an agreement with you.

Therefore, we have prepared a proposed agreement between the two of you whereby you would pay her the lump sum of $10,000 and be relieved of future obligation to pay the $100 per week support payments. This agreement could, in our opinion, be incorporated into the divorce decree rendered in the Jefferson County Circuit Court, but the court costs would run a minimum of $65 to do so. I did provide in the agreement that in the event you or Joyce wanted to have it incorporated into a divorce decree that you had that right. Joyce said she thinks that you would prefer to keep the expenses down and simply pay for the preparation and execution of the agreement, which amount we have set at $250, and not have it incorporated into the divorce decree at this time.

In the event you want to proceed along the lines that Joyce has suggested, we would like for you to sign both copies of the agreement, retain one for your records and return the other copy to us, together with your check in the amount of $65 for court costs and another check for $250 made payable to our firm for our services in this matter.

If you have any questions about it and would like to discuss it on the telephone, please call me. Thank you very much.

Yours truly,

COMMENT:

1. The above letter relates to a matter which has previously been discussed by the lawyer's client and the adverse party. The client, a former wife, and the adverse party, her divorced husband, have agreed to a lump sum settlement of future child support payments.

2. The letter states that the lawyer does not approve of the proposed terms of agreement and that the client nevertheless wishes to enter in the agreement. It is a good idea to indicate this whenever there is an actual difference of opinion between the lawyer and the client. Otherwise it might be assumed that the lawyer concurs in the course of action undertaken by the client.

215.
REQUEST TO CHILD TO CONSENT TO ADOPTION

Dear Paula:

We represent your grandmother, Mrs. Mabel Dykes and her husband, John Dykes, in a proceeding to adopt you and your three brothers as their own children.

Your name will not be changed in the adoption, and a new birth certificate will not be issued for you.

We enclose a copy of the petition for adoption which Mr. and Mrs. Dykes will file if you and your three brothers consent. Richard and Edwin have already signed consents.

We enclose the original and four copies of your consent. If you consent, please go to a notary public and sign the original and all four copies in his presence. Then have the notary sign the original and all four copies, insert the date his commission expires, and affix his seal.

Please return the original and all four copies of your consent to me in the enclosed return envelope. You may keep the copy of the petition for adoption.

If the adoption is completed, the effect will be to make you and your three brothers legally children of Mr. Dykes and your grandmother. The adoption will probably not be completed for about six months.

Very sincerely,

COMMENT:

1. A letter such as the above should be carefully worded to fit the situation involved. In the usual case, it would be wise, as is done here, for the writer to refrain from encouraging execution of the consent.

2. The procedural rules in such proceedings in your jurisdiction should be complied with. It is possible that when minors are involved, a guardian ad litem would need to be appointed to consult and advise with the minors prior to execution of the consent.

216.
REQUEST TO PAY BALANCE OF JUDGMENT OR
ACTION TO BE TAKEN FOR ENFORCEMENT

Dear Mr. Alvarez:

On July 15, 19XX, you paid $600 on the judgment against you held by our client, ABC Company.

You agreed to pay the balance of $1,900 plus interest thereon at 6% per annum on or before July 15, 19XX. We enclose a copy of your agreement.

On July 15, 19XX, the amount owing on the judgment will be:

1. Principal balance		$1,900
2. Interest at 6% per annum from July 15, 19XX, to July 15, 19XX, 365 days		114
3. Total		$2,014

If we do not receive payment as agreed, our client will levy execution or take other appropriate action to enforce payment of the judgment.

Sincerely yours,

COMMENT:

1. The above letter could be changed to invite the addressee to advise of his plans regarding payment. The door could be held open, if desired, to further negotiation regarding terms of payment.

217.
REQUESTING ADVERSE PARTY TO NOTIFY
INSURANCE COMPANY OF ACCIDENT

Dear Mrs. Wallace:

Our firm has been retained to represent Mr. and Mrs. Ralph Turner in their claim for damages against you which resulted from an accident on, at or near Morgan City.

If you carry liability insurance to cover you for this accident, please be sure to turn this letter over to your carrier with the request that they contact the undersigned.

FAILURE TO NOTIFY YOUR INSURANCE COMPANY *IMMEDIATELY* **MAY CAUSE THEM TO REFUSE TO PROTECT YOUR INTERESTS.**

In the event that you do not have insurance, please contact our office as soon as possible.

Yours truly,

COMMENT:

1. The above letter is a standard or form letter addressed to an adverse party requesting him to contact his liability insurance carrier. In the event he does not have insurance, he is requested to contact the writer.

218.
REQUEST FOR CONFERENCE WITH INSURER OR
ATTORNEY CONCERNING PERSONAL INJURY CLAIM

Dear Mr. Teague:

Mr. Wayne Mitchell has consulted me in reference to a fall that he took in your restaurant on March 1, 19XX. Mr. Mitchell was being led by one of your waiters from the bar area to the dining room area when he fell on the unmarked steps leading from the former to the latter. Mr. Mitchell suffered back injuries as a result of the fall and has been forced to incur medical expenses as well as legal expenses that are now being incurred.

I would like to discuss this matter with your insurer or attorney. I would like to do so within a period of seven days from this letter.

Sincerely yours,

COMMENT:

1. The above letter is firm but friendly. The tone of the letter could be changed depending on the facts relating to the claim and the position of the client regarding filing suit.

219.
RECEIPT OF RENT PAYMENT AND REQUESTING ADDITIONAL PAYMENT

Dear Mr. and Mrs. Cornwall:

This will acknowledge receipt of the cashier's check dated September 21, 19XX, in the amount of $340.

This check is being applied to your account with ABC Apartments, Inc., as follows:

$165 for payment of September's rent,
$ 75 toward payment of your arrearage, and
$100 as attorney's fees for our services, which are to be paid by you in accordance with the terms of your lease.

As you know, you previously paid $190 towards your arrearage which had a total of $495 and this now gives you a balance on the arrearage of $230.

In addition, as you know, the October rent is now due and payable, and we will greatly appreciate receiving your check in the amount of $165.

Should you have any questions or suggestions regarding this matter, please let me know.

Sincerely yours,

COMMENT:

1. The above letter written by a lawyer to an adverse party who has failed to make rent payments acknowledges receipt of partial payment. The letter is friendly in tone and should have the effect of encouraging the reader to take care of the matter without the necessity of filing suit.

220.
NOTICE TO TENANT TO VACATE PREMISES

Dear Mr. and Mrs. Lawrence:

As you know from past correspondence, this office represents the management of your apartments with respect to the enforcement of lease provisions and terms. Despite previous warnings, you have breached the terms of your lease. For this reason, the management has reluctantly concluded that it must obtain a new tenant for your apartment.

You are hereby notified that if your past due rent and late charges remain unpaid, your lease is hereby terminated effective five days from the date on which this letter is delivered to you (or is available for you to pick up at the post office). The apartment must be surrendered on the termination date in good condition, broom clean, and free of all furnishings and possessions belonging to you. You should turn in your keys at the manager's office. You will be held accountable for any damages and any cleaning charges, for the balance of any unpaid rent which your security deposit is not sufficient to defray, and for the cost of removing any items from your apartment which do not belong there. Items left in the apartment will be deemed abandoned and will be disposed of by the management without accountability to you. Our state law provides for the collection of double rent from any tenant who holds over after his or her lease is terminated. Therefore, I sincerely hope that you will abide by the terms and conditions of this letter to avoid an expensive and unpleasant confrontation with the sheriff. If you have any questions, they should be directed to this office as the matter is now out of the management's hands.

Yours truly,

COMMENT:

1. The above letter is an example of a firm eviction notice. Many times such a letter is required as the tenant has been given every opportunity to work the matter out through negotiation.

221.
DEMAND TO VACATE PREMISES

Dear Mr. Willison:

As attorney for ABC Company, I hereby demand and notify you that you are required to forthwith leave the following premises, to wit:

> House and lot located at 1615 3rd Avenue, Johnson City for the possession of which premises an action is about to be brought by me, as attorney for ABC Company, against you.

Witness my hand at Johnson City, this the 6th day of February, 19XX.

_____

Attorney for ABC Company

COMMENT:

1. The above letter is an example of a formal demand to vacate premises. The letter could be personalized, if desired, by the writer stating that it is hoped that the tenant will vacate voluntarily or will contact the writer regarding any matters the tenant feels should be considered by the landlord prior to eviction.

222.
NOTICE TO TENANT TO VACATE PREMISES WITHIN TEN DAYS

Dear Mr. LaRue:

On behalf of ABC Company, demand is hereby made that you vacate the premises at 415 Golf Road, Johnson City, no later than ten days from this date. DEF Corporation was the purchaser of the above-described property at a foreclosure sale on August 7, 19XX.

Unless the property is vacated in accordance with this demand, eviction proceedings will be initiated.

Sincerely yours,

COMMENT:

1. The above letter is rather formal and could be softened if desired. The letter could simply state that the tenant is requested to vacate the premises within ten days, and, in the event he fails to do so, the contemplated eviction proceedings will be initiated. The tenant could be requested to advise the writer of any claim he makes to having a right to continued possession of the premises.

2. In the event a friendlier and more personal approach is desired, see letter 223.

223.
NOTICE TO TENANT TO VACATE PREMISES WITHIN TEN DAYS

Dear Miss Kaufman:

ABC Company purchased the property at 300 South Parkway, Johnson City, at a foreclosure sale on September 19, 19XX.

We represent the purchaser. On behalf of our clients we request you to vacate the premises within ten (10) days. Otherwise eviction proceedings will have to be initiated.

If you have any questions, please call me.

Sincerely yours,

COMMENT:

1. This letter could be sent when the lawyer expects the occupants to comply with the demand without protest.

224.
NOTICE TO VACATE PREMISES

Dear Mr. Albert:

You are hereby notified that in consequence of your default in paying the rent pursuant to your lease on the premises now occupied by you at Mayfair Apartments, Apartment 23, Second Floor, Johnson City, the lessor, Mayfair Apartments, Inc., has elected to terminate your lease, and you are hereby notified to quit and deliver up possession of the same within ten days of this notice. Dated this 14th day of October, 19XX.

Yours truly,

COMMENT:

1. The above letter is a somewhat formal notice to vacate premises.

2. The letter could be personalized to appeal to the defaulting party in a friendly way.

3. The lawyer could, if desired, state additional action that will be taken in the event the tenant does not vacate the premises.

225.
**NOTICE TO NEIGHBOR OF CLIENT TO DISCONTINUE ENCROACHING
ON CLIENT'S REAL PROPERTY**

Dear Mr. and Mrs. Gonzales:

This office represents Mr. Alvarez, and he has consulted us regarding the use by you of a portion of his property which adjoins your lot. Mr. Alvarez informs us that you have been storing rock, pipe, and miscellaneous building materials on his lot, that your garden is partially on his lot, that boards have been nailed to trees which belong to Mr. Alvarez, and that you have cut limbs from these trees.

I am sure that you are aware that it is unlawful to make use of the property of another without consent, and I trust that you will discontinue these encroachments. Mr. Alvarez is willing for you to leave the garden until the end of this growing season but requests that you immediately cease all of the other encroachments. After this growing season, it is requested that you do not permit the garden to encroach upon his property.

Encroachments of this nature constitute a trespass under the law of our state, and I know that you will want to comply with the property owner's request to avoid further problems in this connection.

Sincerely yours,

COMMENT:

1. The above letter could be softened, if desired, by inviting the addressee to advise the writer of the basis of any claim he may have to use the property in the manner he has been using it or any claim he may have regarding ownership of the property, depending on the facts.

226.
REQUEST TO BANK TRUST OFFICER TO
APPROVE ASSIGNMENT OF LEASE

Dear Mr. Haley:

On June 1, 19XX, we wrote you to advise you that all of the assets of ABC Corporation, including the above-referenced lease, were being acquired by its parent company, DEF Corporation.

In our letter we stated that a copy of the executed lease would be forwarded to you for your records.

We are enclosing a copy of the executed lease with a place for endorsement by the National Bank of Jefferson City concurring in the assignment. We are also enclosing an additional copy and would appreciate it very much if you would please execute the portion in which the First National Bank of Jefferson City concurs in the assignment and return it to us. The lawyers in Jefferson City representing DEF Corporation have asked us to mail them a certified copy of the assignment as executed. For this reason, we would appreciate it very much if you will please execute it as soon as possible and return it to us.

If you have any questions regarding the matter, please call me.

Sincerely yours,

COMMENT:

1. In the event the reader did not fully understand the transaction involved, the writer could give additional information to the reader regarding the requested execution of the lease.

SECTION 3
LETTERS TO WITNESSES

It is a good idea to correspond with witnesses to a case. This gives them a personal relationship with you as the attorney for your client in connection with the case, and lets them know you recognize them as important. After a conference or interview with the witness, it is often a good idea to write him a letter telling him you have relayed the results of your interview to your client or telling him how much you appreciated the opportunity of discussing the matter with him or simply thanking him for his cooperation and helpfulness. In addition, it is a good idea to write letters to all witnesses advising them of dates set for depositions, trials, and so forth. This should be done even though subpoenas will be issued and served on the witnesses, both for the purpose of lending a personal touch and making sure the witnesses do, in fact, know the dates in connection with a matter.

GROUP A
Giving Notice or Information

227.
NOTICE TO WITNESS OF DATE OF TRIAL

Dear Miss Carpenter:

This is just a note to remind you that Ben Fanning's trial will be June 2, 19XX, at 9:00 A.M. in the Jefferson County Courthouse. If you could be there at 8:30 A.M., I would be most grateful.

Thank you very much.

Very sincerely,

COMMENT:

1. A simple letter, such as the above, can go a long way toward assuring the presence of an important witness at trial.

228.
NOTICE TO WITNESS OF DATE OF TRIAL

Dear Mrs. Campbell:

You will recall that you were previously contacted in the above case, which you have knowledge of as a witness.

To date we have been unable to settle this case, and it has been set for trial here in Lincoln County on November 3, 19XX. We are hopeful that the case will be settled before trial date; however, we have no way of knowing whether or not it will, in fact, be settled.

We, therefore, ask you to tentatively plan to testify as a witness on the date indicated above. Should this case be settled, or your testimony not be required, we will immediately notify you of this fact.

Under court rules it is necessary that we request the clerk of the court to issue a subpoena to be served by the sheriff's office for you to appear as a witness in this case.

If for any reason it will be impossible for you to be in attendance at that time, I would appreciate it if you would notify me immediately so that the proper arrangements can be made. I want to thank you for your cooperation in this matter.

Please contact my secretary the day before the above trial date, and she will bring you up to date on the current status of the trial.

Very sincerely,

COMMENT:

1. It is a good idea to notify all witnesses of the date of trial and to establish some contact with them prior to trial.

2. The language regarding settlement should be deleted in the event no settlement is expected prior to trial.

GROUP B
Requesting Report or Information

229.
REQUEST TO DOCTOR FOR MEDICAL REPORT AND BILL

Dear Dr. Jones:

Our office represents the above client for injuries received on the date indicated.

In order to properly handle this matter, we will need from you a detailed medical report setting forth the following:

(1) Patient's history of injury

(2) Subjective and objective complaints

(3) Interpretation of x-rays and other tests

(4) Treatment rendered the patient

(5) Diagnosis and prognosis (including future treatment)

Also, please send us duplicate copies of your bill for services rendered, and bill us separately for your medical report.

A medical authorization, which authorizes us to receive this information, is enclosed.

Thank you for your cooperation in this matter.

Very sincerely,

COMMENT:

1. Letters such as the above are a convenient means of requesting information from witnesses, especially doctors, hospitals and business companies.

230.
REQUEST TO HOSPITAL FOR MEDICAL RECORDS AND CHARGES

Dear Mr. Parker:

Our firm is representing Mrs. Lois Johnson, who was confined to your hospital on the above date.

We are enclosing an authorization for medical information signed by our client, authorizing you to furnish us information requested below.

Please forward the following:

1. Copy of statement of charges by the hospital.

2. Copy of all hospital records pertaining to our client arising out of this confinement.

Thank you very much.

Sincerely,

COMMENT:

1. The above letter, if appropriate, should contain language requesting the hospital to delete any notation regarding payment which may have been made on the statement of charges.

231.
REQUEST TO HOSPITAL FOR MEDICAL RECORDS

Dear Mrs. Parker:

Our office represents Mrs. Mildred Kaufman for injuries received on the date indicated.

It is my understanding that Mildred was subsequently treated at your hospital for these injuries, and I am requesting that you forward to me copies of her hospital records.

Enclosed is a medical authorization which authorizes us to receive this information.

Thank you for your consideration of this matter.

Sincerely yours,

COMMENT:

1. Consideration should be given, in appropriate cases, to securing the entire medical record of a client at a particular hospital in the event the client has previously been a patient in the hospital. This is for the purpose of distinguishing prior injuries from injuries resulting from the accident in question.

232.
REQUEST TO DOCTOR FOR MEDICAL REPORT IN
WORKMEN'S COMPENSATION CASE

Dear Dr. Paul:

Our firm represents Joseph Mitchell in a workmen's compensation action against ABC Construction Co., his employer.

Enclosed is a medical authorization, signed by our client, authorizing you to furnish us with medical information.

Please furnish us with a report relating to the following items:

    1. Whether or not the patient's disability is permanent or temporary based upon reasonable medical certainty.

    2. The present percentage of disability from a medical standpoint based upon reasonable medical certainty.

    3. Whether or not you have released said patient to return to full time employment and, if so, the date of said release.

    4. If so, whether or not any limitations are placed upon the patient's return to full time employment.

    5. Itemize any limitations.

Thank you for your assistance. Please send us your statement for preparing this report. Please make your statement to the patient for your services, and we will see that these charges are paid out of any settlement obtained arising out of this accident.

Sincerely yours,

COMMENT:

1. The above letter should be changed in the event the lawyer intends to pay the doctor directly for the report.

233.
REQUEST TO DOCTOR FOR MEDICAL REPORT FOR
SOCIAL SECURITY DISABILITY CLAIM

Dear Dr. Mitchell:

We represent Joseph Johnson who, we understand, is your patient, regarding his claim for social security disability. It will be greatly appreciated if we could obtain your medical records regarding Joseph, along with your diagnosis and prognosis of his condition. Enclosed is Joseph's executed authorization for you to release these records to us.

Please forward Joseph's records and your report of his condition to us as soon as possible and include your statement; we will remit promptly.

Thank you for your assistance.

Very sincerely,

COMMENT:

1. The above letter could be personalized by stating the need which the client has for establishing disability or commenting upon his inability to work.

234.
REQUEST TO DOCTOR FOR MEDICAL REPORT FOR
CLIENT'S SOCIAL SECURITY CLAIM

Dear Dr. Morgan:

We represent Rose Jones in her social security claim based on disability. We must show that she is unable to engage in any substantially gainful activity by reason of any medically determinable physical or mental impairment which can be expected to result in death or which can be expected to last for a continuous period of not less than twelve months. The physical or mental impairment is, under social security terms, any impairment that results from anatomical, physiological or psychological abnormalities which are demonstrable by medically acceptable diagnostic techniques.

Rose complained of an acute ruptured disc in her back, arthritis in her shoulders and hips, and a torn cartilage in one of her knees. As you know, she is 53 years of age and has approximately nine years of education. She has worked as a housekeeper and lunch room helper.

It would be helpful to us in preparing the case if you could send to us a detailed report stating in narrative form the following:

1. The dates of all examinations made by you.

2. The complaint and history (medically) of the patient.

3. Your examination.

4. X-ray reports, if any.

5. Your clinical impression (including diagnosis and prognosis).

6. The types of medication the patient is taking and the effects this medication might have on her functioning, as well as the effects and possible dangers of other proposed forms of treatment.

7. Your medical opinion as to whether Rose is unable to engage in work such as that which she previously performed by reason of any medically determinable physical or mental impairment which can be expected to last for a continuous period of not less than twelve months.

I am enclosing the necessary form by which Rose authorizes us to have this information which we have requested. Rose has further advised me that you may bill her account for any charges involved for this report.

Very sincerely,

COMMENT:

1. In the event the attorney intends to pay for the requested report, the doctor could be invited to bill the attorney for the report.

2. Itemizing the specific matters to be covered in the report is a good idea. In the event particular problems are expected, the letter could be further tailored.

235.
REQUEST TO PHYSICIAN FOR OPINION OF DISABILITY OF CLIENT FOR USE IN SOCIAL SECURITY DISABILITY CLAIM

Dear Dr. White:

William Mitchell has for a good many years been a close personal friend of mine. On April 20th of this year he called me and requested that I help him in connection with his application for social security disability benefits.

I wrote to Senator Williams to urge that he do what he can to expedite the processing of Bill's claim. Later I learned, to my surprise, from Senator William's office, that the claim had been disapproved.

I understood when I talked to Bill on April 26, 19XX that he is totally disabled; that he hasn't worked since March 18 of last year when he had his last stroke; that he has been under your care; that your report indicates that he is subject to TIA at any time; and that he cannot drive a car. I further understand that the transient ischemic attacks (TIA) cause him to go into an unconscious state for variable lengths of time.

The social security definition of disability, as provided in the United States Code, is: "Inability to engage in any substantial gainful activity by reason of any medically determinable physical impairment which can be expected to result in death or which has lasted or can be expected to last for a continued period of . . . 12 months."

I checked your report of January 10, 19XX with the medical authority here in Johnson City and was advised that, in accordance with your report, there is no doubt that Bill is totally and permanently disabled. In addition, he has been given disability waiver of premium by the ABC Insurance Company.

I would appreciate it very much if you could make an addition to your existing medical report pointing out whether or not, in your opinion, Bill meets the definition of disability as defined above.

Frankly, Dr. White, I can't imagine an employer employing a person who is subject to going unconscious at any time as stated in your report. In addition, I would think an employee who has unsteadiness or vertigo and is unable to drive a car would not be able to find a job.

I talked to Bill on the phone today, and he told me that you have yourself been out of the office in connection with some illness. I certainly hope everything goes well with you.

Thank you very much.

Very sincerely,

COMMENT:

1. It is thoughtful and helpful in a letter such as the above, in which a physician's opinion is requested regarding disability, to give to the physician the legal definition of disability pertaining to the case.

SECTION 4
LETTERS TO LAWYERS

Letters to lawyers comprise a significant portion of a lawyer's correspondence. Lawyers are, of course, generally friendly, respectful and considerate of each other. A well-written letter to an opposing attorney can set forth your client's position in connection with a dispute, litigation or other matter. Many lawyers feel it is a good idea to send copies of all correspondence written in connection with the client's case or matter to the client. This, of course, would include letters written to opposing attorneys or other lawyers in connection with the matter. It is usually better to write rather than call the attorney representing an opposing or other party so that he has a written record of what you need to know or the information or decision you need from him or his client. If you simply call him on the telephone or see him on the street or at the courthouse, he may forget what was said. In addition, a letter can contain all of the relevant information, argument, law, etc., that he will need to act upon the matter at hand.

Sending copies of lawyer-to-lawyer letters to clients keeps them informed of progress in your handling of the case and cuts down on the number of phone calls from clients who simply want to know what's going on.

265

GROUP A
Giving Notice or Information

236.
**REFERRAL TO PRIVATE ATTORNEY BY LEGAL AID SOCIETY OF
DOMESTIC RELATIONS CASE DUE TO CONFLICT OF INTEREST**

Dear Mr. Bailey:

Mr. Tom Williams has come to this office seeking advice and representation in a domestic relations case in which Mr. Grady Paul of this office represents an adverse party. Mr. Williams appears to be financially eligible for the services of the Legal Aid Society.

Pursuant to your informal agreement last year that you would advise and, if necessary, represent indigent clients in domestic relations cases which cannot be accepted by the Legal Aid Society because of a conflict of interest, I would appreciate your granting Mr. Williams a brief interview. If, after talking to him you conclude that you cannot represent him without charging a fee or making some arrangement for deferring payment of a fee, please refer him back to this office for referral to another private attorney. However, if, during the course of your interview, you elicit information from him that gives you cause to doubt his eligibility for the services of the Legal Aid Society, please relay that information to me at your earliest convenience following the interview.

Thank you for your cooperation.

Very sincerely,

COMMENT:

1. The above letter is a form letter used by a legal aid society to refer domestic relation cases to private attorneys when appropriate.

237.
REQUEST FOR FINANCIAL DATA FOR DIVORCE CASE

Dear Mrs. Thomas:

Pursuant to our telephone conference of February 17, we are awaiting receipt of Mr. Fox's financial data so that we may proceed with this matter. Please forward this information to us as soon as possible as our client is most anxious to conclude the matter. Thank you.

Sincerely yours,

COMMENT:

1. Many times a letter such as the above will produce desired information from the opposing party without the necessity of formal discovery procedures.

238.
TRANSMITTING COPY OF DIVORCE DECREE

Dear Mrs. Brown:

In accordance with your letter dated March 12, 19XX, we are enclosing a copy of the divorce decree, filed November 6, 19XX, in the above-referenced case, together with a copy of the agreement between the parties.

If there is anything further we can do for you in this matter, please let us know.

Sincerely yours,

COMMENT:

1. Generally a letter of transmittal should be used whenever documents or pleadings are forwarded in connection with a case. This is not only a friendly gesture but provides a written record of the action.

239.
STATEMENT TO ASSOCIATE ATTORNEY OF CLIENT'S DESIRE FOR CONTINGENCY FEE ARRANGEMENT

Dear Mr. Parker:

I have checked with our client, Robert Paul, regarding your retainer fee of $750, which you requested in your letter dated April 26, 19XX. Mr. Paul does not wish to commit any further retainer money in the case. He did state, however, that if you would reconsider and take the case on a contingency fee basis, this would be agreeable with him.

Tom, in the event you do not wish to take the case on a contingency fee basis, please return Robert's file to me as he will need it for documentation to IRS.

Thank you very much.

Very sincerely,

COMMENT:

1. If appropriate, the terms of the proposed contingent fee should be outlined in the above letter.

240.
ACKNOWLEDGMENT OF LETTER APPLYING FOR POSITION WITH FIRM AND REQUEST FOR INTERVIEW

Dear Bill:

Thank you for your letter of April 16 enclosing the biographical data. We will be very happy to visit with you when you are in Akron during the period from May 30 to June 5. I would suggest that when you get to Akron you might call Tom Binger who is in charge of the additions to our legal staff. You have a very fine record, and I have no doubt at all that you will continue to do extremely well in your profession. We will be glad to see you when you come to Akron for interviews.

Very sincerely,

COMMENT:

1. In appropriate cases some reference could be made to the future prospect of a position being available with the firm independent of the applicant's qualifications.

241.
CONGRATULATING LAWYER ON OPENING LAW OFFICE

Dear Robert:

I would like to congratulate you and wish you the very best of success on the occasion of opening your office for the practice of law in Jackson.

I wish you would stop by to say hello the next time you are in New Orleans.

Very sincerely,

COMMENT:

1. Letters of congratulations such as the above generate good will and cordial relations among members of the bar.

242.
NOTICE OF REPRESENTING DEFENDANT IN SUIT

Dear Mr. Chapman:

This is to advise you that Coy Jackson, president of ABC Corporation, was served with a copy of the bill of complaint in the above-referenced case yesterday and that I will be representing the corporation in connection with the proceeding.

Just as soon as possible, I will file a responsive pleading in the suit. Also, at any early date I would like to have an opportunity to get together with you regarding this matter.

Thank you very much.

Sincerely yours,

COMMENT:

1. It is a good practice for a lawyer to write the opposing attorney when he enters a case. This not only advises an attorney of the representation but may, in some cases, prevent the taking of a default judgment without notification.

243.
NOTICE TO PLAINTIFF OF REPRESENTATION OF DEFENDANT
INDEPENDENT OF COUNSEL PROVIDED BY INSURANCE CARRIER

Dear Mr. Thomas:

We are representing the defendant Marvin Feldman individually in connection with the suit filed against him by Joseph Cornwall, who you represent.

Marvin's insurance carrier is providing the primary defense for the defendant through Baker, Taylor and Snyder. However, we would appreciate it very much if you will forward us copies of all medical reports, the accident report, and any other documents you feel will be helpful to us in evaluating our client's position in this matter independent of the representation being afforded to him by the insurance carrier.

Thank you very much.

Very sincerely,

COMMENT:

1. Upon entering the case, it is a good idea to advise the opposing counsel of the representation.

244.
CONFIRMATION OF DATE OF DEPOSITION

Dear Richard:

This will confirm the recent telephone conversation between our offices wherein arrangements were made for the deposition of William Schmidt, in our office on October 4 at 2:00 P.M. in the above-entitled action.

This office will provide the reporter for the deposition. Thank you for your cooperation in this matter.

Very sincerely,

COMMENT:

1. Written confirmation of a deposition reminds the addressee of the deposition and provides a permanent record of it.

245.
CONFIRMATION OF DATE FOR DEPOSITION

Dear Mr. Thomas:

This is to confirm that I will take the deposition of George Taylor at your office on June 2, 19XX at 10:00 A.M. I will secure the reporter.

I will have a subpoena duces tecum ready for service on Mr. Taylor at the deposition, along with a check for a statutory witness fee.

Sincerely,

246.
NOTICE OF DEPOSITION

Dear Mr. Brownell:

This letter will confirm the taking of Dr. Albert Carter's deposition on February 20, 19XX, at 2:00 P.M. at his office in the above case.

I have obtained the services of a court reporter.

Sincerely,

COMMENT:

1. Written notice of a deposition serves the dual purpose of advising or reminding the opposing party of the deposition and providing a permanent record of the matter. Misunderstanding can be avoided, as here, by expressly stating or acknowledging which party is to secure the services of the court reporter.

247.
TRANSMITTAL OF NOTICE OF TAKING DEPOSITION

Dear Mr. Kaufman:

Enclosed is a Notice of Taking Deposition. We will change the time if necessary, but this notice is for record purposes.

Thanks very much.

Sincerely yours,

COMMENT:

1. A letter such as the above, transmitting the notice of taking deposition, helps personalize the matter and contributes toward friendlier relations between opposing attorneys.

248.
LETTER TO OPPOSING ATTORNEY ADVISING OF AVAILABILITY OF CLIENT FOR MEDICAL EXAMINATION

Dear Mr. Mason:

In accordance with your request, we will instruct our client to submit to an examination by your physician. This is being done with the understanding that you will furnish us a copy of his report within ten days of the date of examination or your receipt of his report.

Sincerely yours,

COMMENT:

1. The lawyer should, when his client is examined by a physician secured by the opposing party, request a copy of the physician's report.

249.
CONFIRMATION OF ADDITIONAL TIME TO ANSWER COMPLAINT

Dear Tom:

This letter will confirm, pursuant to our telephone conversation of September 13, 19XX, the fact that you have given us 30 additional days in which to answer the complaint served upon our client, Hunter Barker.

We are in the process of securing the attorney who will be representing Mr. Barker in connection with the case. We understand that Joseph Algood of the firm Watson, Story & Algood is probably the attorney who will represent him.

Very sincerely,

COMMENT:

1. It is a good idea to write a letter such as the above to make a permanent record of an agreement regarding negotiation of an important matter with legal consequences such as extentions of time for pleading.

250.
REMINDER TO ATTORNEY REGARDING ANSWERS TO
INTERROGATORIES

Dear Mr. Mitchell:

Your answers to our interrogatories are overdue.

We hesitate to compel your answers by court action and ask for sanctions. However, unless you take affirmative measures to see that we receive the answers within a reasonable period of time, you will leave us no other choice.

We would appreciate your cooperation.

Very sincerely,

COMMENT:

1. A reminder such as the above regarding answers to interrogatories may avoid the necessity of filing a formal motion or petition to the court to require answers.

251.
TRANSMITTAL TO ASSOCIATE ATTORNEY OF MOTIONS TO
REQUIRE ANSWERS TO INTERROGATORIES AND TO PRODUCE

Dear Pete:

I am enclosing a copy of the Motion to Require Answers to Interrogatories and to Produce prepared after we received your letter suggesting it, together with the order of Judge Wilson setting the matter for a hearing on October 8 at 2:00 P.M.

I would appreciate it very much if you would please appear in behalf of the plaintiff on this matter.

Also, I will appreciate it if you will confirm the fact that you will be able to appear for the plaintiff by either calling me or sending me a note.

Thanks very much.

Very sincerely,

COMMENT:

1. It is a good idea to request confirmation that another attorney will appear at a hearing.

252.
CONFIRMATION OF AUTHORITY TO CASH SETTLEMENT CHECK AND
STATUS REPORT OF RELEASES

Dear John:

This letter confirms that you have authorized me to negotiate the check you previously sent me in the amount of $8,000. I will secure a release from Edward Wilson. I will revise the release form so that the release is mutual and forward it to you. You have agreed to secure the signature of Foster Brown on behalf of ABC Corporation and Edward Wilson individually.

Very sincerely,

COMMENT:

1. It is a good idea to write a letter confirming verbal authority given by an opposing attorney or opposing party to cash a settlement check. In appropriate cases the terms of settlement should be recited in written form, either in the letter or enclosed with the letter.

253.
POSITION OF HEALTH DEPARTMENT ON SUBDIVISION DEVELOPMENT
REFUSING TO AUTHORIZE SEPTIC TANKS

Dear Mr. Johnson:

Dr. Ralph Paul, Washington County Health Officer, has referred to us for reply to your letter dated March 18, 19XX, regarding the above reference matter.

The subdivision of land invariably results in the development of homes, businesses, or industry in which sewage is generated in one form or another, and it is for this reason the State Health Department and the Washington County Health Department prescribe certain regulations and criteria dealing with safe disposal of sewage waste. Their main objective or purpose is to protect the public health and provide for the safe disposal of human excreta and other sewage waste. The state and county health departments do this by regulating development of subdivisions and regulating the type, location, capacity, construction, maintenance, and use of them.

Legal authority for the regulation of subdivision development is derived from the State Code, Title _____, Sec. _____ which describes the general jurisdiction of the State Board of Health, as well as the State Code, Title _____, Sec. _____, which prescribes the duties of county health officers. I am also enclosing for your information other material relating to the matter. This material is as follows:

Exhibit 1. Copy of Act 461, State Legislature Regular Session 19XX.

Exhibit 2. Copy of subdivision criteria adopted by the State Department of Public Health, Environmental Health Administration.

Exhibit 3. Copy of Rules and Regulations to protect the public health and provide for the safe disposal of human excreta and other sewage wastes, etc.

Exhibit 4. Copy of U.S. Department of Agriculture Bulletin 267 entitled, "Know Your Soil."

Exhibit 5. Copy of letter from the State Attorney General to Dr. Paul, dated November 12, 19XX.

Exhibit 6. Copy of the Public Health magazine article relating to septic tank problem, which appeared in the May issue.

Exhibit 7. Copy of article appearing in Public Health, relating to the need of an engineering survey and study to determine a proper and adequate method of disposal of waste in connection with subdivision development.

The next part of your inquiry deals with precedents upon which the Washington County Health Department relies in denying or refusing the use of septic tanks for the referenced subdivision.

The referenced subdivision lies basically on top of or astride, a hill or small mountain northeast of the City of Covington in an area that supplies or comprises part of the recharge area for the City of Covington's drinking water. According to our information, no subdivision development has been approved in this area within the past several years due largely to data supplied to the Washington County Health Department by the U.S. Geologists and State Geologists. Both agencies wholeheartedly agree, due to the fact that Covington's water supply lies on top of a rock formation from 50 to 70 feet below surface in an area subject to cracks and crevices as well as sink holes, that development on septic tanks would greatly endanger the drinking water for the entire city.

The eastern side of the referenced subdivision drains into a valley that was engineered years ago and found to be unsatisfactory for septic tanks and is presently being developed on a central sewer system operated by the City of Covington. In fact, both sides of the referenced project are being developed on sewers from the City of Covington, the most recent being a high school which had to run a line over two miles to a sanitary sewer. I understand a sanitary sewer line is available within one mile of the proposed subdivision development. I further understand that the proposed subdivision is substantial in size both with regard to the total area involved and the number of lots.

The only houses being built in the vicinity of the above-referenced subdivision are on lots in subdivisions that were approved before the Washington County Health Department had knowledge of possible contamination of a municipal water supply.

The stated policy of the Washington County Health Department is, and has always been, to administer the public health laws of our state in an equal and impartial way, always remembering that the officers and officials of the department work for people seeking or purchasing homes, representing the largest single investment they will ever make and which should afford a healthy environment for their families.

For your further information, I understand officials of the Washington County Health Department are presently trying to rescue some twenty-three homeowners who have purchased homes on septic tanks that have failed, and the federal government is standing approximately a one-half million dollar loss in connection with another subdivision. In addition, the City of New Sharon has just experienced a three million dollar loss in rescuing homeowners who have been saddled with failing septic tanks.

I hope the above information, submitted in accordance with your request, will be helpful to you.

Very sincerely,

COMMENT:

1. A letter such as the above, going into detail regarding the matter, is often very effective in discouraging litigation.

254.
ACCEPTANCE OF REFERRAL TO COLLECT JUDGMENT

Dear Mr. Berkman:

Thank you for your letter. I appreciate being considered for referral of the case against ABC Corporation.

I will be pleased to assist in collecting this judgment rendered against ABC Corporation.

Our fee will be one-third of the amount collected. We will require a $50 retainer fee, which will be credited toward any fee earned.

We will handle it on a straight time basis if you prefer.

Please confirm.

Very sincerely,

COMMENT:

1. It is a good idea in a letter such as the above to always set forth clearly the fee arrangement.

255.
AGREEING TO SERVE AS AGENT FOR SERVICE OF PROCESS

Dear Mr. Gibson:

We will certainly be happy for you to continue our listing as agent for service on ABC Corporation in our state as long as it will be of any assistance to the corporation.

There will be no charge for the services, and, in the event you decide to dissolve the corporation, we will be happy to prepare and file the necessary notice of dissolution without any charge.

Please let us know any time we can be of any assistance.

Sincerely,

COMMENT:

1. In the event there is a charge for service as agent for service of process, such charges should be set forth in the letter.

256.
EXPRESSING APPRECIATION FOR RECOMMENDING APPOINTMENT TO STATE BAR COMMITTEE

Dear Henry:

I appreciated very much getting your letter advising me that you have given my name to John Weller for appointment to a state bar committee dealing with the practices of publishing houses.

Thank you for thinking of me, and I look forward to serving on the committee.

Very sincerely,

COMMENT:

1. Letters of appreciation to other attorneys help generate good will and cordial relations.

257.
ACKNOWLEDGMENT OF RECEIPT OF PAPERS AND ADVICE OF APPOINTMENT WITH CLIENT TO REVIEW

Dear George:

I have received the papers that you forwarded to me. I have an appointment with my client at Johnson City on May 12, 19XX. I will review all the documentation with him at that time and will then be processing the papers for return to you or for filing with the court.

Sincerely yours,

258.
ACKNOWLEDGMENT OF RECEIPT OF COPY OF LETTER TO
CHAIRMAN OF CALENDAR COMMITTEE

Dear Jim:

I received a copy of your letter dated September 23 to the chairman of the Calendar Committee and also the calendar for the civil term beginning October 1, showing the above case on the motion docket for October 14. I also received a copy of your motion for a jury trial.

This is to advise that I will not oppose your motion. However, I am writing the chairman of the Calendar Committee, and I am enclosing a copy of my letter, asking that the above case be placed on the motion calendar for the term beginning October 1, which, I understand, is the next civil term. At that time I expect to make a motion for summary judgment and, of course, will send you copy of the motion and support documents in ample time.

Sincerely yours,

COMMENT:

1. The above letter could be personalized by some comment or observation made to the opposing attorney either regarding past cooperation in connection with the case or looking forward to seeing him at the next pleading session, hearing, etc.

259.
NOTICE OF CONTINUANCE OF CASE

Dear Bill:

The trial setting of March 14 has been vacated, and trial will be reset after April 1.

Judge Wallace's secretary is ill today and will reset the case when she returns to work. We will advise you of the new setting.

Sincerely,

COMMENT:

1. The above letter could be further personalized by including any new information or observation regarding the case.

260.
TRANSMITTAL OF RESPONDENT'S MOTION FOR NEW TRIAL AND
NOTICE OF HEARING

Dear Arthur:

I am enclosing a copy of the Respondent's Original Motion for New Trial filed in the above matter on February 3. A hearing has been set for March 20 at 9:00 A.M.

Sincerely,

COMMENT:

1. In most jurisdictions the word "respondent" has been replaced by "defendant."

Requesting Information

261.
REQUEST FOR DOCUMENTS AND STATUS REPORT OF
ANCILLARY PROBATE PROCEEDINGS

Dear Paul:

Thank you, and also please thank Ed, for referring the ancillary proceedings of Mr. Wilkinson's estate to my office. Here is what we will need:

1. A certified copy of the will of Mr. Wilkinson;

2. A certified copy of the order, judgment or decree admitting said will to probate;

3. A certificate of the clerk of the court stating that the will was duly admitted to probate. Such certificate should be accompanied by a certified copy of Letters Testamentary.

When all of the above is presented along with an appropriate application for Ancillary Letters Testamentary, which I will prepare and send through you, the Ancillary Letters Testamentary will issue from our court to the executor who is requested in the application (the same person who is the executor in Washington County). There are certain other things which must be done, but they can be easily handled. It would serve no purpose to bring these up at this time. One thing you should know, if the will which is being presented does not require a bond of the executor, then one will not be required here. If the will is silent as to whether a bond is necessary or not, it is probable that the local probate court will require some kind of bond.

Upon receipt of the items requested above, I will proceed with the ancillary probate.

Kind regards to you and the others in your fine law firm.

Very sincerely,

COMMENT:

1. In appropriate cases the fee arrangement should be stated in the letter.

262.
REQUEST FOR SUGGESTED DATE FOR DEPOSITION

Dear Ralph:

This case is now at issue and ready for discovery. We are particularly anxious to move the case toward trial without any unnecessary delay.

Our client is available for deposition and medical examination and is willing to sign any and all work or medical authorizations that are transmitted.

If you desire any additional authorizations signed, please send them within the next ten (10) days, and please select one of the following dates for a deposition. We would like to have it scheduled in our office. We would also like to take the deposition of Joe Taylor.

Our available dates and times are as follows: June 3, June 8 and July 12.

Will you please notify us by return mail which of the foregoing dates is acceptable to you and whether or not you wish for us to arrange for the reporter. In addition to any authorizations that you desire signed, please notify us of the name of a doctor and time, place, etc., for the purpose of a medical examination of our client.

Thank you for your cooperation.

Very sincerely,

COMMENT:

1. A letter such as the above requesting opposing counsel to suggest the date or dates for the deposition is not only a generous courtesy extended to the opposing counsel but may also avoid the necessity of continuing the deposition to a convenient date.

263.
ASKING WHETHER PLAINTIFF WILL PROSECUTE OR DISMISS SUIT

Dear Glen:

The above-referenced case is set for trial in the Superior Court on September 8.

Accordingly, I got in touch with my client to prepare for trial.

However, my client called today and advised me that, according to his information, Roger Wilhite has left Norwich.

We are wondering whether your client intends to maintain the suit or whether you intend to dismiss this suit.

We would appreciate it very much if you would please advise.

Sincerely yours,

COMMENT:

1. Letters such as the above to the opposing attorney requesting his intention with regard to an action may avoid unnecessary work in connection with the action.

264.
REQUESTING MEDICAL REPORT FROM ASSOCIATED LAWYER

Dear Robert:

I have your letter dated November 6, suggesting that we take the deposition of Dr. Winthrop.

I would suggest that, prior to taking Dr. Winthrop's deposition, it would be better for us to get a statement from him regarding his examination and treatment of Paul Shepard.

Accordingly, I am enclosing an authorization to release medical reports. I would appreciate it very much if you would please have Paul sign them and return them to me at your earliest convenience.

In the event you have previously secured a report from Dr. Winthrop, I would appreciate receiving a copy of it. Also I would appreciate a list of the injuries received by Paul in connection with the accident.

Thanks very much.

Very sincerely,

COMMENT:

1. Whenever there is an associate lawyer, which is often the case where lawyers are required in different cities, each should endeavor to cooperate fully with the other. Letters offer a convenient means of such cooperation.

265.
REQUEST FOR COPY OF PROPOSED ORDINANCE

Dear Mr. Bergin:

I understand from W. T. Patterson that you may have a copy of a proposed ordinance that the City of Toledo is considering with regard to the septic tank situation.

I would appreciate it very much if you would please send me a copy of the proposed ordinance as well as any other printed information you may have. I would also like to know the status of the matter.

Thanks very much.

Very sincerely,

COMMENT:

1. A letter is often the most convenient means for requesting information or copies of pleadings and other documents.

GROUP C

Negotiating Agreement or Settlement

266.
STATING POSITION OF CLIENT ON PAYMENT OF ACCOUNT

Dear Mr. Johnston:

Our clients, Audrey Wells & Stanley White, gave us a copy of your letter of June 6 regarding your representation of ABC Corporation.

I understand from talking to Audrey that the agreement to pay Mrs. Austin the sum of $2,500 was a generous one in the circumstances, and there is a long story behind it. At any rate, it was due to the efforts of Mr. White to preserve the business that Mrs. Austin would realize anything out of her original investment in the original business.

I understand from Stanley that the business ran a substantial loss last year, and, while their volume of business has been good it has been quite an uphill struggle to try to finance it. In addition, they tell me they have drawn practically nothing from the business in the way of living expenses since it was started.

With this in mind they have advised me that they will do the best they can to pay Mrs. Austin, and it is their intention to pay approximately $200 a month.

I would appreciate it very much if you would please convey this intention to her and our thoughts that it will be better to do this than to litigate the matter and have both sides spend several hundred dollars in connection with it in attorney's fees.

I am thoroughly convinced of the good faith of Audrey and Stanley in their desire to eventually pay Mrs. Austin the full amount. However, on behalf of our clients I would like to say we will very much appreciate your client bearing with them in the circumstances.

Very sincerely,

COMMENT:

1. A letter such as the above stating the position of the client may be effective in helping to avoid litigation.

267.
AGREEMENT BY CREDITOR TO MONTHLY PAYMENTS ON ACCOUNT

Dear Mr. Jefferson:

In your letter to me of February 18 you stated that your client, Louise Richardson would like to settle her indebtedness to Paul Thompson by making payments of $50 per month beginning April 1, 19XX.

I spoke to Mr. Thompson yesterday regarding this matter, and he is willing to accept this arrangement with the condition, however, that if Mrs. Richardson misses one payment that we will immediately file suit for the balance of the indebtedness.

Sincerely yours,

COMMENT:

1. Letters such as the above confirming agreements regarding payment on account are helpful in providing permanent records and avoiding any future misunderstanding.

268.
PROPOSING TERMS OF DIVORCE AGREEMENT FOR WIFE

Dear Mr. Jacobs:

As I told you when you called today to advise me you are representing Mr. Morgan, I met with Mrs. Morgan for an extended conference today regarding the matter.

Since Mrs. Morgan's last visit in my office on June 16, 19XX, she has, at my suggestion, had one or more conferences with a case worker at the Mental Health Center in Johnson City. She has also, I understand, consulted another person trained as a family counselor.

Mrs. Morgan's position at the present time, in which I concur, is that in the event Mr. Morgan persists in his desire for a divorce and is willing to agree to a reasonable financial arrangement with Mrs. Morgan, she would be agreeable to a divorce.

As you probably know, Mrs. Morgan has a high school education but no special skills from which she could earn more than $90 or $100 a week, and, in addition, she has the two children, aged 3 and 5. For this reason, it appears in the immediate future she will be required to remain at home with the children, and, in any event, the expenses of securing a babysitter would more or less neutralize any account she is able to earn.

I am writing this letter after consulting with her to outline what appears to us to be reasonable terms. One thing I want to emphasize is that we do not know Mr. Morgan's exact earnings. Our understanding is that he is employed at an approximate annual salary of $18,000.

We would appreciate it very much, and would require it as a condition of signing any agreement for a divorce, if Mr. Morgan would disclose to her his exact earnings, including any bonus arrangement he may have with his employer.

As far as custody of the children, Mrs. Morgan would, of course, have primary custody but would be willing to allow Mr. Morgan to have access and visitation of the children at reasonable times on reasonable notice. She is unwilling to specify any further rights to Mr. Morgan at this time.

For alimony for the wife and support for the children, Mrs. Morgan would require the sum of $500 per month or 33⅓ per cent of Mr. Morgan's gross earnings, whichever amount is more. She would require Mr. Morgan to deed the house to her in Johnson City and convey to her his interest in the household furniture and furnishings. In addition, she would like to have the Chevrolet automobile, which she uses, and the approximate amount of $4,000 from the savings account previously maintained by them.

I understand Mr. Morgan has previously expressed to her a willingness to maintain at least $25,000 of life insurance on his life and to name as beneficiary the children. In addition, Mrs. Morgan would like to have Mr. Morgan agree to pay all medical and dental bills incurred by the children, for which, we understand, he probably has insurance coverage through his employer.

We would appreciate hearing from you regarding this matter at your convenience.

Very sincerely,

COMMENT:

1. In appropriate cases, a proposed agreement could be enclosed with the letter.

269.
REQUEST FOR ANSWERS TO INTERROGATORIES

Dear Mr. Abernathy:

You are overdue in returning the answers to interrogatories which I have served upon you. This letter is notice pursuant to our rules of procedure that the answers are now overdue. If I have not received them during the next three days, I will be filing an appropriate notice with the court to require answers and to sanction ABC Company for failure to answer the interrogatories on time.

Sincerely yours,

COMMENT:

1. The tone of the above letter could be softened in appropriate cases to simply request that answers be filed within a specified time or that the writer be advised of any reasons that exist for seeking additional time.

270.
SETTLEMENT DEMAND TO OPPOSING ATTORNEY OR
INSURANCE COMPANY

Dear Mr. Taylor:

I am sure you share our view that both sides have a strong obligation to do their utmost to settle cases at the earliest possible time in order to save court time, preparation time and other expense, as well as avoid the anxieties that come with delay.

Of course, it is possible to settle cases more reasonably at an early date because the expenses involved in litigation are less, and the opportunity to put the money to work for the plaintiff is greater. The nervous tension and anxiety which the uncertainties of litigation hold for all people is also a recognized adjustment.

I am also sure that the same interests apply to your insured. It is my hope that you may be able to spare your insured the anxieties that flow from lawsuits of this type. I am sure that you recognize your obligation under the insurance policy to both defend him and fairly represent him. This has been construed by the courts as an obligation to relieve him of these anxieties at the first reasonably available moment, as well as to avoid the risks of a verdict greater than his policy limits.

Unfortunately for the plaintiff, it is our burden to offer to settle the case within the policy limits in order to transfer liability to the insurance company for any judgment in excess of the insurance coverage. In this case, this poses a severe burden upon the plaintiff inasmuch as the injuries warrant a recovery far greater than the amount of the policy.

Despite this, we are willing to settle this case within the policy limits for the amount stated above.

While you are certainly aware of the obligations imposed upon your company by virtue of the cases, this language may not be known to your insured, and with this in mind and knowing that you will, of course, be sending him a copy of this letter, we wish to quote the applicable law from the leading case in the United States, the California case of *Crisci v. Security Insurance Company*, 58 Cal. Rptr. 13:

> ". . . the rejection of a settlement within the limits, where there is *any danger* of a judgment in excess of the limits, can be justified, if at all, only on the basis of the interests of the insurer, and in light of the common knowledge that settlement is one of the usual methods by which an insured receives protection under a liability policy, it may not be unreasonable for an insured who purchases a policy with limits to believe that a sum of money equal to the limits available, will be used so as to avoid liability on his part with regard to any covered accident. *In view of such expectation an insurer should not be permitted to further its own interests by rejecting opportunities to settle within the policy limits unless it is also willing to absorb losses which may result from its failure to settle.*
> *"The proposed rule is a simple one to apply and avoids the burdens of a determination whether a settlement offer within the policy limits was reasonable."* (Emphasis added)

The California Supreme Court then goes on to say that "the actual judgment itself furnishes an inference that the value of the claim is the equivalent of the amount of the judgment and that acceptance of an offer within those limits was the most reasonable method of dealing with the claim."

What this means, of course, is that the court will now reason back independently of any opposing viewpoints relative to what the claim may or may not be worth, take the actual judgment as finally obtained as conclusive of that value, and therefore any settlement offer within the limits (and below the final verdict) will have been unreasonably rejected. In actual fact, the court is rejecting the "reasonableness-of-the rejection" test and is simply saying that the insurance company now gambles with its own money when it turns down an offer within the limits and not with its insured's money.

It is also to be noted that in the Crisci case, the original defendant was able to recover an additional $25,000 against her own insurance company for mental suffering as a result of her insurance company's failure to settle the case for the amount of the offer.

The Crisci case has now been made the subject of countless seminars throughout the United States, and its principles have been favorably adopted in dozens of other jurisdictions. The law is clear, and I am hopeful that our offers will be recognized by you as a good faith attempt to settle this litigation with no mental anxieties to your insured.

Certainly there are two viewpoints in every lawsuit, and none of us can assume that our own appraisal is the perfect appraisal for a given case on the basis of either liability or damages. The Supreme Court recognizes these variations in judgment but makes clear that where the insurance company guesses wrong, it guesses wrong with its own money once it rejects an offer to settle within policy limits.

The liability facts have undoubtedly been determined by you. The basic injuries are known to you. We see no purpose in holding this matter open beyond the time limit that we specified in the offer. We therefore make our offer one of both time and amount and hope that it will be accepted by you as the fastest and most economical way out of this litigation.

Thank you for your cooperation.

Yours truly,

COMMENT:

1. A detailed letter such as the above is often an effective and persuasive means of negotiating favorable settlement of a case.

271.
SETTLEMENT OFFER BY PLAINTIFF'S ATTORNEY IN
AUTO ACCIDENT CASE

Dear Mr. Kaufman:

I just talked to Roy Campbell today, and he promises me that he will try to get the 19XX tax return finished by March 15, 19XX.

Mr. Campbell has been confined some, and this is part of the delay. He has emphysema that has put him on a limited scale, and I don't believe he will be able to come to court. If we could do his deposition, I will arrange to get permission of Judge Mason to use it.

I will try to have my witness list ready by April 10, 19XX.

I had intended to wait until the economic workup to make a demand, but we are running short, and Dr. Johnson's earnings will be substantial. Accordingly, I can give you a demand to settle the case for $450,000.

Dr. Johnson was age 46, in good health, was sound both physically and mentally, had a good reputation for industry and personal habits and was literally on the verge of really big earnings in the medical profession. In fact, I will be able to show that his earnings were on the increase and that he had not yet reached maximum earnings.

Besides leaving a young widow, he has five surviving children: Joseph Johnson, Jr., David Johnson, Mary Kay Johnson, Elizabeth Johnson and Richard Johnson.

His life expectancy was 33 years.

I won't debate the liability question, but suffice it to say that your truck was on the wrong side of the road on a four-lane highway going through Elkton, and my proof will indicate that the driver was making a minimum speed of something like 50 mph. Other indications of 40 feet of skid marks will indicate that he was going in excess of 40 mph. The speed limit varies as to whether or not it was a congested area, but, in any event, it would be anywhere from 35 to 50 mph. Your driver admits to it being a congested area, which would make it a 35 mph zone, and admits also to going something like, as I recall, 45 mph. My proof will be that he was going much faster.

The attached listing of the signs as you come into the City of Elkton clearly show the four speed limit signs and road construction signs leading on up to the ultimate last two 35 mph speed signs that your driver totally ignored. As you recall from his deposition, he says he didn't recall seeing any, but we not only will have testimony to this effect, but pictures taken 50 feet north of each of these signs as you travel south on the by-pass. We will also have an aerial of the by-pass and an aerial of the skid marks, which show surprisingly well.

In short, Mr. Kaufman, I believe that the demand of $450,000 for the death of a 46 year old doctor, in the prime of life, survived by widow and five children, considering all circumstances in the case, is fair and reasonable. Clearly, the speed of your driver is the cause of this wreck. We will have testimony that the skid marks began more than 40 feet from where the truck ultimately came to rest, and it came to rest at the end of the skid marks. I know your investigation shows that with any kind of reaction time, this puts the truck driver approximately 300 feet north. However, even 200 feet to 300 feet north shows that, had the truck been traveling within the 35 mph speed limit, the wreck would not have occurred.

I had better close before I withdraw my offer.

Very sincerely,

COMMENT:

1. A well written settlement offer, such as the above, is often an effective tool preliminary to personal settlement negotiations.

272.
PROPOSING SETTLEMENT AS PREVIOUSLY DISCUSSED

Dear Ray:

Following receipt of your last letter regarding this matter, I wrote our client and also discussed it with him on the telephone. I understand he is denying liability.

In the event your client is interested in a settlement along the lines previously discussed, we will be happy to further discuss the matter with you.

Thanks very much.

Very sincerely,

COMMENT:

1. Letters regarding settlement negotiations are an effective means of furthering such negotiations and providing a permanent record of them.

273.
TRANSMITTING AND DISCUSSING PROPOSED JUDGMENT

Dear Mr. Brownell:

We received your proposed judgment today and return it herewith.

We also enclose an original and two copies of a proposed judgment which we have drafted and which itemizes the damages. We prefer to have the judgment reflect the amounts allowed for special damages, pain and suffering, and punitive damages, if our client decides to appeal.

If you object to our proposed form of judgment, please send both proposed forms to Judge Tom Brown. We are sending him a copy of both judgments and a copy of this letter.

Sincerely yours,

COMMENT:

1. In many jurisdictions proposed judgments submitted by attorneys for the parties must be formally filed with the clerk of the court.

274.
TRANSMITTING LETTERS AND SETTLEMENT OFFER TO LAWYER FOR CO-DEFENDANT

Dear Tom:

I am enclosing a copy of the letter from Mr. Will Fanning and a copy of a letter from the ABC Company regarding the DEF properties.

I am also enclosing a suggested contribution by the defendants in order to settle this case, given to me by Larry Snyder. You will note that the total contributions suggested by Larry total $130,000, which is the same figure he has given us since the beginning of the case.

It was good seeing you in the courthouse today, and I hope to see you again soon.

Very sincerely,

COMMENT:

1. In the event the lawyer has a recommendation regarding the proposed settlement, it could be included in the letter.

275.
AGREEMENT FOR APPRAISALS OF HOUSE BY TWO APPRAISERS

Dear Mr. Haley:

I have now conferred with our client, Elbert Fanning, and have secured his permission, based on our recommendation, for Paul Jacobs and William Bell to prepare an appraisal of the value of his house. I presume if the two of them differ as to fair value of it, they would each state their independent conclusions.

At any rate, I wanted to let you know that this procedure is agreeable to us. I am sending a copy of this letter to Mr. Fanning for his information, and I presume you will be getting in touch with Paul Jacobs and William Bell.

Thank you very much.

Sincerely yours,

COMMENT:

1. If desired, the above letter could cover any agreement reached as to the use of the appraisals after they are secured by the parties.

SECTION 5
LETTERS TO PUBLIC OFFICIALS

Letters to public officials comprise a substantial volume of correspondence from a lawyer's office. These letters may include letters written to senators, congressmen, state legislators, governors, federal and state agencies, city and county officials, local judges, etc. A letter is often the best means of communicating with a public official. For example, if a call is placed to a United States senator, it is likely that the senator himself will not be reached in connection with the call and an assistant will be reached. Even though you discuss the matter with the assistant, it should be followed or preceded by a letter so that a written document relating to the matter will be available for filing in the office.

GROUP A
Giving Notice or Information

276.
INFORMATION TO DISTRICT ATTORNEY IN
DRIVING WHILE INTOXICATED CASE

Dear Mark:

We are representing Roy Miller in connection with a driving-while-intoxicated charge pending against him in the District Court. He has two reckless driving charges pending; in one he has been represented by Ford & Brown, and in the other, by us.

Roy has three children and is gainfully employed, and they are desperately in need of his support.

I understand that he has quit drinking. Indeed, his wife tells me that he has not had anything to drink for the past three months.

I will appreciate it very much if you would let me know when it will be convenient for us to get together to discuss this matter. We are most interested in working out an arrangement whereby Roy can continue in his job.

Very sincerely,

COMMENT:

1. When a lawyer enters a criminal case, such as the above, a letter advising the district attorney of the representation is thoughtful and also affords the opportunity of stressing important matters on behalf of the client.

277.

NOTICE TO U.S. MAGISTRATE OF REPRESENTATION OF CLIENT TO APPEAR IN DRIVING WHILE INTOXICATED CASE

Dear Mr. Bell:

My good friend Jim Murphy, who is with the Naval Air Command, came to my office today and gave me a copy of his violation notice charging him with DWI at the Navy training station. I understand his court appearance is set for June 7, 19XX.

I will be representing him and will be in court on that day. He had a breathalizer test, and I understand the results were negative. I also understand from Jim that he has 18 years federal service, his age 47, and he has never had any traffic offense of any type at the Navy training station where he has been stationed for six years. Prior to that time he was at the Navy training station in Wilson City.

Jim is a personal friend of mine as I have previously represented a number of the employees at the Naval Air Command. We are most interested in trying to get the charge reduced to reckless driving as Jim is quite concerned about his drivers license, which he must have.

I just wanted to drop you a note about this case and my representation of him prior to appearing in his behalf in court on June 7, 19XX.

Very sincerely,

COMMENT:

1. Depending on local practice, a letter such as the above may or may not be appropriate. Care should be taken to conform to local rules and custom.

278.
NOTICE TO ASSISTANT DISTRICT ATTORNEY OF
REPRESENTING DEFENDANT IN CRIMINAL CASE WITH
PLEA BARGAINING INFORMATION

Dear Roy:

We are representing Albert Johnson in the case of burglary and grand larceny involving the breaking and entering of a beer store between here and Miller City on or about September 15, 19XX.

Three other boys, Micky Williams, Mark Adams and Gene Wilson were indicted in connection with this case. I understand the cases were dropped against Mark Adams and Gene Wilson.

Our client, Albert Johnson, has already served six months in ABC Prison as a result of this case. He had previously served time in DEF Industrial School and was out on probation at the time of the charges in this case. As a result of the charges, his probation or parole was vacated, and he was caused to return to ABC Prison and serve an additional eleven months. You may verify this with Darrell Parker, his parole officer.

Our client is now married, has one minor child, and is gainfully employed in Miller City by the GHI Company. He would like very much to secure probation in connection with this case, and to this end I would appreciate it very much if you would let me know when it is convenient for me to discuss this matter with you.

Again, I want you to know how much I appreciate the cooperation we have always received from you and the district attorney's office.

Very sincerely,

COMMENT:

1. In many jurisdictions plea bargaining has been abolished. Care should be taken to see that your letter conforms to procedural requirements as well as substantive law.

279.

INFORMATION TO DISTRICT ATTORNEY OF CASE OF CLIENT IN JAIL

Dear LeRoy:

I had a long conference with Jimmy Parker at the Mason City Jail on October 2, 19XX, regarding his cases. When I got there, Reverend John Thomas, Vicar of Northside Episcopal Church, was visiting with Jimmy and said that Jimmy is active in the church, and his church is interested in him and wants to do anything it can to help. I told Reverend Thomas that I probably would give his name to you in the event you or the probation officer might be interested in any of the background information regarding Jimmy.

At any rate, Jimmy realizes the situation he is in, and his attitude and spirit seem to be remarkably good and high considering the circumstances. Also, it appears to me from talking with him that his participation in connection with the sale of the dilaudid to the undercover agent, whose name I understand is Gerald Carter, was minimal.

Jimmy is still on probation and has another two or three months to go from his youthful offender's sentence, which I understand was eighteen months.

I would like to meet with you as soon as possible to see if we can work out something on this. Jimmy is very much interested in working with the work release program here. He tells me that Ralph Turner of the probation department has talked with him and says there is no problem of getting him on the work release program, but prior to doing this some disposition needs to be made of his case.

I'd appreciate it very much if you would please let me know when I could see you on this. His case is now set for arraignment on November 17 at 9:00 A.M. before Judge Morganthal.

Thank you very much.

Very sincerely,

COMMENT:

1. A letter to the district attorney handling a criminal case is a convenient means of exchanging information in behalf of the lawyer's client with the district attorney.

280.
REQUEST TO PROBATE REGISTRAR TO FILE PROOF OF
PUBLICATION OF NOTICE TO CREDITORS

Dear Mrs. Carpenter:

Enclosed is the proof of publication of the Notice to Creditors which was published in the *Hale County Record*. Please file this proof in Cause No. 76,316.

Sincerely yours,

COMMENT:

1. The above letter could be personalized with a concluding word of thanks or appreciation.

281.
REQUEST TO CLERK OF COURT TO FILE DIVORCE PETITION AND
RETURN COPY SHOWING DATE OF FILING

Dear Mr. Albert:

Enclosed for filing in the above matter you will find the original and three copies of original petition for divorce. Please file the original and return the copies with the appropriate date of filing stamped thereon.

Enclosed is our check in the sum of $35 to cover the filing fee. Issuance of citation is waived at this time.

Very sincerely,

COMMENT:

1. The above letter could be concluded with a word of thanks or appreciation.

282.
INFORMATION TO DISTRICT ATTORNEY IN RECIPROCAL
ENFORCEMENT OF SUPPORT PROCEEDINGS

Dear Mr. Jones:

We are representing Gerald Smith in connection with the reciprocal nonsupport proceedings begun by his former wife, Adeline Turner. Gerald lives in Johnson City and Mrs. Turner lives in Kansas City.

Gerald Smith is now married to the daughter of a longtime friend of mine.

Mr. Smith and his former wife have three children, namely: Louise, age 17, who does not live with the mother but is living in Omaha and has previously lived with the father; Tina, age 12; and Robert, age 10.

Gerald's weekly income is approximately $230. Mrs. Turner is a housewife but is married to an ABC Company executive who makes approximately $40,000 to $50,000 per year, according to Mr. Smith.

I'd like to get over to see you regarding this case and see if we can reach an agreement on it.

Thanks very much.

Very sincerely,

COMMENT:

1. In criminal or quasi-criminal cases it is helpful to write the district attorney handling the matter and advise him of any facts or law the lawyer deems helpful to his client.

283.
NOTICE TO JUVENILE COURT OF EXPECTED PLEA

Dear Mr. Gonzales:

This is to inform you that we expect Melinda Jones to plead "Not Guilty" and ask for a formal hearing on the date set.

You asked me to inform you ahead of time so that you could subpoena your witnesses.

Very sincerely,

COMMENT:

1. Letters such as the above, in a juvenile case, are helpful in promoting a friendly relation between the lawyer and juvenile court officials.

284.
ACKNOWLEDGMENT TO PROBATION OFFICER OF DATE OF HEARING
IN JUVENILE CASE AND NOTICE OF DESIRE FOR APPOINTMENT

Dear Mr. Taylor:

I received your letter dated February 26, 19XX, advising me that a hearing date has been set in the above-referenced case at 10:00 A.M. on March 19, 19XX.

I would like to get over to see you and review the file prior to that date, if possible. I am asking my secretary, Linda Robinson, to check with your office when would be the best time for me to come over and visit with you.

Thank you very much.

Very sincerely,

COMMENT:

1. Some reference or mention of specific facts or details regarding the minor could be made to give the letter a more personal flavor.

285.
TRANSMITTAL OF MOTION AND BRIEF TO CLERK OF JUVENILE COURT

Dear Sir:

I would like to file the enclosed motion and brief on behalf of my client, Larry Johnson. I was instructed that I could do this by certified mail. If there is any problem involved, would you be kind enough to contact me immediately.

Yours truly,

COMMENT:

1. A letter of transmittal, such as the above, is a convenient means of stating the purpose of transmittal, here, filing. It also makes a permanent record of the filing.

286.
TRANSMITTAL TO CLERK OF COURT OF DEFENDANTS' ANSWERS

Dear Sir:

Enclosed herein for filing and docketing are Separate Answer of Defendant Albert C. Parsons, Separate Answer of Defendant William J. Parsons, and Motion to Strike.

Consistent with my certificate of service and by copy of this letter, I am serving copies of the above documents on counsel for the plaintiff.

I appreciate your cooperation in this matter.

Yours truly,

COMMENT:

1. Transmittal letters advise the addressee of the reason for transmitting and make a permanent record of the action.

287.
TRANSMITTAL TO CLERK OF NOTICE OF FILING INTERROGATORIES,
AND INTERROGATORIES

Dear Mrs. Browning:

Enclosed for filing and docketing are Notice of Filing Interrogatories and Interrogatories to Plaintiff in the above cause.

Consistent with my certificate of service and together with a copy of this letter, I am serving a copy of both documents on counsel for plaintiff.

Very sincerely,

COMMENT:

1. Transmittal letters advise the addressee of the reason for transmitting and make a permanent record of the action.

288.
TRANSMITTAL OF FINANCIAL RESPONSIBILITY FORM TO
DEPARTMENT OF MOTOR VEHICLES

Gentlemen:

We represent Edgar Powell, who was injured in a motor vehicle accident.

On behalf of our client we are filing the Financial Responsibility Form SR-1.

Yours truly,

COMMENT:

1. Transmittal letters advise the addressee of the reason for transmitting and make a permanent record of the action.

289.
LETTER NOTIFYING OFFICER OF SUBPOENA AS
WITNESS FOR DEFENDANT

Dear Officer Johnson:

I represent Mr. Maurice Kaufman, who is the defendant in a suit filed against him by Alice Jones as a result of an automobile accident which occurred on December 26, 19XX, at Haleyville. I have had you subpoenaed as a witness on behalf of Mr. Kaufman.

During the week of trial, which will be February 27th, it is agreeable with me for you to be on call if you will let me know where you can be reached on short notice so that I may notify you when the case is called for trial.

Very sincerely,

COMMENT:

1. It is helpful to notify a police officer or other official who is being subpoenaed in a case of the subpoena and the date of trial.

290.

CONFIRMATION TO COURT REPORTER OF DATE OF DEPOSITION

Dear Mrs. Robins:

This letter will confirm our telephone conversation today wherein someone from your office will be taking the deposition of James Carpenter in our office on January 3, 19XX, at 4:00 P.M.

Enclosed is a copy of the style of the case.

Yours truly,

COMMENT:

1. It is helpful to confirm arrangements for a court reporter in writing to avoid misunderstanding and make a record of the appointment.

291.

REQUEST TO RECORD DEED IN COUNTY LAND RECORDS

Gentlemen:

We are enclosing special warranty deed from David Fisher to Ralph Cornwall for recording in Hale County.

Please advise the amount of recording fee, and we shall send a check by return mail.

Thank you for your attention to this matter.

Yours truly,

COMMENT:

1. If desired, the amount of the recording fee could be ascertained in advance by calling the appropriate office.

292.
TRANSMITTAL OF COPIES OF LEASES TO SMALL BUSINESS
ADMINISTRATOR LOAN OFFICER FOR SBA LOAN APPLICATION

Dear Mr. Brownell:

Copies of the leases, which you requested in the above matter, are enclosed.

Thank you for your assistance and consideration of this application.

Very sincerely,

COMMENT:

1. The above letter could restate the need of the client for the loan or the importance of the loan to the client.

293.
TRANSMITTAL OF COPY OF CERTIFICATE OF INCORPORATION TO
SMALL BUSINESS ADMINISTRATION LOAN OFFICER

Dear Mr. Smith:

Pursuant to my secretary's conversation with you today, enclosed is a stamped copy of the Certificate of Incorporation of ABC Corporation. Please change the applicant on your documents to reflect ABC Corporation rather than ABC Company.

We are in the process of preparing the by-laws and other necessary corporation documents. As soon as these papers are prepared, copies will be forwarded to you.

Thank you very much for your assistance in this matter.

Very sincerely,

COMMENT:

1. A letter of transmittal containing a status report, such as the above to a government agency, is often helpful in processing a matter before the agency.

294.
TRANSMITTAL OF PRELIMINARY TITLE OPINION TO
FARMERS HOME ADMINISTRATION

Dear Mr. Carter:

We have examined title to the property which is subject to the above loan application, and our preliminary title opinion is enclosed.

We are now in the process of attempting to secure the partial release from ABC Bank, releasing said property from the lien of the mortgage from DEF Mortgage Company to Ralph Morganthal, dated April 16, 19XX, and recorded in Mortgage Book 403, page 196, Probate Records of Jefferson County.

However, at the present time Pat Jones is on vacation, but we will secure this release just as soon as possible.

Thank you very much for giving us the opportunity to handle this matter.

Sincerely yours,

COMMENT:

1. There are many situations when a letter is much better than a telephone conversation. The above letter of transmittal of a preliminary title opinion is an example. The letter also includes a status report of the matter to the government agency involved.

295.
TRANSMITTAL OF INFORMATION TO IRS AGENT FOR AUDIT

Dear Mr. Williams:

We have now received the information we requested from Murphy, Wilson and Jones, Certified Public Accountants in Memphis, which we mentioned in our letter to you of February 6, 19XX.

For your information we are enclosing a copy of their letter, together with a copy of their enclosures.

After reviewing their letter and enclosures, if you have any further questions or need any more information on this item, please let me know.

Thank you very much.

Very sincerely,

COMMENT:

1. Transmittal letters advise the addressee of the reason for transmittal and provide a permanent record of the action.

296.

INFORMATION TO IRS AGENT FOR AUDIT OF ESTATE TAX RETURN

Dear Mr. Eversharp:

This letter is in response to the items on which you requested information during your appointment in Harrisburg on October 18, 19XX, with me as attorney for the estate of Edward Hamilton.

We submit the following for information in connection with your examination of the Federal Estate Tax Return filed for the estate:

1. *Schedule K, Items 26, 27, 28 and 29. These items, which are debts of decedent, are as follows:*

Item No.	Description	Amount
26	State income tax 19XX	$ 8,740
27	Federal income tax 19XX	64,392
28	State income tax	3,461
29	Federal income tax 19XX	28,396

You asked for our computations for 19XX and 19XX and stated you are primarily interested in the 19XX return. We have consulted with George, Jason & Watson, Certified Public Accountants, 1618 Randolph Street, Harrisburg, and have requested this information. They have advised us they will send it just as soon as possible. Upon receipt of it, we will forward it to you immediately.

2. *Check drawn by decedent payable to Max Parker for $13,000 dated June 14.*

We have looked into this matter and are willing to concede, on behalf of the estate, that the above check in the amount of $13,000 does represent a gift in contemplation of death.

3. *Schedule D—Insurance on Decedent's Life, Items 22 and 23. These items are as follows on the Federal Estate Tax Return:*

Item No.	Description	Alternate Value
22	ABC Life Insurance Company, Policy No. 1000 Amount $50,000 Payable to Martha Hamilton, wife, beneficiary and owner	None
23	DEF Life Insurance Company, Policy No. 2000, Amount $20,000, Payable to Martha Hamilton, wife, beneficiary	None

We have written to ABC Life Insurance Company regarding the ABC Life Insurance Company Policy No. 1000 listed above, Item 22, but have not yet learned from the company the date of the assignment of this policy from Edward to Martha.

The date of the assignment to Martha of the DEF Life Insurance Company Policy, Item 23, was September 12, 19XX.

a) *Life motives.* Life motives were predominant and decisive. They led Mr. Hamilton to give the policies to Martha. His life motives are evidenced by the following:

(1) The gifts of insurance policies to Martha were very small in relation to

Edward's estate and did not affect his financial independence. They were in keeping with his desire to help Martha establish a separate estate.

(2) Edward had given more to his children over an extended period of time and had a desire to give to Martha to help equalize his prior gifts to his children. The transfers of insurance to Martha were not large in relation to prior gifts to the Hamilton children over the years. Martha, at the time of the transfer, was not independently established, especially in relation to her children.

(3) Edward has a long established practice of generosity to his family, and the transfers in question were part of that practice.

(4) At the time of the transfers in question, Edward did not have any particular concern about his death giving rise to a definite motive, other than the general expectation of death, which all of us entertain. There was no reason to anticipate Edward's death within the forseeable immediate future.

4. Schedule K, debts of decedent, Items 32, 33, 34, 35 and 39. These items are as follows on the Federal Estate Tax Return:

Item No.		Amount
32	ABC National Bank Note dated August 12 for $8,000 signed by Edward Hamilton, Joe Fox and Sally Fox	$ 8,000
33	DEF National Bank of Harrisburg, Note dated January 21, 19XX for $12,000 signed by Edward Hamilton, George Mason and Judith Mason due January 21, 19XX	$12,000
	Accrued interest on item 2	$ 1,120
34	GHI National Bank of Gettysburg, Note dated September 4, 19XX for $3,500 Signed by Edward Hamilton and Wallace Sloan, Due 90 days after date	$3,500
	Accrued interest on item 3	120
35	JKL National Bank, Note dated March 18,19XX for $18,500, signed by Edward Hamilton and George Jackson, due March 18, 19XX	$18,500
	Accrued interest on item 4	1,670
39	MNO National Bank of Scranton, Note made by Phillip Randolph guaranteed by Edward Hamilton, due April 21, 19XX Schedule K-1	$ 2,500

Items 32, 33 and 35 are promissory notes in which Edward joined for the purpose of helping the other parties obtain loans. The other named parties received the proceeds of such loans. As a result of our discussion of these items with you while you were in Harrisburg, we are willing to have these items, namely items 32, 33 and 35, disallowed as debts of the decedent as the estate has not actually paid them. In the event in the future the estate is required to pay one or more of them, we understand at that time a claim for refund may be made.

As to item 34, the estate paid one-half, and Wallace Sloan paid one-half. As we discussed while you were in Harrisburg, we are willing to have one-half of this item be disallowed.

As to item 39, the estate paid this amount in full, and there is no chance of recovery. As we discussed with you, we feel this item should not be disallowed.

We will appreciate hearing from you after you have had an opportunity to consider the information contained in this letter. In addition, as stated earlier in the letter, we will forward to you the information described in paragraph one above just as soon as we receive it from the accountants.

I want to thank you for your courtesy and helpfulness while you were in Harrisburg on your visit.

Sincerely,

COMMENT:

1. A letter such as the above to an official of the Internal Revenue Service states explicitly the position of the client and is helpful in settling complicated matters.

2. Substantive tax matters should be checked against current law.

297.

**TRANSMITTAL OF PAYMENT OF ADDITIONAL ESTATE AND
GIFT TAXES PURSUANT TO AGREEMENT WITH IRS AGENT**

Dear Mr. Ethan:

Enclosed is a check drawn on the estate of Edward Hamilton, payable to Internal Revenue Service for $8,000 as follows:

1. Agreed increase of estate tax pursuant to form 1273.		$ 5,000
2. Gift tax of Edward Hamilton, deceased, pursuant to form 3233.		1,500
3. Gift tax of Martha Hamilton pursuant to form 3233.		1,500
	Total	8,000

Also enclosed are executed forms 898, covering gift tax assessments, and 890B, covering estate tax assessments.

It has been a pleasure working with you on this matter.

Very sincerely,

COMMENT:

1. Letters such as the above transmitting payment give the explicit reason for the payment and provide a permanent record of it.

298.

TRANSMITTAL OF PROTEST OF IRS AGENT'S EXAMINATION REPORT

Dear Mr. Howard:

Enclosed is a protest with respect to the above-captioned matter in response to the determination made in the Internal Revenue Agent's examination report in this matter. Also enclosed are copies of two letters in support of the protest and two copies of the power of attorney authorizing me to represent the taxpayer involved.

A conference before the Appellate Division of the Regional Commissioner's Office has been requested, and Mr. Cornwall of your regional office has been designated as the Appellate Conferee.

Sincerely yours,

COMMENT:

1. Appropriate procedural rules should be complied with in a letter such as the above. The letter might also, if desired, state explicitly the action requested.

299.
REQUEST TO IRS FOR EXTENSION OF THIRTY DAYS FOR
FILING PROTEST

Dear Mr. Campbell:

As indicated to you on the telephone, we would very much appreciate an extension of thirty days' time for filing the protest in the above case. The accountant has just recently been able to provide us with the necessary bookkeeping data, and we will need additional time in which to review this information and properly prepare the protest.

Copies of a power of attorney are enclosed.

With many thanks.

Very sincerely,

COMMENT:

1. Many times a written request, such as the above, should follow a verbal request on the telephone for the purpose of making a permanent record.

300.
TRANSMITTAL TO CLERK OF TAX COURT OF THE UNITED STATES OF
PETITION OF TAXPAYER AND REQUEST FOR DESIGNATION OF
PLACE OF TRIAL

Dear Sir:

Enclosed are five copies of a petition on behalf of the above-named taxpayer, together with a check for the filing fee to the Treasurer of the United States in the amount of $35. Also enclosed is a request for designation of place of trial.

Yours truly,

COMMENT:

1. Transmittal letters advise the addressee of the reason for transmittal and make a permanent record of the action.

301.
NOTICE TO STATE DEPARTMENT OF REVENUE OF
AGREEMENT WITH IRS OF FEDERAL ESTATE TAXES DUE

Dear Mr. Worthington:

We have reached an agreement with the Internal Revenue Service regarding the additional tax due by the Elmer Brown estate.

We are enclosing a copy of form 890-B indicating that we have agreed to an additional tax of $12,296. I understand this will result in an increase in the credit for state taxes as well as state taxes due of $1,400.

Just as soon as we get the final audit report, we will forward it to you.

Thank you very much.

Very sincerely,

COMMENT:

1. The letter above is essentially a status report. Such status reports are helpful in coordinating matters when more than one government agency is involved.

302.
FILING FRANCHISE TAX RETURN WITH
STATE DEPARTMENT OF REVENUE

Dear Mr. Taylor:

Thank you very much for your letter of June 1, 19XX, regarding the above-referenced corporation.

We are enclosing a copy of the domestic corporation franchise tax return which we filed with your office about March 5, 19XX. We are also enclosing a copy of the cancelled check, which was endorsed by your office representing payment of one-half a year's franchise tax for 19XX.

If we can be of further assistance, please let us know.

Very sincerely,

303.
NOTICE TO PROBATE JUDGE THAT CLIENT DOES NOT
DESIRE TO REDEEM PROPERTY SOLD AT TAX SALE

Dear Judge Black:

This is to advise you that rather than redeem the lands sold at the tax sale on August 5, 19XX, and purchased by William Bledsoe and Roy Bledsoe, we have arranged to purchase this property from them and have secured an assignment of the certificate for land sold for taxes.

Accordingly, we do not desire to redeem this property and would appreciate it very much if you could please return our check in the amount of $2,800 forwarded to you for this purpose previously.

Thank you very much.

Very sincerely,

304.
LETTER TO CLERK OF COURT ENCLOSING PLEADINGS

Dear Sir:

Enclosed for filing is a Motion to Dismiss in the captioned case on behalf of Mary Ann Baker. Please date stamp the copy of this letter and return it to me to evidence for my file, the filing of the original.

Yours truly,

COMMENT:

1. Transmittal letters notify the addressee of the reason for transmittal of a document or other pleading and make a record of the action.

305.
TRANSMITTAL TO BANKRUPTCY CLERK OF COMPLAINT AND ORDER

Dear Mr. Brown:

Enclosed herein are the complaint in duplicate and the proposed order in connection with the above captioned matter in triplicate, together with our check payable to the United States District Court in the amount of $50.

If you have any questions, please call me. I certainly appreciate your cooperation.

Very sincerely,

COMMENT:

1. Transmittal letters advise the addressee of the reason for transmittal and make a permanent record of the action.

306.
FILING BANKRUPTCY PETITION WITH COURT CLERK

Dear Mrs. Miller:

Transmitted herewith for filing are the original and two copies of a petition in bankruptcy for John Banks and the original and two copies of a petition in bankruptcy for Louise Banks.

Thank you very much.

Very sincerely,

COMMENT:

1. The above letter, if desired, could invite the clerk to examine the documents filed and to advise if anything further should be done in connection with filing them.

307.
TRANSMITTAL TO BANKRUPTCY CLERK OF AFFIDAVIT OF SERVICE

Dear Mr. Pauling:

Pursuant to Bankruptcy Rule 704(g), enclosed for filing is an affidavit of service, together with the original executed certified mail receipt, which demonstrates that the summons and complaint in the above-styled matter have been properly served on the trustee in bankruptcy.

Also, pursuant to the "Notice to Attorney for plaintiff" attached to the face of the order which was entered April 13, 19XX, I am serving, together with a carbon copy of this letter, a copy of said order on the attorney for the bankrupt.

Very sincerely,

COMMENT:

1. Appropriate procedural rules should be complied with in letters such as the above.

308.
NOTICE TO BANKRUPTCY JUDGE OF ADVERSARY PROCEEDING IN
BANKRUPTCY CASE

Dear Judge Walker:

We represent George Parker who does business in Haleyville under the name Parker Brothers Contracting Company, and we previously forwarded to you claims in bankruptcy in the above-referenced cases in the matters of Alex Johnson, Bankruptcy No. 167,928, and Ralph Peabody, Bankruptcy No. 167,929.

We are enclosing a copy of an adversary proceeding which we are attempting to initiate against the bankrupts, their trustees in bankruptcy and also against the ABC Bank and Trust Company of Panama City. The ABC Bank and Trust Company of Panama City admittedly owes jointly to the above named bankrupts and our client the sum of $14,968. Of this amount, our client was due to get $6,712 and the above-named bankrupts were due to get the sum of $8,256. The parties have heretofore been unable to work out the matter, and we are filing this adversary proceeding in the bankruptcy court in order to protect the position of our client. I am most hopeful that the matter can be worked out when the trustees in bankruptcy are appointed and the matter is looked into, and it is ascertained that our client is due to get the sum mentioned above.

I am hopeful that attorney's fees can be held to a minimum. In the event it is necessary for me to be admitted specially for purposes of making this pleading in your court, please let me know and I will take the necessary steps. Also, in the event the matter must be set for a hearing and evidence produced on it, I would anticipate flying out there and appearing for the hearing.

I would appreciate it very much if you would please advise me when the trustees are appointed and give me their names and addresses, as well as any thoughts you may have in connection with the matter.

I do want to mention that this is the first adversary proceeding I have had in bankruptcy, and I will appreciate any suggestions you may have as to the proper procedure.

Thank you very much.

Sincerely yours,

COMMENT:

1. Letters directly to the judge involved are often helpful in keeping the judge informed of the status of the case.

309.
REQUEST TO RECORD ABSTRACT OF JUDGMENT IN
COUNTY RECORDS

Dear Sir:

I am enclosing an Abstract of Judgment in the above matter, which I should like to have recorded in the judgment records of Washington County. Please return the abstract to me after it has been recorded.

I am enclosing our check in the amount of $18 to cover recording fees.

Very sincerely,

COMMENT:

1. The above letter could be concluded with a word of thanks or appreciation.

310.
PERMISSION OF CLIENT TO U.S. SENATOR TO OBTAIN INFORMATION

Dear Senator Hall:

I understand a letter of permission from me to you is necessary as a result of Public Law 93-537, The Privacy Act. You have my permission to proceed in connection with this case and to request and secure any and all information about it from any government agency, or any other source which might be relevant and helpful to you with my case.

Paul Ireland of Ireland, Carpenter and Mitchell, 100 Main Street, Phone 608-5334, is representing me in connection with the case, and you have my further permission and request to discuss, advise and inform him regarding any and all matters and information in connection with my case.

Please know that I am deeply grateful to you for all of your help in my behalf with my claim.

Very sincerely,

COMMENT:

1. The above letter was prepared by the lawyer for the client to comply with the Privacy Act.

311.
EXPRESSING SUPPORT TO REPORT OF CHAIRMAN
OF SUBCOMMITTEE

Dear Mr. Bell:

Thank you for the copy of your letter dated April 1, 19XX, addressed to Senator Wilson.

I have read the letter, together with the attached report, with a great deal of interest, and I would like to congratulate you on the fine job you have done as chairman of the subcommittee.

I am in general agreement with the recommendations of the committee except that I am not aware of the reasons for the recommendation that the Small Business Administration reduce its maximum direct lending limit to $250,000.

I do like the recommendation that loans of under $50,000 under the direct loan program be made under relaxed credit criteria and that the agency operate in this loan size area under a liberal and aggressive philosophy.

Again, Mr. Bell, I want to congratulate you for the fine job you have done on behalf of the Subcommittee on Financing and Investment.

Sincerely yours,

312.
NOTIFYING CONGRESSMAN OF ILLNESS OF CONSTITUENT

Dear Congressman Brown:

I talked to Edith Chambers the other day and found out her husband, Henry, has been in the veterans' hospital in Atlanta and has had an operation to try to improve the circulation in his leg.

I understand that at one time Henry was not sure whether they would have to remove his leg or not because of the poor circulation, and I was happy to hear from Edith that the operation was a complete success and that Henry should recover and have the use of his leg.

Thought you might like to hear this news and perhaps drop a note to Henry regarding the successful outcome of his operation.

Very sincerely,

COMMENT:

1. If appropriate, the address of the person involved should be given.

GROUP B
Requesting Information

313.

REQUESTING INFORMATION ABOUT CORPORATION FROM
SECRETARY OF STATE

Gentlemen:

Please advise if ABC Company is or was a corporation as of July 1, 19XX, and, if so, please advise the date of incorporation, or, if dissolved, the date of its dissolution, the address of the principal office in your state and the names and addresses of the officers, directors and resident agent.

If ABC Company is not reflected exactly as captioned, please advise if your records reflect the name and address of a company or corporation similar in name.

In the event that this corporation is not now incorporated under the laws of your state, kindly advise if it is registered to do business in your state, in which state it is incorporated, and the name and address of its resident agent. Thank you.

Very sincerely,

COMMENT:

1. If appropriate the need for the information requested could be stated or some comment about it could be made.

314.

REQUEST TO SECRETARY OF STATE WHETHER
NAME IS AVAILABLE FOR NEW CORPORATION

Dear Mr. Johnson:

Please inform the undersigned whether or not the above-referenced name is available for domestic corporation use in our state.

We have a client interested in incorporation under this name, and, if the name is available, we would like you to reserve this name for our client for your customary period of 90 days.

Very sincerely,

315.
REQUEST TO SECRETARY OF STATE WHETHER CORPORATION IS INCORPORATED OR QUALIFIED TO DO BUSINESS IN STATE

Dear Mr. Johnson:

Please inform me whether or not the above-referenced corporation is incorporated in our state or has qualified to do business in our state and, if so, the date.

We would also like to know the correct name of this corporation.

Also please inform us of the name and address of the current statutory agent designated for service of process if the corporation is a foreign corporation qualified to do business in our state.

We appreciate your services in this regard.

Yours truly,

COMMENT:

1. A letter is generally the most effective means to request information from a govenment agency.

316.
REQUEST TO BANKING COMMISSION FOR NAME OF REGISTERED AGENT FOR SERVICE OF PROCESS

Gentlemen:

I would appreciate it if you would provide me with the name of the registered agent for service of process of the following lending institutions:

1. ABC Bank
2. DEF Savings and Loan Association

Thank you very much.

Sincerely yours,

317.
REQUEST TO DISTRICT ATTORNEY TO ADVISE WHEN ASSISTANT
DISTRICT ATTORNEY IS ASSIGNED TO CRIMINAL CASE

Dear Mr. Powell:

Our client, Mike Mitchell, was arrested on March 3, 19XX, for obtaining drugs by fraud. He appeared before the District Court for a preliminary hearing this morning, but the hearing was postponed until April 16, 19XX, because an assistant district attorney has not yet been assigned to the case.

We have checked with the Mental Health Center and are in the process of making application for the Umbrella program. When an assistant district attorney has been assigned to the case, we would appreciate it if you would call us and let us know. We are most anxious to work with him in connection with having Mike placed in the Umbrella program.

Thanks very much.

Very sincerely,

COMMENT:

1. When handling a criminal case, it is a good idea for the lawyer to get in touch with the district attorney who will represent the state in connection with the case.

318.
REQUEST TO BUREAU OF VITAL STATISTICS FOR COPIES
OF DEATH CERTIFICATE

Gentlemen:

We are enclosing a check in the amount of $6 and would appreciate it very much if you would please send us three certified copies of the certificate of death of Ralph Thomas who died in Cleveland on or about September 1, 19XX.

Thank you very much.

Sincerely yours,

COMMENT:

1. Generally when a death is involved in a matter, the lawyer should secure an official copy of the certificate of death from the appropriate state or county office.

319.
REQUEST FOR CORONER'S REPORT

Dear Mr. Wilson:

Our clients are the survivors of Mary McAllister.

In addition to an autopsy report, it is our understanding that the coroner also performed an investigation into the circumstances and facts surrounding the death.

We would appreciate it if you would send to us not only the autopsy report, but also the coroner's investigation, as well as any transcripts or statements taken.

Please find enclosed signed authorizations from the survivors, as well as a check for the full amount of the cost of obtaining the records.

Very sincerely,

COMMENT:

1. The above request for coroner's report is an example of the effective use of a letter to secure information regarding a case.

320.
REQUEST FOR ACCIDENT REPORT FROM
STATE DEPARTMENT OF PUBLIC SAFETY

Gentlemen:

We are representing Roy Campbell in connection with an automobile accident which occurred on January 6, 19XX, on U.S. Highway 5 near Wheeling, between a 1975 Ford Pick-up driven by Roy Campbell and a 1977 automobile owned by Joseph Murphy of Haley City, and driven by Alice Brown.

We are enclosing our check of $3 and would appreciate it very much if you would please send us a copy of the accident report.

Also, we will appreciate it very much if you would please send us a supply of form 513 for use in connection with automobile accidents.

Thank you very much.

Very Sincerely,

COMMENT:

1. Letters such as the above may be used effectively to gather a great deal of information for use in connection with a case.

321.
REQUEST TO DEPARTMENT OF PUBLIC SAFETY FOR ACCIDENT REPORT

Gentlemen:

Enclosed please find our check for the State Highway Patrol Accident Report on the following accident:

Date of Accident: October 20, 19XX
Location: Tampa, Florida
Names and addresses of Drivers of Vehicles:
   Joseph Cornwall, 111 3rd Avenue, Jacksonville, Florida
   Mr. Richard Alvarez, 6970 Main Street, Tampa, Florida

Thank you for your cooperation in this matter.

Very sincerely,

COMMENT:

1 The lawyer should always secure any available accident report in connection with a case he is handling.

322.
REQUEST TO POLICE DEPARTMENT FOR POLICE REPORT

Gentlemen:

Our client was involved in an accident in which a police report was made.

We believe that your police department was the investigating agency.

Enclosed is an authorization signed by our client authorizing you to furnish us with a copy of that report. Please find enclosed a check for $2 to cover the costs of copying.

Please use the enclosed return envelope for the purpose of sending us the police report. Thank you for your cooperation in this matter.

Sincerely yours,

COMMENT:

1. The lawyer handling the case should always secure a copy of any police report or accident report made in connection with the case.

323.
REQUEST TO LICENSE DEPARTMENT FOR NAME OF
OWNER OF AUTOMOBILE

Gentlemen:

Our client, Edith Blackston, was in an automobile accident on July 4, 19XX, which accident occurred on U.S. Highway 4 near Elmhurst.

We understand that a 1976 Cadillac automobile, license number EB 6703, contributed to or caused the accident.

We would appreciate it very much if you could please let us know the name of the owner of the automobile in accordance with your records for the issuance of the license plates. In the event there is a charge for this service, please let us have your bill for it.

Thank you very much.

Very sincerely,

COMMENT:

1 Letters, such as the above, are an effective means of discovering information in connection with a case.

324.
REQUEST TO CITY CLERK FOR LIEN STATEMENT OF
PUBLIC IMPROVEMENT ASSESSMENTS

Dear Mr. Bell:

The following is a lien statement for public improvement assessments. Please sign this statement and return it to me. Thank you for your cooperation.

CITY OF Stephenson, Iowa

To Whom It May Concern:

This is to certify that the City of Stephenson has no liens and no liens are pending or in process against
    Address: 1911 West Elm Street
    Legal Description: lot 6, Block 2, Mayfair Village Subdivision, 4th Addition
Assessed to: William McKenzie and wife, June McKenzie

Except

This certificate does not apply to any liens of record in the Office of the Probate Judge of Jefferson County, Iowa, nor to city taxes which are collected by the tax collector of Jefferson County.

Yours truly,

COMMENT:

1. The above letter and certificate should be tailored to conform to local practice.

325.
REQUEST TO STAFF MEMBER OF U.S. SENATE COMMITTEE FOR
INFORMATION ON SBA LEASE GUARANTY PROGRAM

Dear Mr. Mitchell:

I would appreciate it very much if you could have someone secure all the information that has been printed in connection with the SBA Lease Guaranty Program.

I have a client who is very interested in the program and would like to review all of the material I can get together regarding it.

Why don't you come to see us soon, and thanks very much.

Very sincerely,

COMMENT:

1. Rather than request all information that has been printed, the request could simply be for all information that is available or all printed information that is available.

2. The letter could also state the reason for the request or use that will be made with the information. Sometimes this is helpful in ascertaining the information that is sought.

326.
REQUEST TO SMALL BUSINESS ADMINISTRATION FOR
SBA LOAN INFORMATION

Dear Mr. Chapman:

One of our clients has asked us to write you and try to secure any information or literature which you have regarding SBA loans.

We would appreciate it very much if you would please send anything you have available directly to Mr. Horace Jones, of ABC Corporation, 111 Main Street, Lansing, Michigan.

Thank you very much.

Sincerely yours,

COMMENT:

1. The letter could specify the specific type or size of loan contemplated. Sometimes further details are helpful in ascertaining what information is relevant or appropriate.

327.
REQUEST FOR INFORMATION FROM U.S. SENATOR ABOUT
HOUSING PROGRAM

Dear Senator Worthington:

My good friend, Elmer Potter of the homebuilders association here in Cleveland asked me to write you and find out all that I could with regard to the new housing program under which purchasers get money for houses up to approximately $15,000 for one percent, and the government pays the balance of the interest on their loans.

I would appreciate it very much if you would please refer this letter to the appropriate agency with the request that they forward me all printed information they have regarding this program.

Thank you very much.

Very sincerely,

COMMENT:

1. The letter could state, if appropriate, the purpose for which the client desires the information. Sometimes this is helpful in ascertaining what information is appropriate.

328.
LETTER TO IRS REQUESTING CLIENT'S TAX RETURNS

Gentlemen:

The above-named person is our client.

We are currently handling legal matters for our client which necessitate that we obtain records from the Internal Revenue Service.

We would appreciate it if the Internal Revenue Service would furnish us with copies of our client's tax returns for the past five years.

Enclosed is a check to your department for $25.

Please note the notarized authorization attached hereto.

Very sincerely,

COMMENT:

1. When a client has lost or misplaced his income tax returns, and they are necessary to the lawyer handling the case, the returns may be requested from the Internal Revenue Service. The letter should be addressed to the regional office where the client filed the returns.

2. A letter similar to the above could be addressed to the appropriate social security national, district, or branch office to request social security records.

329.
REQUEST TO VETERANS ADMINISTRATION FOR COPY OF
SERVICE RECORDS

Gentlemen:

Mr. Paul Jones, whose claim number is described above, has asked us to assist him in connection with his VA claim.

We would appreciate it very much if you could please send us photostatic copies of all records pertaining to Mr. Jones from the time of his entering service until the time of his discharge.

In the event there is a charge for this service, please let us have your bill, and we will be happy to pay it.

Thank you very much.

Very sincerely,

COMMENT:

1. In many cases where personal information is requested, a power of attorney or written authorization may be requested prior to disclosure of the information or records.

330.
REQUEST TO VETERANS ADMINISTRATION FOR CLIENT'S MEDICAL
RECORDS WITH ENCLOSURE IDENTIFYING CLIENT

Gentlemen:

We enclose an authorization signed by our client for information contained within his medical or army records.

We would appreciate it if you could identify the location of those records.

We leave space for your reply on the bottom of this letter.

Thank you for your cooperation.

Sincerely yours,

ENCLOSURE

Client's Name:
Service Serial No.:
Date of Birth:
Social Security No.:
Period of Service:
Various Addresses:

COMMENT:

1. It is helpful to a lawyer to have all medical records relevant to a client's claim, or the claim made against the client.

331.
REQUEST TO SUPERVISOR OF DEPARTMENT OF PENSIONS AND SECURITY FOR EXPLANATION OF AUTHORITY FOR ACTION

Dear Mr. Barnes:

I am enclosing a copy of a letter I have received from Mr. LaRue, in which he requests my advice regarding a conversation he had with Mr. Murphy of your office.

I understand that Mr. Murphy has advised Mr. LaRue that he must deed a trailer located on his property to his wife's mother, Mrs. Wilbur Morganthal. I understand that the reason assigned why Mr. LaRue should deed the trailer to his mother-in-law was for her financial security. Mrs. Morganthal's only income, according to my information, consists of social security benefits and old age benefits.

I would appreciate it very much if you would please have Mr. Murphy advise us of his authority to require this conveyance by Mr. LaRue.

Thank you very much.

Very sincerely,

COMMENT:

1. The above letter could be softened in tone by stating the reason the request is made for the disclosure of authority to act as has been in connection with the matter.

GROUP C
Requesting Support or Action

332.

TRANSMITTAL OF ARTICLES OF INCORPORATION TO SECRETARY OF STATE AND REQUEST FOR CERTIFICATE OF INCORPORATION

Dear Sir:

Enclosed are duplicate originals of the Articles of Incorporation for ABC Blueprint, Inc., duly signed and verified pursuant to provisions of our state Business Corporation Act; in addition, a check in the amount of $50 is enclosed for your filing fee.

We request that a Certificate of Incorporation be issued.

Yours truly,

COMMENT:

1. The above letter could be concluded with an expression of thanks or appreciation.

333.

TRANSMITTAL OF ARTICLES OF INCORPORATION TO SECRETARY OF STATE AND REQUEST FOR CHARTER

Dear Sir:

Enclosed in duplicate are the Articles of Incorporation of ABC Corporation. Also enclosed is a check in the sum of $46 in payment of the filing fee.

Please issue the charter for this new corporation as soon as possible and send it to me.

Thank you for your time and attention to this matter.

Very sincerely,

COMMENT:

1. The above is a good example of a friendly and effective letter of transmittal which gets the job done as well as makes a permament record of the action.

334.
TRANSMITTAL OF ARTICLES OF ASSOCIATION TO SECRETARY OF STATE AND REQUEST FOR CHARTER

Dear Mrs. Clark:

Enclosed with this letter you will find submitted in duplicate Articles of Association for the above-captioned professional association. Both documents are originally signed. We have also enclosed a check in the amount of $100 in payment of the filing fee.

We would like to request that you handle these Articles of Association in the normal fashion and return to our office the charter for the new professional association.

Very sincerely,

COMMENT:

1. Letters of transmittal need not be lengthy, as the above effective letter illustrates.

335.
REQUEST TO PUBLIC SERVICE COMMISSION FOR
ASSISTANCE AND ADVICE ON APPLICATION FOR
AMENDMENT OF HOUSEHOLD GOODS PERMIT

Dear Mr. Albert:

I am writing you to request your help and advice in connection with a forthcoming application for amendment of a household goods permit on behalf of my long-time friend and client, Mary Brown, doing business as Brown Moving Company, which is agent for ABC Movers, Inc., as a common carrier for movement of household goods between points within a 15 mile radius of Millersville on the one hand, and, on the other hand, all points in our state.

Mary Brown, a long-time friend and client, is a very fine businesswoman. She has been in the household goods moving business for a number of years and is an active member of the association. She has a substantial business, substantial assets, and is adequately financed. As in all other businesses, she finds it necessary to aggressively pursue new business and to render improved service to her clients and customers.

Her forthcoming application for expanded authority is directly connected to the conduct of her business. At the present time I understand that approximately 25% of her business involves movement of new and transferred employees for the DEF Corporation to and from our state to 3 locations in Ohio, such as Cleveland, Akron and the DEF Corporation plant over in Sandusky. I understand her rates are attractive and that DEF Corporation enjoys doing business with her. Several times, she tells us, she has been given to understand from the people that they would appreciate it if she could handle moves intrastate in our state for new employees and transferred employees from points within the northern part of our state to other points where there are military installations. On account of the restrictions in her permit, she can only handle intrastate moves to and from Millersville. Ironically, she can handle any kind of interstate moves through her agency with United Movers, Inc.

In order to give full and satisfactory service to her regular customers, as well as other customers, she finds a real, present and growing business need to secure authority to make intrastate moves to and from other points in the northern part of our state in addition to Millersville.

I am in the process of getting together full information in connection with this forthcoming application and would like very much to come to Hamilton and visit with you briefly to discuss it on June 16, if that date is satisfactory with you. I am hopeful also of discussing it with Mr. Whitmore and Mrs. Lopez while I am there.

I will appreciate it very much if you will please let me know whether it will be convenient for me to visit with you on June 16 regarding this matter.

Very sincerely,

COMMENT:

1. The above letter is a good example of acquainting the reader with the facts of a matter prior to seeing him personally about it.

336.
REQUEST TO DISTRICT ATTORNEY TO DISMISS POSSESSION OF MARIJUANA CASE

Dear Mr. Shelby:

The above case is set for trial before Judge Wilson Jones on April 4 at 10:00 A.M.

I have carefully looked into the circumstances involved in this matter, and it is my opinion that there is no substantial case against our client, Barry Jacobs. The case was made pursuant to the fruits of a search warrant at the place where Barry and his younger brother, David reside. Barry was home, and marijuana was discovered on the premises. However, the marijuana belonged to David, and he will so testify.

In addition, we are in the process of handling David's case, where we anticipate he will admit his involvement in family court as he is a minor.

I have talked to both Barry and David at some length, and if both of them are telling me the truth, it appears that Barry is absolutely without guilt in connection with this case.

I would like to get together with you before the trial to go over this case and see if you might want to nolle pros this matter.

Very sincerely,

337.
DISTRICT ATTORNEY'S LETTER REGARDING EXTRADITION

Dear Mr. Schmidt:

As you may know, we have in custody in the Morgan County Jail at this time Max Williams, wanted as a fugitive from justice from your state. Mr. Williams appeared in court (with his attorney) on November 3, 19XX. At that time he informed the court that he would refuse to waive extradition to your state. As a result, if you wish to have Mr. Williams returned, it will be necessary to begin extradition proceedings by obtaining a governor's warrant. Since a hearing date has been set here in Morgan County for January 29, 19XX, it is imperative that this procedure is begun immediately.

If you have any further information with respect to this defendant and this case, please contact me.

Very sincerely,

COMMENT:

1. District attorneys and other law enforcement officials find letters a convenient means of transacting business with each other. The above letter is used by a district attorney when the defendant refuses to waive extradition, to inquire whether the state from which a fugitive has fled wishes to begin extradition proceedings.

338.
REQUEST FOR NEW BIRTH CERTIFICATE FOLLOWING
FINAL DECREE OF ADOPTION

Dear Sir:

Enclosed is a certified copy of the final decree of adoption of the above-referenced minor child, together with a copy of her birth certificate.

As the final decree of adoption indicates, Jane Kennedy has been adopted by John Bolton and Louise Bolton, and the minor's name was changed by court order to Jane Bolton.

Please issue a new birth certificate in the name of Jane Bolton and return to me.

I have enclosed our check made to your order in blank. You are authorized to fill in the amount of your charges for the birth certificate.

Sincerely yours,

COMMENT:

1. The amount of the charge for filing a document in a governmental office may be ascertained in advance by calling on the telephone. This is usually preferable to enclosing a check in blank or requesting billing. Many offices will not file documents without receiving payment. Also, there is some danger in sending checks in blank.

339.
REQUEST TO U.S. SENATOR FOR ASSISTANCE WITH
SBA LOAN APPLICATION

Dear Senator McCampbell:

I am writing on behalf of ABC Oil Company requesting your assistance in its obtaining an SBA Loan. Ralph Wilson, the owner, has done very well as a distributor for DEF Corporation. DEF Corporation wants to establish him as one of their distributors in the Fort Worth area. This represents quite an opportunity for Ralph since his profits will increase greatly even on his present volume of business, and, in addition, his prospects for growth are excellent. To be a distributor requires, however, that Ralph purchase a substantial amount of equipment and have the minimum financial resources as required by DEF Corporation.

Enclosed is a letter which is self-explanatory from Hugh Merrill and Austin Fitzhugh.

Joe Madison, the commercial loan officer of XYZ Bank, is backing Ralph 100% and doing everything he can to help secure a favorable approval from the SBA. Mr. Phil Burton at the SBA District Office in Dallas is processing the loan at the present time.

We will appreciate very much anything you can do in Ralph Wilson's behalf in connection with the SBA Loan application.

Very sincerely,

COMMENT:

1. Congressmen and senators are often helpful in connection with claims and applications and other matters pending before federal agencies. A congressional inquiry is often helpful in cutting red tape and securing prompt consideration of the matter. The lawyer should realize whenever he writes a congressman or senator that his letter or a copy of it will probably be transmitted to the agency involved for action. The letter should be drafted with this in mind.

340.
REQUEST TO U.S. SENATOR FOR ASSISTANCE WITH
CLIENT'S LINE OF CREDIT GUARANTY APPLICATION TO
SMALL BUSINESS ADMINISTRATION

Dear Senator:

Our good friends Joe McCoy and Jerry Kaufman of ABC Builders have applied through the Bank of Covington for a line of credit guaranty in connection with their construction business.

ABC Builders is one of the finest builders in the area, and they have been getting a number of large jobs. For example, very recently I understand they got a job in the neighborhood of seven hundred or eight hundred thousand dollars for some work out at Lawrenceburg.

Their volume of business has for some time been over one million dollars a year, and, although I don't have the existing figures before me, I would estimate they probably will do two million dollars worth this year. They are greatly in need of this line of credit guaranty from the SBA to facilitate their construction activities.

We will very much appreciate anything you can do to help expedite approval of the line of credit guaranty application by the state director of the Small Business Administration in Jefferson City. I am going ahead and forwarding a copy of this letter to George Parsons and Wilbur Jones of the state directors office for their information. Thank you very much.

Very sincerely,

COMMENT:

1. In appropriate cases, when a letter is written to a United States senator or congressman, copies of the letter may be forwarded to government agency officials in order to expedite consideration.

341.
LETTER TO U.S. SENATOR REQUESTING SUPPORT FOR HOME LOAN APPLICATION

Dear Senator:

I am enclosing a copy of a letter we have sent to the county supervisor of the Farmer's Home Administration in Memphis in behalf of our client and friend, Sue Carpenter, who is employed by the Chamber of Commerce in Jackson.

Sue took a bankruptcy in April, 19XX, and was discharged in bankruptcy in September, 19XX, and she is concerned that the record of the bankruptcy will have an adverse effect on her application for housing assistance from the Farmer's Home Administration. She has an absolutely outstanding record in paying her debts and has secured a bank loan from ABC Bank of Jackson subsequent to the bankruptcy. She has steady employment and has supported her three children solely by herself. Her ex-husband has never contributed anything to the support of the children.

I would appreciate it very much if you would please contact the Farmer's Home Administration officials and urge favorable action on her application for housing assistance. I know that a new home for her and her family will mean a lot to her, and I can comfortably predict that she will be able to make all of the payments and will do all that is required of her in connection with the loan and mortgage.

Thank you very much for all you may be able to do to help her.

Very sincerely,

COMMENT:

1. Many times it is a good idea to continue to pursue an important matter after the federal agency has given unfavorable report or rejected a claim. Letters are an effective means of reasserting or, in effect, appealing an adverse decision by a government agency.

342.
REQUEST TO SENATOR FOR SUPPORT OF PREVIOUSLY REJECTED
LOAN GUARANTY APPLICATION

Dear Senator Thomas:

George Murray, loan officer with the Northern district office in Omaha, wrote William Brownell, president of Bank of Omaha, on September 3, 19XX, regarding the application of Phillip Dorter for an SBA loan in the amount of $250,000.

Mr. Brownell stated that, upon review of the application submitted, the SBA does not feel that the funds requested could be justified at this time.

I met at the bank today with George Murray, Tom Gibson and Phillip Dorter. George said he really wanted the loan application to be approved and he felt since the property owned by Phillip in Omaha has been appraised for $338,000, the major stockholders are willing to sign personal guarantees, and he has a favorable feeling for the business, that this loan should be approved.

George is interested enough in helping secure approval of the loan that he made an appointment while I was in his office to see William Brownell in Omaha at 2:30 P.M. on September 30, in behalf of the application. I understand from Phillip that the application is being reprepared, the amount requested is being reduced and other things are being done in connection with the application which they hope will facilitate approval of the loan.

I told George that in view of his tremendous interest in the loan and his belief and faith in Phillip Dorter and their program, that I would write you and request that you bring it to the Senator's personal attention with the further request that you contact Mr. Brownell in Omaha regarding the application.

Anything you can do will be appreciated.

Very sincerely,

COMMENT:

1. A request to a senator or congressman may be the means in effect of appealing an adverse decision by a government agency.

343.
LETTER TO LOAN OFFICER REQUESTING APPROVAL OF APPLICATION FOR HOME LOAN

Dear Mr. Jacobs:

Shirley Jones, a client of ours who works for ABC Corporation, with offices in Jefferson City, discussed with me today her application for a home loan under one of your programs.

Shirley was quite concerned that a bankruptcy proceeding, in which she was discharged in bankruptcy on March 18, 19XX, might affect her application. I would like to strongly recommend her for the proposed loan. Following the bankruptcy, Shirley has paid all of her creditors without exception. In addition she has secured a loan from DEF Bank of Jefferson City, the loan officer being John Brownell in Jefferson City. She has a satisfactory record of paying this loan.

Prior to the bankruptcy Shirley's ex-husband had never contributed to the support of her three children, and she found herself unfortunately in a position where she was not able to pay her debts. On our recommendation, she did take the bankruptcy. However, I would like to vouch for her good character, her integrity and her willingness to pay her just debts.

I do think she would be quite a good risk for this loan program, and I know it would mean a lot to her to be able to secure adequate housing for her family. She has had very steady employment with ABC Corporation and is quite a conscientious person in every respect.

All consideration you can give to favorable action on her application will be very much appreciated. In the event you need any further information which we might give you, please let me know.

Sincerely yours,

COMMENT:

1. Letters such as the above are effective means of dealing with government agencies and officers.

344.
TRANSMITTAL TO IRS OF APPLICATION FOR APPROVAL OF
MASTER PROFIT SHARING PLAN

Dear Mr. Ireland:

We are enclosing a Sponsor Application, Form 4461, in behalf of the ABC Bank of Seattle, for approval of its Master Profit Sharing Plan.

In connection with the application, we are also enclosing an executed Power of Attorney, Form 2848, designating the undersigned to represent the bank in connection with this matter, a duplicate copy of the executed plan, participation agreement, enrollment agreement, and master retirement trust.

The undersigned has made a study of the Pension Reform Act, and I am hopeful that the enclosed documents are in full compliance with it.

We are most anxious to secure your approval at the earliest possible date. We will very much appreciate your interim advice regarding the length of time estimated to be necessary for review of this matter by you.

We forwarded copies of the plans and related documents to your office on September 10, 19XX, and were advised that there was in effect at that time a temporary suspension of issuing determination letters. We later were advised that the plans should be resubmitted on the forms revised as of April 15, 19XX. This submission is on the revised form 4461.

Thank you very much for your consideration.

Sincerely yours,

COMMENT:

1. As illustrated in the letter above, letters of transmittal may be used to bring any additional matters to the attention of the addressee that the writer desires.

345.
TRANSMITTAL OF APPLICATION FOR APPROVAL OF MASTER MONEY PURCHASE PENSION PLAN TO COMMISSIONER OF INTERNAL REVENUE

Dear Mr. Caplin:

We are enclosing a Sponsor Application, Form 4461, in behalf of the ABC Bank of Seattle, for approval of its Master Money Purchase Pension Plan.

In connection with the application, we are also enclosing an executed Power of Attorney, Form 2848, designating the undersigned to represent the bank in connection with this matter, a duplicate copy of the executed plan, participation agreement, enrollment agreement and master retirement trust.

The undersigned has made a study of the Pension Reform Act, and I am hopeful that the enclosed documents are in full compliance with it.

We are most anxious to secure your approval at the earliest possible date. We will very much appreciate your interim advice regarding the length of time estimated to be necessary for review of this matter by you.

Thank you very much for your consideration.

Yours very sincerely,

COMMENT:

1. Care should be taken in letters of transmittal of such things as applications or requests for information that appropriate powers of attorney or letters of authorization are enclosed.

346.
REQUEST TO JUDGE FOR CONTINUANCE OF CASE BECAUSE OF CONFLICT WITH TRIAL OF ANOTHER CASE

Dear Judge Taylor:

In checking my calendar for the coming weeks, I noticed that the above-referenced case is scheduled for final hearing in your chambers on the 12th day of October, 19XX at 9:00 a.m. Please be advised that I will be in Salt Lake City the entire week of October 12, trying a lawsuit.

I would appreciate it very much if you could change the date of this hearing to the next available date. Thank you very much.

Respectfully yours,

COMMENT:

1. A copy of the above letter should be sent to the opposing attorney and anyone else who needs to be advised of the request for continuance.

347.
REQUEST TO JUDGE FOR RULING ON MOTION TO DISMISS

Dear Judge Wilson:

I am enclosing a copy of the motion of our client Roy Miller, in which he seeks to be dismissed as a party plaintiff in the above-referenced case, now pending in your court.

I am hopeful that it will be possible for you to issue an order dismissing Roy Miller as a party plaintiff in this action without the necessity of a hearing and the expense of our coming to Washington, D.C. In this regard, I am sending a copy of this motion to the attorneys in the Justice Department representing the Government in this case, as well as to the attorneys for the plaintiff, with the request that they advise the court and the undersigned in the event they wish to contest the granting of this motion of dismissal, within fifteen days.

In the event I do not hear from them to the contrary within fifteen days, I will again write you and request that the order be entered without a hearing.

In the event you feel there must be a hearing on this motion, regardless of whether or not it is opposed, I will appreciate it very much if you would please let me know.

Thank you very much for the consideration of the request contained in this letter.

Respectfully yours,

COMMENT:

1. Whenever you write directly to a judge about a case, you should always send a copy to all opposing and other attorneys in the case. Many times a letter directly to the judge is an effective means of bringing the matter to his personal attention.

348.
LETTER TO JUDGE WITH SECOND REQUEST FOR CONTINUANCE

Dear Judge Parker:

I filed a motion in the Clerk's office for a continuance in the above-referenced case, which is set on your docket for the 3rd of October at 9:00 a.m. and cited a number of reasons for said motion. I sent a copy of my motion to the attorney for the defendant and they have this morning called me to inform me that they would gladly go along with the motion for continuance. They asked me to please contact you and let you know that they are in agreement for said case to be continued.

Therefore, I respectfully ask again that you grant my motion for continuance.

Sincerely yours,

COMMENT:

1. In a delicate matter, such as that covered by the above letter where a continuance has once been refused and a second request is made, the request can be made effectively in the form of a letter.

349.
TRANSMITTAL TO COURT CLERK OF MOTION TO WITHDRAW
AS ATTORNEY AND REQUEST TO HAVE JUDGE
SIGN ORDER APPROVING WITHDRAWAL

Dear Mr. Harbin:

Enclosed is our motion to withdraw as attorney in the above cause, together with an order and copy approving withdrawal.

Please file the motion and have the presiding judge sign the order and return a certified copy to me.

Very sincerely,

COMMENT:

1. The above letter, if appropriate, could state or summarize the reasons for withdrawal.

350.
REQUEST TO CLERK OF COURT TO MIMEOGRAPH BRIEF OF DEFENDANTS-APPELLEES

Dear Mr. Murphy:

I am enclosing the brief of defendants-appellees to be mimeographed under your supervision, along with check for $85 to cover estimated costs. I shall appreciate it if you will please mimeograph the necessary number of copies promptly. I have today mailed a copy of the brief to the attorney for the plaintiff-appellant.

If there are additional costs, please advise me, and I shall immediately send a check.

Sincerely yours,

COMMENT:

1. Letters are an effective means of coordinating matters with clerks of court.

351.
REQUEST TO SHERIFF TO LEVY ON PROPERTY PURSUANT TO EXECUTION

Dear Sheriff Canelli:

I am enclosing an execution in connection with the above matter, which I should like to have levied upon any non-exempt property of the defendant located in Washington County. Mr. William Thomas' address is 334 Edgemont Drive.

Please advise me if you are able to locate any property upon which to levy. I am enclosing our check to cover your fee for services.

Sincerely yours,

COMMENT:

1. The above letter could describe any property known to the writer for the information of the sheriff.

352.
REQUEST FOR CIVIL SERVICE COMMISSION RECORD FOR
USE IN APPEAL TO U.S. DISTRICT COURT

Dear Mr. Brownell:

Please send us the official copies of the record in the above-listed two cases involving our client, Joseph Jacobs. We need these official records for a suit we have filed in the United States District Court for the Southern District of California in behalf of Mr. Jacobs in connection with the matter.

We need these files just as soon as we can get them so would appreciate your expediting this request.

Thank you very much.

Sincerely yours,

COMMENT:

1. A letter is generally the most effective means of requesting official records from government agencies.

353.
REQUEST TO OFFICIAL IN SOCIAL SECURITY DISTRICT OFFICE TO
EXPEDITE CLIENT'S DISABILITY CLAIM

Dear Mr. Thomas:

I appreciate very much the courtesy you gave me on the telephone by locating the file of my friend John Mason and discussing the matter with me. I am enclosing a copy of the letter I have just written to Dr. Miller asking for an additional medical report in connection with John's disability condition.

I called John on the telephone today and suggested he or his wife go into the office and file the application for reconsideration as we discussed. I am certain they will be down there shortly. Anything you can do to expedite consideration of this matter will be greatly appreciated as I understand John is presently destitute, having been unable to work since October, 19XX.

Thank you very much.

Very sincerely,

COMMENT:

1. In dealing with a large agency which handles a multitude of cases and matters, letters are the most effective means of transacting business and asserting claims.

354.
TRANSMITTAL OF COMPLAINT OF UNFAIR LABOR PRACTICE TO
LABOR DEPARTMENT AREA DIRECTOR

Dear Mr. Powell:

You advised us in your letter of June 1 regarding the filing of an unfair labor practice complaint in behalf of Local 1304, AFGE, AFL-CIO, that the complaint must be filed on forms prescribed by the assistant secretary in accordance with Part 203, Chapter II, Title 29, Code of Federal Regulations. You were also kind enough to send us the applicable Rules and Regulations and the prescribed forms.

Enclosed are the original complaint, four copies of the complaint, and two copies of the supporting documents, which are being filed in accordance with Part 203 of the Rules and Regulations. I trust these papers are now in proper order.

Thank you very much.

Sincerely yours,

COMMENT:

1. When transmitting complaints or petititions involving adverse parties to a government agency, care should be taken to forward copies to all parties or their attorneys.

355.
REQUEST TO OFFICE OF SERVICEMEN'S GROUP LIFE INSURANCE TO PAY CLAIM FOR DEATH BENEFITS

Dear Ms. Shelby:

I wrote you on April 20, 19XX, regarding the efforts of Mr. Capehart's widow, Martha, to prove coverage of the Servicemen's Group Life Insurance at the time of Mr. Capehart's death. This was on August 8, some 63 days after his release from active duty.

My heart goes out to Mrs. Capehart in this case because of the personal tragedy here. I sincerely hope you will approve payment of this claim.

The following information is submitted in response to your letter of May 4, 19XX.

1. The Statement of Disability you enclosed has been completed and signed by the physician, Dr. Wilson. This statement shows that Mr. Capehart retrogressed prior to death; that he was totally disabled; that mentally he was not competent to endorse checks and direct the use of the proceeds; that disability continued until death and that his death was due to disability.

2. Also enclosed is a letter from Dr. Wilson stating that for practical purposes Mr. Capehart was totally disabled for some time before he went into the VA Hospital.

3. Martha tells me that he was sick for weeks and would not admit it to himself or to her. He obviously had, although undiagnosed, the severe chronic ulcerative colitis condition at the time of his release from active duty just 63 days before his death. He never found permanent work and never made the transition from being in the service. He was not mentally able to attend to his business affairs or convert his insurance before his death. His disability was comparable to the disability of a person with terminal cancer. His physical condition grew progressively worse, and he died as a result of his service connected disability, which disability remained with him and steadily grew worse until his death.

4. The VA Regional Office in Atlanta wrote Martha on November 27, 19XX, that Mr. Capehart was rated by the VA as being 100 percent disabled due to service-connected causes at the time of his death on August 8, 19XX. This certificate was furnished to help her get commissary store and exchange privileges. (She was able to get them.) A copy of the letter is enclosed.

Ms. Shelby, you will notice on the Attending Physician's Statement of Disability, that Mr. Capehart's symptoms first appeared in August, 19XX (he was released from service in June, 19XX). He was not able to attend to his business matters. He never really found work due to his disability of which he died so quickly after release from active duty. On behalf of Martha, I sincerely hope with the enclosed information you will approve payment.

Very sincerely,

COMMENT:

1. The above letter is a good example of documentation of a claim made in letter form.

356.
REQUEST TO U.S. SENATOR TO EXPEDITE PROCESSING OF
SOCIAL SECURITY DISABILITY CLAIM

Dear Senator Williams:

My long time friend Gary Johnson called me from Topeka today and told me that he has had two strokes in recent months, with the most recent one being over Thanksgiving. He also told me that he is totally disabled and unable to work and that he has put in an application for social security disability through the Topeka Social Security Office.

Gary said the application will be processed in the Topeka Social Security Office. He is most interested and anxious to have this application expedited and processed as soon as possible as his family is without funds for their livelihood.

I would appreciate very much anything you can do to contact the Topeka social security officials and request that they expedite processing of Gary's application.

Senator Williams, I very much appreciate your doing this, and I want to thank you also for Gary for anything you may be able to do to help him with this matter.

Very sincerely,

COMMENT:

1. Congressmen and senators are often able to do a lot in helping to expedite matters before government agencies.

357.

INVITATION TO U.S. SENATOR TO SPEAK AT LAW SCHOOL

Dear Senator Carter:

I am enclosing an invitation from Bill Brownell, president of the Student Bar Association of the Law School at the University of Tennessee, inviting you to speak at the law school, preferably in either April or May of this year, or at any time during the academic year.

If nothing else, you are getting this invitation in a rather round-about way. Let me explain.

Lydon Parker, who is the Chief Justice of the Tennessee Supreme Court and, incidentally, who is doing a tremendous job in law reform in Tennessee, suggested to Bill that he get me to write you a letter urging that you accept the invitation with the idea that it might help get you to accept. I think the way the Chief Justice connects me with you is that Charles Fanning, who you may remember as an instructor at Yale Law School, and who later became dean of the law school at Tennessee (before going back to Yale where he is now), told him at one time you and I were very good friends (and erroneously told him that we were roommates while we were at Yale Law School).

At any rate, both the Chief Justice and the students of the law school at the University of Tennessee would very much like you to come down. I hope it will be possible for you to accept. Of course, if you are able to accept, I will look forward to saying hello and to hearing you.

I suggest that you respond directly to Bill Brownell at his address at the Student Bar Association indicated on the attached letter. Please just send me a copy of your reply.

Hope you can make it.

Very sincerely,

COMMENT:

1. Many times a letter is the most effective and useful means of transmitting an invitation to speak or appear on a special occasion.

358.
RECOMMENDATION OF STUDENT TO SENATOR FOR SUMMER JOB

Dear Senator Jameson:

I would like to recommend Joan Mason for a summer job in your office. Mary and I consider the Mason family to be valued friends. George is a respected community leader here, and his daughter has already begun to show those qualities of leadership and genuine interest in her community.

I have enclosed Joan's resume and will be pleased if you will consider her.

Very sincerely,

COMMENT:

1. Letters are a convenient means of recommending applicants for employment.

SECTION 6
LETTERS TO FRIENDS

Letters to friends are often overlooked, but at the same time they are most important. The thoughtful lawyer should write letters of congratulation to his friends when they are in order, letters of condolence upon the death of some member of the friend's family and other letters according to the occasion. Lawyers can reach their friends easily through the medium of letters. Other types of letters to friends include thank you letters and social letters.

GROUP A
"Thank You" Letters

359.
ACKNOWLEDGMENT OF CONGRATULATORY LETTER ON
ADDITION OF MEMBERS TO FIRM

Dear Jim:

You were mighty thoughtful to write that nice note with respect to the addition of Bill Thomas and Joe Wilson to our firm. My partners join with me in expressing our appreciation.

With warmest personal regards.

Very sincerely,

360.
EXPRESSING THANKS FOR NEWS ARTICLE

Dear Maury:

It was a delightful surprise to receive your letter and attached column.

I am was so pleased with it that I showed it to Gary and then took it home to June to read. Your article was so well written, and I deeply appreciate the nice things you had to say about my book.

Incidentally, they are using it in the eleventh grade in the public schools of Kentucky, and I understand the students like it.

The other day I had occasion to go to Lexington Junior High School and speak to six of their eleventh grade classes about law, and I really enjoyed it. They were using the book there.

Maury, I hope you will drop by to see me the next time you are in Lexington. Thank you so much for your letter and the column.

Very sincerely,

COMMENT:

1. Letters of appreciation are helpful in promoting cordial and warm relations between a lawyer and his clients and friends.

361.
THANK YOU FOR GIFT

Dear Mr. Jones:

I want to thank you very, very much for the glasses which you gave to June and me. I assure you they will be put to good use at our home. We really needed some glasses, and those were very lovely.

You are most thoughtful, and I am deeply grateful to you for it. I consider you and Christine to be very good friends, as well as clients, and I want you to know that I am almost as pleased as you are that your business is doing so well.

I think it might be a good idea to call my secretary, Joan, and set up an appointment for you to come in, in view of the new insurance that you have taken out, and let's review your estate planning situation just to see that everything is the way you want it. It's a good idea to do this about once a year.

Please give my best to Christine. I certainly hope your plans to open the branch store in Albany will work out and that the new store will give a substantial boost to your overall sales.

Sincerely yours,

COMMENT:

1. It is, of course, highly appropriate for a lawyer to write a letter of thanks to a client or other person who has given him a gift.

362.
LETTER OF APPRECIATION TO REFERRING LAYMAN

Dear Mr. Ireland:

Thank you very much for referring Peter Bell. We shall do our best to handle the case in a satisfactory manner.

We want you to know that we very much appreciate the confidence that you have in us. We'll do our best to justify it.

Very sincerely,

COMMENT:

1. The above is a very thoughtful letter from the lawyer to the person who has referred a case to the lawyer.

GROUP B
Congratulation or Commendation

363.

ACKNOWLEDGMENT OF RECEIPT OF ANNOUNCEMENT OF INCORPORATION OF INVESTMENT BANKING COMPANY

Dear Jason:

I was very pleased to receive your announcement of the incorporation of the ABC Investment Banking Company.

I hope if you are up this way any time, you will drop in to see me, and, in the meantime, if I get any matters I feel may be of interest to you, I will either refer them to you or get in touch with you.

You have my best wishes for success.

Very sincerely,

COMMENT:

1. It is very thoughtful for a lawyer to write a letter of commendation or congratulation on appropriate occasions.

364.

CONGRATULATIONS ON ELECTION AS PRESIDENT OF SAVINGS AND LOAN ASSOCIATION

Dear Randy:

Heartiest congratulations on your election to the presidency of ABC Savings & Loan. Under your leadership, ABC will continue to grow as it has during the years when Albert was president. You will maintain, and develop to even greater degree, the great record which Albert has made during the twenty-two years of his leadership.

It is a great privilege to be a depositer of ABC Savings & Loan, and, more than that, I appreciate and cherish your friendship.

With every good wish for your continued success, and I know the years that lie ahead will be years of progress and success for ABC Savings & Loan and all of its friends. With kindest regards, as always.

Very sincerely,

365.
TRIBUTE TO WRITER OF EDITORIAL ON PATRIOTISM

Dear Randall:

John Belew in Concord was kind enough to send me a copy of your guest editorial which appeared in the *Manchester Guardian*, together with a copy of his letter to you dated May 8.

I am very grateful to John for letting me share the joy I know he felt when he read your article. It is beautiful. I have done a little writing, and so I know that first, it required word power to express the ideas so well, and second, and most important, it required the underlying thoughts and emotions with regard to our country which you so beautifully expressed.

Especially admirable is your ability to look through form to the substance of our country, your ability to be sentimental without being mawkish, your ability to avoid being defensive, and your ability to perceive the whole and not be obsessed by problems.

Reading your article brought me happiness.

Very sincerely,

GROUP C
Social Letters

366.
REPORT OF EFFORTS TO HELP SECURE SPEAKER FOR PROGRAM

Dear Bill:

I enjoyed very much meeting you and talking with you while you were in Cleveland.

I thought your letter to Senator Jones was very well written, and I have, today, dictated a personal letter to him expressing my hope that he can accept the invitation. I also took the liberty of using Judge Hocker's name in behalf of the invitation, and I am hopeful that the reply will be favorable.

I suggested in my letter that he reply directly to you at your address at the University. I also asked him to send me a copy.

Good luck and I hope the next time you are up this way you will drop in to see me. In the event I get down to the University I will certainly try to look you up.

Very sincerely,

SECTION 7
LETTERS TO OTHER ADDRESSEES

Letters to other addressees cover a multitude of correspondence from a lawyer's office addressed to addressees not listed above. Examples would be letters giving notice or information to accountants, mortgage companies, insurance companies, etc.

Other letters in this category include letters giving a title opinion to a bank, to a mortgage company, or to a party other than a client. Further examples include letters requesting information or action from companies or individuals other than addresses heretofore covered.

GROUP A
Giving Notice or Information

367.

**REQUEST TO CREDITOR TO WITHHOLD ACTION TO COLLECT
ACCOUNT PENDING SETTLEMENT OF DIVORCE CASE**

Dear Mr. Hacker:

Our client, Catherine Bell, has given us a copy of your medical bill which you sent her regarding an account in the amount of $840.

Please be advised that we are representing her in connection with a divorce proceeding with her husband, Mr. Wilson Bell. They have two minor children, and at the moment Catherine is destitute. Just as soon as we can make satisfactory arrangements regarding a division of the property between the parties and the wife's financial support, Catherine has advised us to tell you that this matter will be taken care of.

We will appreciate your bearing with us on this matter.

Very sincerely,

COMMENT:

1. By writing other parties, the lawyer can often assist the client prior to a claim or a matter being forwarded to opposing attorneys for handling.

368.

CANCELLATION OF CLIENT'S PURCHASE CONTRACTS

Dear Mr. Wilson:

We hereby cancel the attached purchase contracts between Paul Murphy, seller, and Delbert Parker and wife, Mary Parker, purchasers.

These contracts relate to Lot 4, Block 5, Fairmont Subdivision and Lot 23, Block 17, Fairmont Subdivision, Second Addition.

This cancellation is in accordance with the written provisions of the contracts whereby seller is entitled to possession of the property, and neither party shall have any further right, remedy or liability.

It will not be necessary to send us a letter of cancellation as this letter will serve that purpose.

Yours very truly,

COMMENT:

1. Care should be made in cancelling a contract to comply with any provisions contained in the contract.

369.

REPORT TO AUDITORS OF OPEN ENGAGEMENTS FOR CLIENT AND IMPENDING LITIGATION AND CLAIMS

Dear Mrs. Thomas:

We have been advised by ABC Electronics Company that you are making your usual examination of their accounts and that we should furnish you with a list of all open engagements we are handling for ABC Electronics Co. as of June 30, 19XX, together with a description of any other matters to which we have devoted substantial attention in the form of legal consultation involving impending litigation or claims by or against, or a contingent liability of, the company or any of its subsidiaries at June 30, or arising subsequently.

We are now representing ABC Electronics Co. in connection with a lawsuit filed on or about March 18, 19XX, wherein ABC Electronics Co. is plaintiff and DEF, Inc. and GHI, Inc. are defendants.

This suit consists of a complaint for injunctive relief to restrain the defendants from infringing plaintiff's trade secrets. A temporary restraining order was issued by the Circuit Court of Lincoln County, where the suit was filed, restraining the defendants from divulging information relating to plaintiff's trade secrets data, knowhow, techniques, etc. The suit does not specifically seek money damages, and none are anticipated at the present time. There is no counterclaim of any type against ABC Electronics Co.

At the present time, we are not representing ABC Electronics Co. in connection with any other matter involving impending litigation or claims by or against or a contingent liability of ABC Electronics Co. as of June 30, 19XX, or arising subsequently.

In the event you would like to have additional information regarding this matter, please let us know.

Sincerely yours,

COMMENT:

1. Accountants often write lawyers requesting information in connection with audits of clients. It is a good idea for the lawyer to maintain a file of answers to such letters as they will probably receive them year after year regarding the same clients.

370.
TRANSMITTAL TO BANK TRUST OFFICER OF COPIES OF WILLS

Dear Mr. Clark:

Enclosed are copies of the wills of Mr. and Mrs. Randolph Kaufman in which the bank is named as Trustee.

I am forwarding these copies to you for your review and any suggestions which you may have.

Mr. and Mrs. Kaufman are presently in the process of changing the beneficiary on their life insurance coverage to the bank, as Trustee.

Very sincerely,

371.
TRANSMITTAL TO BANK TRUST OFFICER OF CORRECTED CODICILS
AND AMENDMENT TO REVOCABLE LIFE INSURANCE TRUST

Dear Mr. Wallace:

Thank you for your letter of September 18 regarding the codicils to the wills of Mr. and Mrs. Jacobs, as well as the First Amendment to the Revocable Life Insurance Trust Agreement of Mr. Jacobs.

We appreciate your pointing out the correct date of the trust as May 23 instead of May 8. These documents have been redone and reexecuted with the correct date. They are enclosed with this letter.

Thank you very much for your help in connection with this matter.

Sincerely yours,

372.
TRANSMITTAL TO INSURANCE COMPANY OF POLICY CERTIFICATE

Dear Mr. Jennings:

As requested in your letter of December 3, 19XX, enclosed is a copy of the policy certificate.

Your prompt attention to this matter will be appreciated.

Thank you.

Very sincerely,

373.

TRANSMITTAL TO INSURANCE AGENT OF CLIENT'S INSURANCE POLICY

Dear Mr. Clayton:

Pursuant to Dr. and Mrs. Bell's request, we are enclosing the original ABC Insurance Company Policy Number 1000.

Please let us know if there is anything further we may do to be of assistance to you with this matter.

Sincerely yours,

374.

TRANSMITTAL TO INSURANCE COMPANY OF POLICY AND CHANGE OF BENEFICIARY FORM

Dear Mr. Mayhall:

Pursuant to your letter of April 27, 19XX, we are enclosing the above-described policy and the executed change of beneficiary form.

Thank you very much.

Yours very sincerely,

375.

REPLY TO INSURANCE COMPANY WITH REQUESTED INFORMATION

Dear Mr. Irving:

In reply to your letter of May 6, we submit the following answers in seriatim:

(1) Policy 1000
(2) Policy 604
(3) Policy 8460
(4) Policy 1246
(5) Policy 1580
(6) Policy 1340
(7) Policy 1250

If you need any further information, please advise.

Sincerely,

COMMENT:

1. The above letter, if appropriate, could state or restate the action desired.

376.
AUTHORIZATION TO SAVINGS AND LOAN ASSOCIATION FOR
WITHDRAWAL FROM GUARDIANSHIP ACCOUNT

Dear Mrs. Johnson:

Please allow Mrs. Gurley to withdraw $500 for the purpose of paying expenses in behalf of Jason. These funds are in a guardianship account for his benefit.

Your cooperation in this matter is greatly appreciated.

Very sincerely,

COMMENT:

1. Letters such as the above are effective in transmitting consent or instructions, as well as in making a permanent record of the action taken.

377.
NOTICE TO APPLICANT FOR LEGAL ASSISTANT POSITION THAT
FIRM DOES NOT HAVE ANY OPENING

Dear Mrs. Macon:

I very much appreciate your writing me, and I was very much impressed with your resume. Your background looks strong, particularly in view of the fact that you have a college degree and have completed the Lawyer's Assistant Program at Emory University.

I am sorry that we simply don't have an opening at this time.

Very sincerely,

COMMENT:

1. The lawyer should always acknowledge a written application for employment. It is a good idea to write all applicants for employment following interviews after a decision is made so·that unsuccessful applicants will be properly advised.

378.

TRANSMITTAL OF RELEASE TO INSURANCE COMPANY PURSUANT TO SETTLEMENT OF CASE

Dear Mrs. Clark:

Enclosed is a signed release in the case of Wilma Powers vs. Brownell Van Lines, Inc.

The release is signed by Wilma Powers and her husband, George Powers, and I have delivered the settlement check to them upon receiving the signed release.

I am glad we have concluded this matter.

Sincerely yours,

COMMENT:

1. Some expression of appreciation may be appropriate in letters such as the above.

379.

NOTICE TO INSURANCE COMPANY OF PERSONAL INJURY CLAIM AGAINST THEIR INSURED

Dear Mrs. Paul:

Please be advised that our firm represents the above-referenced individual concerning an accident which occurred on the above date, involving your above-named insured. I am presently attempting to obtain possession of our client's medical records, and, as soon as I have been able to do so, I will again contact your office in an effort to settle the matter without litigation.

Please feel free to contact me concerning this matter.

Your cooperation in this matter will be greatly appreciated.

Sincerely yours,

COMMENT:

1. The above letter could be personalized by using specific names and details regarding the claim.

380.

REPORT TO INSURANCE ADJUSTERS OF PERSONAL INJURY CLAIM

Dear Mr. Poundstone:

I am now in a position to submit a claim for $24,000 in the above matter.

I have shown you heretofore the medical statement of his major doctor, Dr. Hamilton of the Department of Plastic Surgery at the Bellevue Hospital, whose summary was as follows:

"In summary, this man sustained a tripod fracture of his left malar bone requiring open operative reduction and internal fixation. His prognosis referable to this injury is good in that although he will be left with some scarring and perhaps bony irregularity, there should be little, if any, persistent functional impairment."

More recently he has been examined in the Bellevue Hospital eye clinic, and his sight is now in line and hopefully will be all right.

The ineradicable defects resulting from this injury are, and will remain, an out-of-line countenance, a drooping of the whole right side of his face, most noticeable in his right eye and in the right side of his mouth, all causing indistinct speech. This disfigurement is his permanent burden.

His medical costs are as follows:

1. Hospital costs June 5, 19XX to June 8, 19XX	$1798.20
2. Private clinic, Department of Anesthesiology	196.00
3. Dr. Hamilton's report	25.00

So far I have no filings for:

Clinic charges on July 12, 19XX, July 18, 19XX (removal of fixation wires), July 26, 19XX and August 12, 19XX. Should charges for services on these occasions be made while we are negotiating a settlement, they will be included.

This young man recently turned nineteen and had his heart set upon an overseas Job Corps assignment. He has passed all physical examinations and was in line for consideration by the authorities. The accident in June ruined this chance, and he cannot start over again on an application until after he attends his next checkup with Dr. Hamilton in November. This means he has had a seven months occupational frustration.

I have analyzed this young man's case from the point of view of a jury trial, should the matter be taken to court. Hospitalization for ten days; major orthopedic and plastic surgery; subsequent difficulties with sight, eating, and speech; post-operative visits to the hospital and home therapy; very real pain and general mental and physical suffering; his employment dislocation; and his permanent disfigurement— these are the principal factors.

True, William Kelsey comes from a low income bracket of our society, but—as Mr. Jefferson pointed out so eloquently—he is the equal of any other man under the law. Suppose he had been a Ford, a Kennedy, even a Kissinger. Moreover, his serious and inexcusable injury was caused by a grossly negligent person who was substantially under the influence of intoxicants.

I have reviewed Mr. Kelsey's case carefully with him and with the senior members of his family, and I am authorized to make without prejudice an out-of-court settlement offer in the sum of $24,000, plus medical costs.

Should your company wish to have its own medical men examine Mr. Kelsey for question or confirmation of the injuries I have reported, I shall be glad to arrange for such an examination. Also, I shall be happy to supply as best I can the answers to any questions you may have.

I shall look forward to hearing from you reasonably soon.

Sincerely yours,

COMMENT:

1. The above letter is a good example of what can be done in a letter in connection with negotiations for settlement.

381.
TRANSMITTAL OF TITLE EXAMINATION TO BANK PRESIDENT

Dear Mr. Fanning:

Enclosed is the title examination for the mortgage from Dr. and Mrs. Thomas. If you desire an opinion reflecting your mortgage after it has been recorded, please let me know, and I will be pleased fo furnish it.

I appreciate so very much your referring Dr. Thomas to us. It was a pleasure to get to know him and to represent him in this matter.

With kindest personal regards.

Sincerely yours,

382.
**TRANSMITTAL TO BANK MORTGAGE LOAN DEPARTMENT OF
LOAN CLOSING PAPERS**

Dear Mr. Alvarez:

The above referenced loan was closed on October 16, 19XX, and in this respect I am enclosing the following:

1. Original note.
2. Copy of sales and loan closing statement.
3. Certified copy of mortgage.

If we can be of further assistance in this matter, please notify us.

Very sincerely,

COMMENT:

1. The above letter could be concluded with an expression of thanks or gratitude.

383.
TRANSMITTAL TO MORTGAGE COMPANY OF
LOAN CLOSING PAPERS

Dear Mrs. Whaley:

The above referenced loan was closed on April 18, 19XX, and in this respect I am enclosing the following:

1. Our Check No. 3807 in the amount of $1,240, with voucher attached.
2. Our Check No. 3808 in the amount of $284, with voucher attached.
3. Three copies of note.
4. Two copies of mortgage.
5. Homeowner's insurance policy, No. 1100, with paid receipt attached.
6. Two copies of FHA Firm Commitment.
7. Copy of deed.
8. Tax information letter.
9. Employment and credit affidavit.
10. Flood insurance letter.
11. Three copies of sales and loan closing statement.
12. Original and two copies of disclosure statement.
13. Two copies of mortgage terms.
14. MC-13.
15. Title Insurance Policy No. 2000 issued by ABC Title Company.

If we can be of further assistance to you, please call us.

Very sincerely,

COMMENT:

1. The above letter could conclude with an expression of thanks or gratitude.

384.
REPORT TO BANK PRESIDENT OF CONFERENCE WITH
SMALL BUSINESS ADMINISTRATION LOAN OFFICER ON
APPLICATION FOR SBA LOAN

Dear Mr. Hamilton:

Horace Williams and I had a very successful visit with Joe Norton of SBA in Dallas yesterday regarding the loan application of Norton Industries, Inc. for a $350,000 SBA Loan. Joe Norton's telephone numbers are: 841-3000 and 841-3001.

In the loan application we mentioned that ABC Bank has given Norton Industries, Inc., a temporary line of credit of $100,000 in anticipation of this loan. Joe Norton said that he would like to have a letter from you regarding the matter of the line of credit and the fact that the temporary loan of $75,000 will be repaid out of the loan proceeds. Horace and I both think it will be a good idea for you to call him and get very clear in your mind the exact kind of letter he would like to have on it. He posed no problems regarding the matter and merely said that he would like to have documentation in the file about it.

I am enclosing for your information a copy of a letter I wrote to Horace outlining other things we need to do to meet all of the requirements of the SBA as outlined by Joe Norton in our conference in order to have a complete application.

Again, Brad, I want to thank you for all your help and cooperation in connection with this matter. You are the best banker in town to work with on an SBA loan application, and I know that Horace and Joe Norton appreciate your help in expediting this application.

Very sincerely,

COMMENT:

1. Letters such as the above are effective in reporting the status of a matter to interested parties.

385.
REPORT TO AUDITORS OF INCOME TAX DEFICIENCIES ASSERTED BY IRS AGAINST CLIENT

Dear Mr. Bailey:

In connection with the audit of ABC, Inc., you have indicated to us that you need to have a statement from us as counsel for ABC, Inc., with respect to the income tax deficiencies asserted against ABC, Inc. by the United States Treasury Department.

Federal income tax deficiencies have been asserted by the Treasury Department against ABC, Inc. as follows:

1. For calendar year of 19XX $34,000
2. For calendar year of 19XX $28,760

Negotiations for settlement of the above mentioned tax deficiencies have been going on for quite some time, and, in our opinion, there is a very good prospect of settlement of the asserted deficiencies at a figure very substantially below the total asserted deficiencies.

Very sincerely,

386.
LETTER TO ACCOUNTANT REGARDING TAX PROBLEM OF CLIENT

Dear Mr. Miller:

I am enclosing some material regarding the tax liability of ABC, Inc., in connection with the bad debt deduction taken on the $6,000 note of Tony Hamilton paid by ABC, Inc. as guarantor.

These authorities are as follows:

(a) Exhibit 1. IRS Code Section 166.
(b) Exhibit 2. Reg. Sec. 1.166-8.
(c) Exhibit 3. Rabkin and Johnston, Discussion of Guarantor.
(d) Exhibit 4. Research Institute of America, Discussion and Citation of Authorities Regarding Guarantors' Bad Debts.
(e) Exhibit 5. General Discussion of Guaranty, Suretyship and Indemnity.

In the event Tony Hamilton used the proceeds of his loan in his business, it appears payment of the loan as guarantor by ABC, Inc. would fall within IRS Section 166 (f). I called Wilson Garrett on this point and am trying to reach Tony Hamilton to find out what he did with the proceeds of his loan. Wilson said he thinks he used most of it to pay back taxes. This poses an interesting question as to whether payment of back taxes by an individual engaged in a dental practice would be use of funds for business or for payment of a personal obligation. I understand the IRS was about to lock his doors, and I would think this would make it more like a business consideration.

At any rate, I think the critical factor is whether the transaction was entered into for profit by ABC, Inc. or not. If it simply represented a gift to a relative or friend, no deduction for a bad debt would be permitted. *Hoyt v. Com'r*, 145 F.2d 634. However, Wilson says there is no question that he entered into the transaction for profit.

The fact that the transaction was entered into for profit and there was consideration for the guaranty of ABC, Inc. I think would control, and, accordingly, a bad debt deduction should be allowed. The fact that ABC, Inc. subsequently assigned the obligation it received from Tony Hamilton as consideration for the guaranty should not make any difference. I have found absolutely no authority for such a distinction to be drawn in connection with proposed disallowance of a bad debt.

Pete, after you have had a chance to review the enclosed material, if you want me to do anything further on this, let me know.

Very sincerely,

COMMENT:

1. Letters like this are especially helpful in tax matters in expressing the position of a client, discussing the relevant law, and discussing the facts involved.
2. All tax law legal authorities should be checked against current law.

387.
REPORT REGARDING SPEAKER FOR BAR ASSOCIATION MEETING

   Dear Mrs. Jackson:

   Due to a lack of response from Paul Thomas, president of the Wilmington County Bar Association, to my letter of April 18, 19XX, regarding our efforts to have Max Randolph as a speaker for one of our monthly meetings, I conclude there is not much interest in the matter.

   Let me know if you think there is anything further I should do. I do want to congratulate you, both for your willingness to work hard and the public spirit you have which prompts you to do so.

   Very sincerely,

COMMENT:

1. It is helpful in letters which give a negative report or undesired information to conclude on a strong positive note. The above letter does this.

388.
NOTICE TO CLIENT'S EMPLOYER OF TIME REQUIRED BY
CLIENT IN CONFERENCE AND IN COURT

   Dear Mr. Rich:

   Please be advised that Mr. Albert Boswell has been in my office for consultation on Monday afternoon, April 4, April 11, April 13, and today, April 24. Mr. Boswell is due in court this Monday, April 27 at 9:00 a.m. before Circuit Judge Watson.

   If any additional information is needed, please advise.

   Very sincerely,

389.
RECOMMENDATION OF PHOTOGRAPHER TO PUBLISHER

Dear Mr. Hudson:

This will confirm our telephone conversation today when I told you of the work my good friend Joe Wells is doing in the field of photography.

Specifically, in the event you have any need for a photographer in connection with the preparation of a book or other material, I think Joe could do a good job for you.

I wanted to write you this letter so you would have his name and address which are:

> Joseph H. Wells
> 304 G Gunnison Lane
> Evanston, Illinois

Thank you very much.

Very sincerely,

GROUP B
Giving Assurance or Opinion

390.
ADVICE ON SALE OF STOCK

Dear Boswell:

In connection with the sale of 1000 shares of common stock (the "Stock") of ABC, Inc. for the account of Joseph Hacker and Edith W. Hacker, please be advised of the following:

1. The broker did no more than execute the order or orders to sell the Stock as agent for Joseph Hacker and Edith W. Hacker and, in connection with such sales, the broker received no more than the usual and customary broker's commission.

2. The broker has not solicited or arranged for the solicitation of customer's orders to buy the Stock in anticipation of or in connection with the sale of the Stock; *provided, however,* that the foregoing did not preclude inquiries of other brokers or dealers who had indicated an interest in the company's common stock within the preceding 60 days.

3. After reasonable inquiry, we are not aware of circumstances indicating that Joseph Hacker or Edith W. Hacker are underwriters with respect to the Stock or that the sale of the Stock is part of a distribution of securities of the company.

Sincerely yours,

COMMENT:

1. The above letter should be ended with a complimentary closing. The lawyer could further personalize it by making some comment regarding the matter which would be of interest to the reader.

391.
LETTER FOR CLIENT ON SALE OF STOCK

Dear Mr. Jackson:

The undersigned has sold 3000 shares of common stock (the "Stock") of ABC, Inc. (the "Company") through Miller, Reeves & Rhodes on April 27, 19XX. Midland Securities Trust Company, the transfer agent, has requested our opinion to the effect that such sale was not in violation of Rule 144 under the Securities Act of 1933, as amended. In connection with such request, we have reviewed Rule 144 and represent and certify the following:

1. No shares of the Company's common stock have been sold by or for the account of the undersigned or any other related "person" [as that term is defined in Rule 144 (a) (2)] during the six months prior to April 22, 19XX, nor subsequent to the sale of the Stock to the date hereof.

2. The undersigned did not solicit or arrange for the solicitation of orders to buy the Stock in anticipation of, or in connection with, such sale.

3. The undersigned did not make, and will not make, any payment in connection with the offering or sale of the Stock to any person other than Walker W. Parker.

4. The undersigned has caused to be transmitted to the Securities and Exchange Commission, 500 Capital Street, N.W., Washington, D.C. 20549, three signed copies of the Notice of Proposed Sale of Securities pursuant to Rule 144 (Form 144).

5. The undersigned does not intend to sell additional shares of the Company's common stock through any means, except in compliance with the Federal securities laws.

6. The undersigned has been the beneficial owner of the Stock for more than two years prior to sale, and the consideration for such Stock was given more than two years prior to the sale.

Yours very truly,

COMMENT:

1. The above letter could conclude with a request for any action that is desired. In addition, complimentary remarks could be made such as an expression of thanks for consideration.

392.
CERTIFICATION TO MORTGAGE LENDER THAT
PROPERTY IS NOT IN FLOOD PRONE AREA

Dear Mr. Chapman:

This is to certify that I have checked with the planning commission of the City of St. Louis and determined that the property owned by the above-referenced clients, which is located at the above-referenced location, is not located in a flood prone area. I have also determined that the community has qualified for the Federal Insurance Program, although it is not in a flood prone area.

Sincerely yours,

GROUP C
Requesting Information

393.
REQUEST TO INSURANCE AGENT FOR STATUS OF CLAIM

Dear Mr. Eaton:

Enclosed is a copy of our letter of June 13, 19XX, to you regarding the above-referenced matter. We would appreciate being advised of the status of this claim. Thank you very much for your assistance in this matter.

Very sincerely,

COMMENT:

1. Letters are a good means of requesting the status of a claim as well as giving the status of a claim.

394.
REQUEST TO INSURANCE AGENT FOR NEW POLICY NUMBER FOR
BUY-SELL AGREEMENT

Dear Mr. Cornwall:

I thought we had a very good meeting this morning regarding the buy-sell agreement for ABC, Inc. I think the decisions regarding permanent life insurance were sound and farsighted. I am also thankful to you for bringing the matter to a head and emphasizing the importance of actually executing a buy-sell agreement.

I would like to have the new policy numbers for use with the revised agreement. Please let me have them just as soon as you get them.

Thank you very much. I know that Pat, Horace, and Bill are grateful to you for your interest and for the professional manner in which you have approached the problem.

Sincerely yours,

395.
REQUEST FOR INFORMATION FROM CLIENT'S INSURANCE COMPANY REGARDING SUBROGATION

Dear Mr. Williams:

We have been retained to represent Alberto Alvarez in a personal injury matter.

Your company provides insurance coverage for our client.

Shortly, a complaint will be filed in this matter.

The purpose of this letter is to notify you that the complaint will seek reimbursement for the amount of the deductible loss borne by our client. It will not in any way seek an amount to which you are entitled by subrogation.

Some insurance companies have instituted a procedure whereby they seek reimbursement from a negligent third party for payments made to their insured. We would appreciate being advised whether your company has such a "trust agreement" and whether you will seek such reimbursement. If you do, then please be advised that such recovery will be reduced by a reasonable attorney's fee if made through our efforts.

Sincerely yours,

COMMENT:

1. It is a good idea at the beginning of a matter to resolve all questions regarding subrogation and attorney's fees regarding recovery of amounts which may be subject to subrogation.

396.
REQUEST TO MORTGAGE COMPANY FOR INFORMATION FOR EQUITY SALE OF HOUSE

Dear Mrs. Taylor:

We are handling an equity sale for the above-described property. I shall appreciate your forwarding to me a statement of the outstanding principal balance, the date of the last paid installment, and the status of the escrow account, including any overage which may exist in the escrow account at the present time.

It is our understanding you will have the requested statement in the mail to us within 24 hours after this request is received by you.

Thank you for your attention to this matter.

Sincerely yours,

COMMENT:

1. The statement in paragraph two regarding reply within twenty-four hours should be deleted unless appropriate.

397.
REQUEST TO MORTGAGE COMPANY FOR
MORTGAGE INFORMATION FOR EQUITY TRANSFER

Dear Mrs. Murphy:

Our firm is handling a transfer of title to the above-referenced property, and the mortgage held by your company will be assumed by the purchaser.

Please furnish the undersigned the following information:

1. Outstanding principal balance as of the date of August 7, 19XX.
2. Amount of transfer fee charged by your company.
3. Whether or not the transfer and assumption must be consented to or approved by your company.
4. Date of last payment and payment period covered by last payment.
5. Status of escrow account indicating surplus or deficiency.

Very sincerely,

COMMENT:

1. The above letter could be concluded with an expression of thanks.

398.
REQUEST TO MORTGAGE COMPANY FOR INFORMATION FOR
SALE OF HOUSE SUBJECT TO MORTGAGE

Dear Mrs. Paul:

Our office is handling an equity sale of the above-described property, and I shall appreciate your furnishing to us the following information regarding the loan which is secured by this real estate:

1. The outstanding principal balance;
2. The current status of the escrow fund, including any excess or deficiency;
3. The date of the last payment;
4. The amount of the monthly payment; and
5. The amount of your transfer fee.

Thank you for your attention to this matter.

Sincerely yours,

COMMENT:

1. Many matters such as the above are customarily handled with a letter requesting information.

399.
REQUEST TO MORTGAGE COMPANY FOR AMOUNT TO PAY MORTGAGE IN FULL

Dear Mr. Jones:

Our firm is handling a sale of the above-referenced property, and the mortgage held by your company will be paid in full.

Please furnish the undersigned the following information:

1. Payoff as of November 16, 19XX, including any penalty, additional interest, late charges or other charges.
2. Advance notice required to pay off mortgage.
3. Status of escrow account indicating surplus or deficiency.
4. Per diem interest charged after November 16, 19XX.

Sincerely yours,

COMMENT:

1. The above letter could be concluded with an expression of thanks.

400.
REQUEST TO BANK PRESIDENT FOR STATUS OF APPLICATION FOR LINE OF CREDIT GUARANTY BY SMALL BUSINESS ADMINISTRATION

Dear Mr. Capehart:

Some time ago our client, Wallace Jones, asked us to check with you regarding the status of the application for a line of credit guaranty which we prepared.

I would appreciate your advice on this and am hopeful we can move forward with it.

Yours sincerely,

COMMENT:

1. A letter such as the above is a tactful way of requesting the addressee to take action on the matter which has been pending before him for some time.

401.
REQUEST TO WORKMEN'S COMPENSATION CARRIER FOR
RESULTS OF INVESTIGATION OF ACCIDENT

Dear Mr. Goodwin:

Our client was injured in an accident which is covered by the workmen's compensation laws of the State of Iowa.

It appears, from our preliminary investigation, that the negligence of a third party contributed to and caused the injuries to our client.

We are informed and believe that you have made an investigation into the circumstances of the accident and injury.

We would appreciate it if you would make the results of that investigation known to us. The lawsuit we are filing on behalf of our client probably will result in reimbursement to your insurance company for the amount it has paid out in workmen's compensation benefits.

We believe it is in our mutual interest to cooperate in the pursuit of this claim.

Very sincerely,

COMMENT:

1. The above is a good example of the effective employment of a letter to secure information regarding a claim.

402.
REQUEST TO EMPLOYER BY LEGAL AID SOCIETY FOR
PAY INFORMATION TO HELP DETERMINE ELIGIBILITY FOR
LEGAL ASSISTANCE

Dear Mr. Malone:

The Legal Aid Society is attempting to determine the eligibility of Rudy Valentine and his wife for free legal services in a matter in which they have requested the society's assistance. If this applicant is one of your employees, you can hasten the determination of his or her eligibility for legal services by furnishing us the following information concerning your employment of the applicant:

RATE OF PAY:
IF HOURLY WAGE, AVERAGE NUMBER OF HOURS WORKED PER WEEK:

Please return the completed form in the enclosed stamped, self-addressed envelope.

Your cooperation and assistance in establishing the applicant's eligibility are greatly appreciated.

Very sincerely,

COMMENT:

1. It may be appropriate, or even required by law, to enclose a written consent to the employer, signed by the employee, to furnish the information.

GROUP D

Requesting Action

403.
TRANSMITTAL OF CHECK TO BANK TO PAY LOAN OF CLIENT

Dear Mr. Miller:

Enclosed is a check for $1,750 from our client Michael Thomas in payment of Loan Number 3420. (This loan number was given to us by phone on September 18 by your loan department.)

We would appreciate it if you would mail us the note, marked paid. Also, will you check and see if this note was filed with the State Uniform Commercial Code Division. If so, please file a termination statement.

Thank you very much.

Very sincerely,

COMMENT:

1. Letters transmitting payment are helpful in specifying the items paid and make a permanent record of the payment.

404.
REQUEST TO EMPLOYER TO AID IN COLLECTION OF EMPLOYEE'S ACCOUNT

Dear Mr. Chapman:

Your employee, Rowen Pillsbury, owes my client the sum of $2,400. We have gone to a great deal of trouble without getting any recent payments.

As you know, garnishment is a lot of extra bother for all concerned.

If you would give this party a gentle nudge and aim him in our direction, it would be a gracious favor.

Very sincerely,

COMMENT:

1. Care should be taken to see that any substantive law which restricts letters such as the above is complied with. The above letter could conclude with a request for any action that is desired.

405.
REQUEST TO CORPORATION SERVICE COMPANY TO FILE CERTIFICATE
OF AMENDMENT WITH SECRETARY OF STATE

Dear Mrs. Smith:

I am enclosing a copy of a letter dated February 17 regarding ABC Corporation, signed by Joseph Johnson, tax department of your office.

We have prepared and the company has executed a Certificate of Amendment to the Certificate of Incorporation increasing the B Common, par value $100 stock to 40,000 shares.

We would appreciate it very much if you would please file this Certificate of Amendment with the Secretary of State of Delaware and let us have your bill for costs and expenses in connection with filing this certificate.

In the event you have any questions or suggestions, please call me.

Thank you very much.

Very sincerely,

COMMENT:

1. Letters of transmittal should accompany documents transmitted for filing for the purpose of specifying the action desired as well as making a permanent record of it.

406.

REQUEST TO INSURANCE COMPANY FOR CHANGE OF BENEFICIARIES

Dear Mr. O'Donnell:

In our last correspondence to you dated November 6, we requested that Mr. Frank McIntyre's alternate beneficiary be changed to the Trustee named in his Last Will and Testament dated the 25th day of April, 19XX. In response to our letter, we received the enclosed beneficiary changes to Mr. McIntyre's policies number 1108 and 1109 changing his beneficiary to: "Joan McIntyre, if surviving the insured, otherwise to Trustee named in my Last Will and Testament dated the 25th day of April, 19XX." Please be advised that "Joan McIntyre" is unknown to Mr. McIntyre and that the primary beneficiary on his policies should remain his wife, Martha Williams McIntyre.

We would appreciate your issuing a new beneficiary change form stating Mr. McIntyre's beneficiary as follows: "Martha Williams McIntyre, if surviving the insured, otherwise to the Trustee named in insured Last Will and Testament dated the 25th day of April, 19XX."

Your prompt attention to this matter will be appreciated.

Sincerely yours,

COMMENT:

1. The matter of changing the beneficiaries of insurance polices is very important. Lawyers should take care to see that all changes of beneficiaries requested by their clients are actually made on the records of the insurance company. Letters such as the above are helpful in this regard.

407.
REQUEST TO INSURANCE COMPANY FOR FORMS TO
ASSIGN LIFE INSURANCE POLICIES

Gentlemen:

We are preparing assignments on the following life insurance policies:

Policy No.	Date	Face Amount
1000	June 4, 19XX	$50,000
2000	August 18, 19XX	$75,000
3000	September 12, 19XX	$100,000

These assignments are from William Mason to Linda Nix Mason, and further, from Linda Nix Mason to ABC National Bank, as Trustee of ABC, Inc. Employees Trust.

Please send to us for this purpose, your blank forms used in the assignment of life insurance policies.

Thank you very much.

Sincerely yours,

COMMENT:

1. Insurance companies generally have forms for use in connection with assignment of their policies as well as change of beneficiaries. The lawyer should secure such forms and carefully complete them for the client or have the insurance agent do it and verify that it has been done.

408.
TRANSMITTAL OF LETTERS TO INSURANCE COMPANY AND REQUEST
FOR REVIEW AND ACKNOWLEDGMENT OF CLAIM FOR BENEFITS

Dear Mr. George:

Enclosed is a copy of a letter we received from Mr. Conrad Mason of your office, advising us of the termination as of March 23, 19XX, of the above policy number.

Please find enclosed correspondence dated August 16, 19XX, from your company stating that coverage had been extended to February 14, 19XX, under the policy for Mr. Williams.

Also, enclosed is correspondence from your company dated September 12, 19XX, stating that Mr. Williams has $50,000 of life insurance on the ABC, Inc., Group Plan which he had with the corporation.

Please review these documents and call me upon your receipt of them.

Very sincerely,

COMMENT:

1. A letter such as the above might state explicitly the action desired unless it is clearly understood.

409.
TRANSMITTAL TO INSURANCE COMPANY OF PROOF OF
DEATH FORM AND REQUEST FOR PAYMENT OF CLAIM

Dear Mr. Jacobs:

Please find enclosed the executed proof of death form which you forwarded to our office on April 27. Also enclosed is a certified death certificate.

Your prompt handling of this claim will be appreciated.

Thank you.

Very sincerely,

COMMENT:

1. Life insurance proceeds are generally claimed and handled by correspondence between lawyer and the insurance company.

410.
REQUEST TO NEWSPAPER FOR PUBLICATION OF NOTICE OF
APPOINTMENT OF ADMINISTRATOR WITH CHECK FOR PAYMENT
ENCLOSED AND REQUEST FOR PROOF OF PUBLICATION

Dear Mr. Sims:

Enclosed is our check made to your order in the amount of $35 for publication of Notice of Appointment of Administrator in the above-referenced estate.

Please publish the notice with the correction of spelling. After the completion of publication, please furnish me the Proof of Publication.

Yours very truly,

411.
ORDER TO PUBLISHERS FOR LAW BOOK

Gentlemen:

Please send us one copy of *Legal Anecdotes*.

Upon receipt, we will send our check to pay for the book.

Thank you very much.

Sincerely yours,

412.
TRANSMITTAL OF PAYMENT IN FULL OF MORTGAGE LOAN AND
REQUEST TO SATISFY MORTGAGE OF RECORD

Dear Mr. Bancroft:

Enclosed is our Check No. 1102 in the amount of $27,640, as payment in full of the above-referenced loan.

Please have this mortgage satisfied on the Probate Records of Washington County, Alabama, as soon as possible so that we might complete our title work on this property.

Mr. Whitworth's forwarding address is 3807 Mason Road, Indianapolis, Indiana.

Very sincerely,

COMMENT:

1. The above letter could be concluded with an expression of thanks or gratitude.

413.
STATUS REPORT TO CONSULTANT AND REQUEST FOR
ASSISTANCE IN CIVIL SERVICE COMMISSION CASE
APPEALED TO U.S. DISTRICT COURT

Dear Mr. Culbert:

In Federal Court in Denver, on April 18, Judge Harold Dillard suggested that we prepare a memorandum or study guide specifically pointing out errors in the record before the Civil Service Commission in Mr. Porter's two cases.

I believe you could help us on this. While we do not have the entire official record, we have enough of it so we can essentially recreate it from the records that Mr. Porter has provided both to us and you. I would appreciate it very much if you would please address your time and attention to this.

One thing in particular is the matter of the incorrect documentation in his 201 file as being an error; another is the matter of the Civil Service Commission using letters from Ralph Gray and others against Brad Taylor without disclosing to him the letters that were in the file or the contents of letters. We did not discover the contents or these letters until we were in Denver reviewing the file in connection with his petition for reconsideration of the file. Another possible error in the file is the matter of Mr. Porter requesting while his case was being considered that the Civil Service Commission disclose to him adverse claims being made by the agency. This was never done to my knowledge.

Also, other irregularities in the record may occur to you. It is extremely important that we establish the errors in the record as this must be done to sustain our appeal to Federal Court. For example, it may well be that all the additional evidence we want to adduce in the case will be in the form of an additional hearing ordered by the court to be conducted by the Civil Service Commission. Judge Dillard indicated pretty well that the court itself would not get into the factual disputes in the case but would stick to Civil Service Commission records or proceedings which may be required to perfect or correct the record.

Just wanted to drop you this note to give you a status report and direct your attention to specific help you may give us in the case. My secretary has made an appointment for you, Mr. Porter, and me to get together on June 12 at 3:00 p.m., and I look forward to seeing you.

Very sincerely,

COMMENT:

1. Letters such as the above are an effective means of making a status report to other interested parties.

414.
RECOMMENDATION OF STUDENT FOR ADMISSION TO COLLEGE

Dear Mr. Pickwick:

I would like to strongly recommend for admission as an undergraduate at the University of Maryland, Mr. Paul Pope, of Baltimore. Paul's mother, Mrs. Fred Pope, is a long-time friend of mine, and I had quite a long discussion with her recently regarding Paul.

Paul will graduate from the Getty Academy in Annapolis on June 8 of this year. I understand his average for the four years there is either 3.5 or 3.6 and that he ranked number 6 out of 48 students. In addition to his scholastic attainments, he is a member of the varsity swim team, president of the Trident Club, which is a major organization, and was section editor of the annual. He is also a member of the Key Club, a member of the Debate team and is prefect in his dorm.

I believe that Paul will be a credit to the University of Maryland and hope it will be possible for him to be admitted as an undergraduate this fall.

Very sincerely,

COMMENT:

1. Letters are the customary means of recommending students for admission to college and professional schools.

Appendix (a)   History of Lawyers' Letters

Ancient societies in Mesopotamia, Egypt and elsewhere developed important concepts of property, marriage and government. Early laws evolved into codes which were carried and transmitted from generation to generation by memory until writing was invented in Mesopotamia about 6000 years ago. The first writings were inscribed on wet clay tablets with wedge-shaped styluses. The tablets, which were baked as hard as pottery, were the chief writing materials for thousands of years, and messages inscribed on the tablets, addressed and delivered to someone, were among the first letters. Letters were later carved on bronze, bone or wood and usually protected by a wax coating. Gradually skins of animals and papyrus replaced the clay and other materials.

Postal systems began in about 3000 B.C.; however, "letters" were memorized by couriers or runners who carried the messages to their addressees. Herodotus wrote about the Persian postal system of 500 B.C.: "there is no mortal thing faster than these messengers . . . neither snow nor rain nor heat nor gloom of night stay these couriers from the swift completion of their appointed rounds." Many of the messages carried by the early postal systems undoubtedly involved legal, as well as political and military, matters.

Hammurabi, who ruled Babylonia for 43 years, probably between 1850 and 1750 B.C., compiled one of the first great law codes. A stone slab bearing the carved Code of Hammurabi was discovered in Susa, Iran, in 1901. The Code, based on older collections of Sumerian and Akkadian laws, contains nearly 300 legal provisions, including such matters as false accusation, witchcraft, military service, land and business regulations, family laws, tariffs, wages, trade, loans and debts. Letters of legal nature probably began about the same time law codes were reduced to writing.

Letters were common when the Bible was written. For example, the English Bible describes a letter in II Samuel 11:14: "The following morning David wrote a letter to Joab and sent Uriah with it. He wrote in the letter 'Put Uriah opposite the enemy where the fighting is fiercest and then fall back, and leave him to meet his death.' "

Examples of letter style are found in Ezra 4, Acts 23:36-30, and elsewhere in the Old Testament, and one-third of the New Testament consists of letters. The book of Revelation contains an interesting letter to the "seven churches that are in Asia."

By the fourteenth century the legal profession had become a highly sophisticated profession. The four inns of court were established in London by the beginning of the fifteenth century. The inns of court, namely Lincoln's Inn, Gray's Inn, The Inner Temple and The Middle Temple, are referred to in *Coke's Reports* as the most famous universities for the profession of law and are referred to along with the universities of Oxford and Cambridge.

A system of oral pleading and memorized messages no doubt preceded written pleadings and lawyers' letters in the British legal profession. The development of printing about 500 years ago had a tremendous impact on the development of the common law forms of action and other pleadings and instruments of practice in England. Perhaps printed form letters were used on occasion. Lawyers, however, had to write personalized letters by hand for centuries since the typewriter did not come into use until around 1875.

Lawyers' letters and the legal profession in the United States probably paralleled the growth of America's postal system. Richard Fairbanks developed one of the earliest colonial mail systems in the United States in 1639. He received and dispatched ship mail at his home in Boston and was paid one cent for every letter he handled. The Boston Post Road was built to accommodate an early American postal system beginning in 1672. Finally, in 1775, the system was more formally established when Benjamin Franklin was appointed the first Postmaster General under the Continental Congress. At that time there were about 75 post offices and 2000 miles of post road in America. George Washington insisted on developing an efficient mail service when the United States was formed. The United States Constitution grants to Congress authority to "establish post offices and post roads."

Good handwriting was a major criterion of a lawyer from the beginning of the educated legal profession in England and the United States until about 1875 to 1900, when the typewriter became widely used by lawyers. Except for printed forms, all legal pleadings, letters and other instruments of practice were handwritten by lawyers before the advent of the typewriter. If you search the court records in your county back to about 1900, or a few years earlier, you will probably find the change from handwritten to typed records. You will undoubtedly find the same change from handwriting to typing if you examine the letters appearing in the files of lawyers practicing around 1900.

The typewriter drastically changed lawyers' letters as well as lawyers' methods of practice. The typewriter, indeed, gave rise to the legal secretarial profession. Few lawyers bothered to secure secretaries when letters were handwritten. The typewriter, however, introduced a division of labor between writing or dictating letters and transcribing or typing them.

Electric typewriters and magnetic card, magnetic tape, and other automatic and computer-operated typewriters have accented the division of labor until today scarcely a lawyer would think of writing and preparing a letter without the assistance of his secretary or legal assistant. Modern dictating and transcribing equipment has largely displaced the need for shorthand stenographers in letter writing. Shorthand, however, is still used in many law offices in dictating and preparing letters and is especially useful when a letter needs to be dictated, typed and mailed as soon as possible. Dictating machines are of two types, mechanical and magnetic, which record the voice on discs, belts, wire or tape. Cassette tape dictating equipment has become very popular with lawyers and is beginning to replace early equipment for the dictation of letters and other instruments of practice.

Lawyers have doubled and redoubled their output of letters many times over through the use of dictating and transcribing machines. The economy of labor is obvious. The lawyer's secretary or legal assistant may transcribe dictation while the lawyer is dictating other material or performing other tasks. Letter writing and other tasks may also be delegated to legal assistants through dictated instruction.

Automatic typewriters with memory and computer-operated features are the way of the future in law offices. With such equipment a sole practitioner or law firm may devise a system of forms covering standard letters as well as pleading and practice instruments. The personal touch may still be included through the skill of whoever composes the message.

Modern equipment and tools are the answer for today's and tomorrow's lawyer who must produce letters with greater speed and in greater volume. The importance of volume of a lawyer's letters can only increase as the demand for legal services increases among the people of the United States and the world.

Appendix (b)   Analysis of Lawyers' Letters

In military terms, a lawyer's letter is a strategic weapon. The letter is a long range effort comparable to artillery, not for close hand-to-hand combat. There are times when a conference or a telephone call are essential, but the busy lawyer will find that a well-written letter is one of his most effective means of communication.

In the long run, letters save time, and they can also save the lawyer from the embarrassment of not having tended to a matter. How many times has a lawyer or his secretary tried and tried to reach a client by telephone and then gone on to other things, letting a matter slip. A letter—taking about five to ten minutes time—gets the job done.

Letters, once they are struck, have lasting qualities. People do tend to believe anything they see in print. When people read a story in the newspaper, for instance, they often feel the story has some validity independent of underlying facts simply because it appears in print. Letters have the same tendency. They are also permanent. Conference discussion and telephone conversations fade into oblivion with the passage of time unless they are recorded and preserved. A spoken word has its immediate effect; afterwards it is only a matter of memory. Unfortunately, no one's memory is infallible. In contrast, letters are a permanent record, and the exact words are available ten years later if you need them. Also, it is often advisable and necessary to restate your understanding of a conversation to the other party in this permanent way.

Conversations can go awry at times, and all you needed to say doesn't get said. In a letter you can say all you have to say, with the added advantage of the reader having to hear you out. This fact alone often makes it important to send a letter.

If you keep track of how many letters are written in your office in an average week, you will be surprised at the number. Because so many are written, the study of the art of letter writing deserves time and thought. This analysis of a lawyer's letters is not intended to be pedagogic or definitive. The sole aim is to give you some ideas, some points of departure to assist you in considering your office and ways to improve your letters.

EXAMINE YOUR LETTERS

What do the letters written in your office look like? Most of your letters are probably one or two pages long. Standard ingredients are date line, inside address, reference, salutation, body of letter, complimentary closing, signature, stenographic reference and enclosure line. Block form is becoming more prevalent, and some lawyers are omitting stenographic references. This is all a matter of form and style. Standardization is desirable.

While the mechanics and style of letter writing are important, the art of composing the body of your letter is more important. The art of composing a good letter cannot be reduced to a set formula. There are no hard and fast rules. Always you, the letter writer, are the artist. You make the rules.

MOST IMPORTANT PART OF A LETTER

Each of your letters has a personality. Each is a creature of your thought and imagination. Each begins with a decision you make to write. What, then, is an important consideration when you start to create a letter? Overwhelmingly, the most important consideration is the person you expect to be the reader. Never neglect to carry in your mind the best possible understanding of, and respect for, your reader. People seldom write letters to themselves; your letter is for your reader.

Think about who you have selected to be your reader. You want to inform him, urge him to take some action or form some opinion. The more you know about your reader, the better you can compose your letter, tailored especially for him. Good letter writers know their readers just as good speakers know their audiences.

PURPOSE OF YOUR LETTER

What is the purpose of your letter? Why are you writing it? What is its mission or objective? What do you wish to accomplish? The purpose of a letter is closely related to the reader. Your letter, for example, could be intended to scare or frighten your reader, although such a letter ordinarily is not in good taste. A well-written message persuasively communicates its purpose loudly and clearly to its reader.

Subject matter, of course, is important, although it is not more important than the intended reader and purpose of your letter. Subject matter refers to the underlying transaction, claim, proceeding or situation. The subject matter of your letter, for example, may be an automobile accident case, a marital dispute, the preparation of an estate plan, a real estate transaction, or the organization of a corporation. You must thoroughly understand the facts and law relating to your subject matter. This is a big order, as every lawyer knows. Subject matter of law is coextensive with human personality and human relations. The subject matter of your letters, likewise, is coextensive with your law practice.

HOW TO WRITE A GOOD LETTER

Letters may be thought of as written instruments of practice comparable to pleadings and other legal documents. Unlike other legal instruments, however, lawyers' letters are intended primarily as a means of communication between one person and another. Letters are informal and flexible enough to reach into nearly all areas of information, consultation and negotiation. For this reason letters are the most flexible and versatile of all written instruments of practice.

Ordinarily a letter does not go into great detail. It is usually more like a poster. For example, the typical letter is not intended to serve the purpose of a treatise, brief or memorandum. Many letters are comparable to telephone conversations, or more like face-to-face discussions than formal writings. At the same time, however, a letter may be more precise, may contain more detailed information, and may convey more carefully conceived thoughts and ideas.

A letter, in contrast to a conversation, is a one-way communication. Like oral communication, however, a good letter should ordinarily be warm and human. It should be a projection of you, your personality, your ideas and your way of doing things. It should be sincere. It should be clear, and it should be simple.

THE BODY OF A LETTER

The body of your letter should be creative, original, spontaneous and ingenious. Keep in mind that there is little chance the letter you write will be superior to the affection, warmth, respect, sincerity and thought you give in composing it. The English language offers you a formidable tool for communicating original thought. Avoid word choices and patterns which do not come naturally to you. Do not memorize or standardize phraseology, either your own or someone else's, unless it conveys precisely the message you wish to write. Simply talk to your reader. Tell him your thoughts and load your letter with your originality and spontaneity.

A sentence is simply a group of words which express an idea. How do words come to you? You would not write your sentences like those in a poem, which strictly measured feet. But alliteration, assonance and consonance may be used. Words of contrast vividly convey an idea. Metaphors and similes are powerful. Remember the first and last words in a sentence occupy important positions. The first and last sentences in a paragraph occupy strategic positions.

You, the writer, should have a comprehensive picture of the subject matter you write about. Specific things and names of specific things have more flavor and meaning than generalities. Thoughts and ideas, on the other hand, are more important than miscellaneous details. The details you do include should be subordinate to and support the basic thoughts and ideas.

SENTENCES AND PARAGRAPHS

Sentences are divided into paragraphs to give your reader a rest. There is no general rule for the most suitable length of a paragraph. Too many short ones may be as irritating as long ones are tedious. A paragraph is more a unit of thought than length. Each sentence in a paragraph should be related in subject matter and treatment.

The first paragraph and last paragraph of the body of your letter are most important. The first paragraph, whether long or short, usually announces to your reader the purpose of your letter. The last paragraph of your letter may simply contain concluding or complimentary material. The last strong paragraph, however, should conclude or recapitulate your basic purpose and state simply and specifically what you want the reader to do, think or know.

The middle paragraphs of a well-written letter should develop the purpose into logical parts. These paragraphs should set forth in an orderly and interesting matter, relevant information, thoughts and ideas. Each paragraph should develop one basic thought or topic. The development should make the general purpose and subject matter more specific. Specific details, names, places, examples, etc., help make the subject matter and purpose of the letter more precise and definite. Logical, orderly, informative and interesting development of the middle paragraphs add depth and strength to your beginning and concluding paragraphs.

Your last strong paragraph should move your reader. The full force of your letter should be felt here. Such a paragraph may be followed by a sentence or short paragraph expressing personal warmth, regards and friendliness. Closing matter, however, should never detract from the overall impact of your letter.

THE TONE

Lawyers' letters have a tone. Indeed, they may carry many of the qualities of music. The words of your letter may radiate warmth, graciousness and friendliness. They may likewise convey fear, anger, frustration, or confusion. A base letter can crystalize and personify rudeness. You must carefully draft your letters to avoid unintended coldness, rudeness or unfriendliness. Your overall tone should be controlled throughout.

THE LAST ACT OF YOUR LETTER

Remember always that the effective letter is one which accomplishes its purpose. The first act is performed when you write the letter. Never forget, however, that the last act—the response you desire—must be performed by your reader.

Appendix (c)   Style for Lawyers' Letters

A letter that looks good will create a favorable impression on the reader. Never underestimate eye appeal. Although what you have to say in the letter is most important, composition, construction and outward appearance have an effect on the reader.

The outward appearance of your letters is greatly affected by the letterhead imprint on the paper you use for your letters. The letterhead identifies the lawyer or law firm. Your letterhead should be attractive and supply your readers with essential information, such as name of lawyer or firm, address, telephone number, names of lawyers in firm, etc. You should use good quality paper for your letters. Extra sheets, when a letter exceeds one page, should be of the same paper stock but without the letterhead imprint. The name of the addressee, date and page number (referred to as continuation lines) should be typed at the top of each additional page of a letter. Three lines of text, as a minimum, should appear in addition to the complimentary close and signature on the final page of a letter.

Each letter should be thought of as a picture. Composition is as important in letter writing as in art. For example, the side margins in a brief letter should be larger to display the letter in a manner pleasing to the eye. Ample blank space should always appear in the top, side and bottom margins of each page. The date line normally comes first after the letterhead imprint. The inside address appears next, followed by the reference line, salutation, body, complimentary close, signature, stenographic reference and enclosure lines. In addition, letters may contain file numbers, attention lines, postscripts, and other elements.

The inside address serves to identify who the letter is to, since envelopes are usually thrown away. The inside address also helps in filing and may be used with window envelopes.

The salutation used sets the tone of your letter. "Dear Nick" sounds friendlier than "Dear Mr. Jones," but either is friendlier than "Dear Sir."

The body of your letter is the most important part. The composition of the body of your letter should be neat and uniform. Ordinarily, long paragraphs should be avoided. A good combination of short and longer paragraphs is usually more pleasing to the eye. Capitalizing looks better than underlining to give emphasis. The general rules of legal citation should be adhered to in your letters when legal authorities are cited.

Customary forms for the complimentary close are: "Yours truly," "Yours sincerely," "Yours very truly," or simply "Sincerely" or "Very sincerely" to express greater intimacy. "Respectfully yours" may be used in correspondence with judges and other officials.

Basic letter forms are distinguished by indentation. Paragraphs of handwritten letters, for example, are indented for visual clarity. Indentations are a burden instead of a help in typewritten letters. Visual clarity is served equally well by double-spacing between paragraphs. These line separations are becoming more common than indentation in lawyers' letters. They look better and save time in typing.

Full block, modified block and indented forms are the three styles in use. The full block form is easiest to type since all typing under the letterhead is aligned along the left margin. Full block form should be considered as an economy measure to save time, thus money.

The style in widest use for lawyers' letters at the present time is the modified block form. The modified block form is distinguished from the full block form by alignment of certain elements such as the date line and the complimentary close and signature to the right to help balance the letter.

The indented form features full indentation or partial indentation. This was most common when letters were handwritten. Paragraphs and other sequences of lines in salutations and complimentary closings are indented in the full indentation form. Various forms of modified indentation have virtually replaced full indentation of letters. In time the typewriter will probably render nearly all forms of indentation obsolete.

The envelope is the first part of your letter to be seen. Your firm's name and address should be imprinted on the envelope. The outside address is normally typed in block form. It may be indented, but indentation is probably a waste of time. The outside address contains the name and title of the addressee, the street address or post office box number, the city, state and zip code. On foreign mail the name of the country replaces the state.

The zip code is a five-digit number designed to aid accuracy and speed in mail delivery. The first numeral of the zip code identifies one of the ten national service areas. The second and third numbers indicate the service area and post office. The last two numbers identify the station from which the mail is delivered.

The zip code should appear on the last line of both the address and return address following the city and state. Not less than two nor more than six spaces should appear between the last letter of the state and the zip code. No comma or other punctuation appears before or after the zip code.

Appendix (d)   Dictation and Writing Techniques

Effective dictating and writing techniques are time savers and money makers for your firm. A good command of English and knowledge of the rules of grammar are essential. Practice is essential to help you develop your own technique, and dictation and writing should be allocated high priority for your professional time.

Ordinarily your letters should be dictated through your secretary or preferably on dictating equipment. Before dictating a letter, you should have the appropriate file and other materials at your desk. Consider first who you are writing to and the purpose of your letter. Instruct your secretary as to the date, addressee, reference and salutation, if necessary. You may include the file number, depending on the practice of your office.

Talk your dictation just as you would say it if your reader were in front of you. Begin your letter by stating the purpose. Let your reader know at the beginning whether your purpose is to give him information, a recommendation or opinion, or to secure information or request action or decision by him. In a longer letter the middle paragraphs will develop your purpose by giving examples, illustrations, or other material which makes the matter clearer to your reader. Your last paragraph, other than complimentary matter, should state precisely what you want your reader to know, think, feel, do or believe. Speak clearly and naturally, as though you are talking to the person you are writing to. Speak at about the same speed you do in natural conversation. Be careful not to speak too rapidly. You will want to pause from time to time to reflect on what you want to say next. Try to be specific. Give facts, names, and details. Depending on the skill of your secretary, you may want to give grammatical instructions indicating paragraphs, sentences and punctuation. It is a good idea to spell any word or name with which your secretary may be unfamiliar.

Most letters should be typed directly from your dictation, ready for mailing. It is quite time consuming to make corrections and for the secretary to type more than one draft. You may find it helpful to write loose notes on a legal pad to aid you in dictating more detailed and involved letters. Such notes may also be helpful to your secretary in transcribing your dictation. You should consider offering them to her for this purpose.

You should instruct your secretary, either before or after dictating each letter, how many copies you want and where each is to go. It is generally a good idea to send a copy of all out-going letters involving a matter to your client. The secretary should prepare a copy of the letter for the file without specific instructions.

You can probably dictate about three times as many letters as you could write by hand in the same time. If you haven't perfected your dictating technique, work at it since it will be very much worthwhile and will make you much more efficient in your law practice. Lawyers with well-developed techniques find it considerably easier, as well as quicker, to dictate a letter than to write one by hand.

Appendix (e)   Paralegal Techniques

The volume of letters which must be written by the average lawyer is constantly increasing. One of the more direct ways a good paralegal or legal assistant can save a lawyer time and make him more efficient is by actually writing letters for him. A legal assistant with a basic understanding of the transaction or matter involved should be able to draft acceptable and usable letters relating to the matter. Many letters involve routine or standard matters which may be handled more efficiently by the legal assistant than by the lawyer himself.

A lawyer may easily monitor letters written for him by his legal assistant. The lawyer is fully aware of what the legal assistant has written, and, unless the letter meets his approval, it simply is not mailed. If a letter has been mailed, the lawyer can easily advise the appropriate parties of the situation. This would not be true of a telephone conversation handled by a legal assistant since things may be said by the assistant of which the lawyer is not aware and with which he might take issue if they were brought to his attention.

The legal assistant should be thoroughly familiar with the lawyer's style and personal preference with regard to tone and approach used in a letter. If the lawyer's style is to be very warm, friendly, cordial, informal, etc., the legal assistant should know this. On the other hand, if a lawyer's style is to be more formal and businesslike, the legal assistant should be aware of the lawyer's preference. It may be difficult to decide who wrote a particular letter—the lawyer or the legal assistant—after a period of collaboration where there is a good understanding between the two of style, purpose and way of doing things. The ultimate objective for the legal assistant is to be able to serve the lawyer so well that one can hardly tell the work product of the legal assistant from the work product of the lawyer. Of course all of the work done by a legal assistant, including letters written for a lawyer, are subject to the lawyer's supervision, and the lawyer is responsible for whatever the legal assistant has done or written.

The lawyer may take two approaches to his legal secretaries and legal assistants with the aid of modern dictating equipment. First, he can dictate correspondence, pleadings and other legal documents verbatim. On the other hand, the lawyer can simply dictate what he wants done—instructions to do this or that or write a letter along such and such a line. It is best that the lawyer use the second approach and make full use of qualified assistants, thereby delivering the maximum legal services to his clients.

Index

423